Ministers and Elders

The Birth of Presbyterianism

Steven Paas

Kachere Theses no. 24

Kachere Series, Zomba 2007

Copyright© 2007 Steven Paas

All rights reserved. No part of this publication may be reproduced, stored in a retrieval system, or transmitted in any form, nor by any means, electronic, mechanical, photocopying, recording or otherwise, without prior permission from the author.

ISBN: 978-99908-87-02-0

Layout and Cover: Willem Hendrik Paas

Cover Illustration: Map of part of Western Europe and the main players in the history of early Presbyterianism, respectively Thomas Cartwright (England), John Knox (Scotland), Martin Bucer (Strasbourg), and John Calvin (Geneva).

Printed by Lightning Source

This book is a publication of the **Kachere Series**, the publishing arm of the **Department of Theology and Religious Studies of the University of Malawi.**

Kachere Series,
P.O. Box 1037, Zomba, Malawi
Distributed by African Books Collective
www.africanbookscollective.com

Table of Contents

Table of Contents 3
Preface 8
Chapter 1 11
Prelude to the Reformation 11
   1. Desire for Reform 11
      a. Church-rule in The Middle Ages 11
      b. Organisational Demands 12
   2. Pre-Reformation England 13
      a. The Celtic Church 13
      b. The Normans 14
      c. John Wycliffe 16
      d. Prelude to Change 17
   3. Papacy Decapitated and Episcopacy Retained 18
      a. Proto-Puritans Dissatisfied 18
      b. Anglicanism Challenged 20
Chapter 2 22
Church-Rule: By Whom and How? 22
   1. Authority and church-government 22
      a. Authority of the Scriptures 22
      b. Emergence of Presbyterian Thought 23
      c. Christ Defines the Church-Structure 27
      d. Three Phases 28
   2. Continental Models demand Completion 30
      a. The Gap is too Wide 30
      b. Waves of Exiles 30
Chapter 3 33
Continental Reformers and the Church 33
   1. The Ideas of the Reformers 33
      a. Break with Rome 33
      b. The Lutheran position 34
   2. The Reformers and the Radicals 35
      a. No Divine Right for Elders? 35
      b. Anabaptist Radicalism 36
      d. Radical and Magisterial Reformers 38
   3. Martin Luther 40
      a. Communio Sanctorum 40
      b. Princes Rule the Church 40
   4. Huldrych Zwingli 42

    a. A Christian Commonwealth 42
    b. Supremacy of the State 43
  5. Martin Bucer 44
    a. Relative Obscurity 44
    b. Christology and Pneumatology 45
    c. Christ is King through the Spirit 46
    d. No Absolute Office – Equality of Believers 47
    e. Presbytership, the Basic Office 49
  6. John Calvin 50
    a. Comparison with Bucer 50
    b. Elders and Ministers 54
    c. Calvin's Context 56

Chapter 4 59
Reception of Continental Thought 59
  1. Original interest in Luther 59
    a. Early Influence 59
    b. Cranmer and Luther 60
  2. The Bishops Focus on Zwingli and Erastus 60
    a. Congenial Climate 60
    b. Church and State in Unity 61
    c. New Influx of Ideas 63
  3. Bucer: a Sympathetic Refugee 64
    a. Claimed by all 64
    b. Articles and Canons 65
    c. Bucer Misunderstood 66
  4. Shift to Calvin 68
    a. Varied Reception 68
    b. Different Situations 70
    c. Not Violent but Adamant 75
    d. Differentiated Approach 76

Chapter 5 78
The Edwardian Prayer Book 78
  1. Hooper and the Vestments 78
    a. Changing Climate 78
    b. Church-robes rejected 79
    c. Puritanism leads to Presbyterianism 81
  2. John Knox and the *Black Rubric* 83
    a. Kneeling at the Eucharist 83
    b. Refusal of Bishopric 84
  3. Puritans and the *Prayer Book* 85
    a. Protestant Direction 85
    b. Bucer's *Censura* 87
    c. Form and Government are Essential 88
    d. No Compromise 90

Chapter 6 92
Restoration of the Papacy and Exile **92**
  1. The old Henricians resume Power 92
     a. Pragmatists 92
     b. Persecutions 93
  2. The Marian exile 94
     a. Refuge on the Continent 94
     b. More than Vestments 95
     c. The Puritans in Frankfort 96
     d. Knox and Geneva 98
Chapter 7 100
The Vestments' Controversy **100**
  1. The Precisians Disappointed 100
     a. Erastian and Theocratic Views 100
     b. Via Media 102
  2. The Elizabethan Settlement 103
     a. Act of Uniformity 103
     b. Provoking a Breach 105
  3. The Ejectment of Nonconforming Ministers 106
     a. Birth of the name 'Puritan' 106
     b. Continental Reformers Displeased 107
     c. Open Defiance 108
  4. The first Congregations ruled by Elders 109
     a. Shift from Dress to Rule 109
     b. Circumstantial Separatists 110
Chapter 8 113
The Admonition Controversy **113**
  1. The appearance of Thomas Cartwright 113
     a. Cartwright as a Scholar 113
     b. Cartwright's First Debate with Whitgift 114
     c. The First Exile: Geneva 115
     d. The Wandsworth Enterprise 116
     e. The Second Exile: Heidelberg 118
     f. Cartwright and Browne 119
  2. The *Admonitions* to Parliament and the *Explicatio* 121
     a. The House of Commons 121
     b. The First Admonition 121
     c. The Second Admonition 123
     d. Travers' *Explicatio* 126
     e. Travers' *Directory of Church-government* 130
Chapter 9 132
Failure of the Grand Design **132**
  1. The Use of Legal Means 132
     a. The Grand Design 132

    b. The Prophesyings 132
    c. Browne and Harrison 135
    d. Greenwood, Barrowe and Penry 136
    e. The Dedham Papers 137
    f. Expulsion or Subscription 139
    g. Whitgift's Inquisition 140
  2. 'A godly Discipline outside the Law' 142
    a. Presbyterian Experiments 142
    b. The Martin Mar-Prelate Papers 143
    c. The Proto-Presbyterian network Discovered 145
    d. Cartwright's Trial 146
    e. Separatists in Exile 147
    f. Anglican attacks: Bancroft, Hooker 148
    g. The Grand Design kept alive 151
    h. Followers of the Genevan Example 152

Chapter 10 154
Attacks from Two Sides 154
  1. Godly Discipline 154
  2. No Imitator 154
  3. Inconsistent or Planned? 155
  4. Elevation of the Minister 157
  5. Change of Strategy 159

Chapter 11 160
Defence against the Right 160
  1. Rotten Pillar or Apostolic Model 160
  2. Sacrificing Priest or Preaching Minister 160
  3. Government by Elders Disputed 166

Chapter 12 173
Defence against the Left 173
  1. Struggle within Puritanism 173
    a. Cradled in Presbyterian Climate 173
    b. Separatists differed from Anabaptists 174
  2. Church of Christ or False Church 175
    a. The Church is Founded on Christ 175
    b. The Objectivity of the Church 176
  3. The Position of the Minister Disputed 176
    a. Full Consent 176
    b. Eldership and Democracy 177
  4. Debate with Anne Stubbe 178
    a. Imperfect, yet True Church 178
    b. The Voice of Christ is heard 180
  5. Fading Authority of the Elder 181
    a. Do Elders Preach and Teach? 181

   b. Clericalist Tendency 182
6. Cartwright and Calvin 184
   a. The Same Principles 184
   b. Shifts of Emphasis 185
7. Theocratic Vision weakened 185
   a. Not a Lost Cause 185
   b. Vision of the Church Changed 186
8. Conclusion 187
Table of Events **188**
Bibliography **191**
Index **193**

Preface

Jesus Christ is King of God's Church. However, who governs the Church under Him? How is the Church to be ruled? These problems have intrigued me for many years. In most Protestant churches, the *elder* and the *minister* are the principal actors in the governmental structure. I have served in both offices, respectively in The Netherlands and in Central Africa (Malawi). The difference in cultural context and denomination -African Presbyterian and Dutch Reformed- made the picture more complicated, but also encouraged me to continue investigating the origins and characteristics of Presbyterian church-rule. Concerning the authority of these two offices, I see three series of important questions.

First, are they deriving authority directly from God, or indirectly from the congregation? This question leads to another one. Are they hovering *above*, or being *opposed to*, the congregation, executing authority independently from it, or is their authority *dynamically interwoven* with and *dependent on* the authority of the congregation?

Secondly, are they basically *one* office, i.e. the *eldership*, or are they in principle *two* different offices, the elders only for ruling, disciplining and pastoring, and the ministers in exclusive addition to that for preaching and teaching the Word of God? Consequently, there is another question. Are ministers having authority together with the elders, or are they a separate authority, hovering above the elders?

The third series of questions regards the congregation, and is derived from the questions on elders and ministers. It concerns the authority of members, either individually or collectively. Some deny this right as an offence against the authority from above from God, which they consider as being reflected in ministers and elders only. Others claim this right, as a legal expression of the authority of God who planted the Church and gave gifts to any believer, stressing the office of priesthood of all believers.

In Presbyterian and other denominations, the government of the Church has often become an imitation of the ruling structures in state and society. Depending on the prevailing culture and political climate, the minister is the principal leader. He may behave as an autocratic ruler, or he may have adopted the style of a modern manager, in a more democratic way. Under him, the elders are a body of executives, sometimes not much more than just counselors; more often, in various degrees, they are participants in decision-making and leadership. In most cases, there is not much room for initiative and leadership emerging from the congregation. Basically, no independent authority is allowed to the congregation because of the classical thought that the Church does not only include believers but also hidden unbelievers or 'hypocrites'. Churches that believe in 'perfect membership', look differently on the characteristics of the Church, but in practice, this principle has not produced independent congregational authority either. In general, office bearers often do not encourage initiatives by 'common' believers and practically tend to leave little room for the development of leadership gifts in the congregation.

How do these questions and situations relate to the Word of God? The present book does not offer final answers to this question, but tries to throw light on the historical context. It is a result of my research of the beginnings of the tradition of Presbyterian church-rule. It focuses on the Elizabethan era of the English Church, when Presbyterianism emerged as a reaction against autocratic one-man-rule on the one hand, and against 'radical' conceptions of rule-by-many on the other hand.[1] Instead of these two extremes, Presbyterians liked the idea of church-rule by limited groups of office-bearers. Their adage was: 'a few of the best rule the rest'.

I trust that this survey of the earliest history of Presbyterianism will assist to make the present situation more transparent for members of today's churches of Calvinist and Reformed persuasion and for members of other churches as well. Like in those years before 1600, the Church in the 21st century ought to find Biblical solutions for the problem of the structure of the Church and its government. The Church is the Body of Christ. The governmental structure should reflect that reality. Such a Biblical structure strengthens the Church to act as Christ's missionary agent. It will enable the Church to answer adequately to the challenges world, showing it where its real needs are. A Biblical governmental structure of the Church mobilises and empowers Christians to be co-workers in the proclamation of the Gospel. The message of salvation should reach anyone who does not yet know Him who is the Way, the Truth and the Life. This *Great Commission* requires a Church that allows any believer to have his or her rightful place and task.

Zomba 2007

Steven Paas

---

[1] The present book overlaps part of my publication in Dutch on the same subject, *De Gemeenschap der Heiligen: Kerk en Gezag bij Presbyteriaanse en Separatistische Puriteinen 1570-1593*, Zoetermeer: Boekencentrum, 1996 [The Communion of Saints: Church and Authority with Presbyterian and Separatist Puritans 1570-1593]. The latter study contains an extensive survey of a special group of Separatists, headed by John Greenwood and Henry Barrowe, who wrote their church views while in prison, shortly before their execution. The Elizabethan Presbyterians claimed to be followers of Calvin in the line of Scripture. Their attacks on the Separatists included disapproval of Greenwood and Barrowe. In my research of Greenwoodian and Barrowist writings, I have summarised and evaluated their ideas.

Chapter 1

Prelude to the Reformation

1. Desire for Reform

a. Church-rule in The Middle Ages

How is the Church of Jesus Christ to be governed? What should be the structures of the Church and its congregations? These were no questions for the European Church of the late Middle Ages. Representatives considered its organisation in a Papal and Episcopal structure as the only valid derivation from the New Testament and Tradition. The Church was seen as a monolithic organization, led by the hierarchy of pope and bishops, who represented the clergy as divided from the mass of lay-people. The pope was considered to be Christ's authoritative representation on earth, not only in the Church, but also - as the *Decretals of Gratianus* († 1150) put it- the absolute lord of all kings, princes and civil magistrates.

How much room did this all-embracing pretension leave to the sense of hidden fellowship with the Lord, which is the secret of the Church? It is clear that the Roman power structure put less emphasis on the invisible aspects of the Church than on its being a visible society. The stress on the visibility of the Church implied its need of powers of oversight and government, to be exercised upon its members and upon the whole of medieval life.

However, as time wore on, the pressures, under which these Papal pretensions sought to realise and to maintain themselves, grew heavier and the monolithic structure began to erode. International and external developments led to a situation in which the intrinsic value of a *corpus christianum* headed by the Pope of Rome, gradually came to be doubted by many and to be fiercely rejected by some.

Friction within the hierarchy -because of the moral decay of the Papacy itself- was stimulated by the *Conciliar Movement*. Conciliarists wished to replace absolute Papal power, by the authority of a general council, manned by bishops. The reform-council of Pisa (1409) succeeded in ending the rule of the 'pseudo' Avignon Popes, but the problem of Papal authority was not solved. The Council of Constance (1414-1418), initiated by the Habsburg Emperor, unsuccessfully tried to limit Papal power by pushing the Church into a national direction. The original victory by the conciliarists did not prevent the revival of Papal power. They elected a new pope -Martinus V- who held firmly to his exclusive traditional position. The Council of Basel (1431) was also a failure for the conciliarists. Pope Eugenius IV disbanded it. Further councils, in Ferrara

(1438) and Florence (1439), saw the victory of curialist supporters and absolute Papal rule. By 1449 the *Conciliar Movement* had died and with that those elements within the clerical hierarchy who favoured reform of the Church's governmental system.[1]

However, among the lower clergy, the clerical and lay orders and the masses of lay people, the reform movement was getting momentum. The desire for reform was much favoured by the changing political, economical and social climate. The times of highhanded popes, e.g. Innocentius III (1198-1216) and Boniface VIII (1294-1302), who were able to defy and submit even kings and emperors, seemed to be gone. Boniface's bull *Unam Sanctam* (1302), in which he claimed the authority over the 'spiritual' as well as the 'secular sword', had lost much of its impact to the rulers of Europe. Even the emperor of the Habsburg Empire, though for political reasons in favour of Roman Catholic unity, saw the necessity of reforms, including the limitation of Papal power. The rulers of the territorial states and independent cities supported a policy of decentralisation of the empire and, by consequence, they were much interested in reform, not only of the political system but also of the Church. Besides, national states like France and England, became more centralised, more independent and stronger. The thriving city-states along the Rhine, and in The Netherlands, grew in power and would soon be centralised in new national states. Reforms were in the interest of their kings and princes, who were out to expand their power. Limitation of Papal authority within their boundaries fitted the policy of national magistrates.

Thus, mainly outside the ranks of the leading clergy a mighty cry for comprehensive reforms was heard. This cry took shape in the movements of *Renaissance* and *Humanism*, which demanded the recognition of the natural rights of man, as their leaders had learnt them from the Greek philosophers of Antiquity. These demands ran parallel to, but were not naturally connected to, the burning desire for a Reformation based on the principles of the Church of the New Testament and of the early Fathers.

b. Organisational Demands

In the Protestant Reformation of the 16th century, all aspects of Christian faith and Christian organisation were at stake. First, there was the central question of salvation. How can sinful human beings be acceptable for God? A reinterpretation and rearrangement of the doctrines of justification and

---

[1] B. Lohse, *Martin Luther, eine Einführung,* München: Beck 1981, describes in chapter 1, parts 12-15 the impact of the *Conciliar Movement* as a prelude to the Lutheran Reformation. The 5th Lateran Council, (1512-1517), which took place when the conciliarists had already been defeated, showed that the Church was unable to reform itself.

sanctification, in defiance of Roman doctrines, was the result of the activities of the Reformers. The second area of change pertained to the organisational aspects of the Church. On the one hand, there were the questions of supremacy and government with regard to the Church. This involved the position of Papacy, and the relationship of the 'Kingdom of God' and the 'Kingdom of the world', and the relationship of the Church and the State. Paramount in this, was the problem whether Christ meant to govern his Church by means of a hierarchy of bishops and priests, which left no room for the authority of the spiritual body of lay-members. Does Scripture require authority from the top, or authority from the bottom? Often these two possibilities were represented as a dilemma, in a manner as if they would exclude one another. Of course, this dilemma focused the attention on the government and discipline of local and regional church bodies. Would the strict division into the classes of clergy and laity be maintained? Would this mean that lay-members, even if they belonged to the increasingly influential middle class or to the local magistracies, had no say in the government of their own congregations?

According to some Protestant Reformers, these organisational aspects of the Church were indifferent matters that could be organised according to the rule of expediency. They were of the opinion that church-organisation and church-government did not touch the main question of salvation. However, to others the faith and the organisation of the Church were very much interwoven. The doctrines of salvation and faith are neither to be separated from the question in which way the Church should be governed and disciplined, nor from the views on the relationship of Church and State.

The struggle for a Reformation of the Church in its organisational aspects was not fought everywhere in Europe with similar intensity and comprehensiveness. The desire for abolition of the Papacy was a common denominator among Protestants, but with regard to the position of bishops, and Episcopalian systems, and the position of the magistrates, there were many different and often opposed opinions.

England is the only country of Europe where perhaps all these organisational aspects of the ecclesiology-struggle played an important role, even in the later stages of the Reformation.

2. Pre-Reformation England

a. The Celtic Church

The Protestant Reformation in England can be characterised by its *Anglicanism*, by its *Puritanism*, and by its *Presbyterianism*. These elements at the same time constitute different aspects and different stages in English Reformation.

Anglicanism refers to the abolishment of the Papacy and its replacement by the supremacy of the King and under him, the Bishops. Puritanism reflects the absorption of the continental Reformers' ideas on salvation. Presbyterianism is a variation of Puritanism. It means a continuation of the Reformation into the direction of a complete abolishment of the old Episcopalian structures of supremacy and church-government, and the introduction of ruling bodies with lay-involvement.

The roots of these three characteristics are already visible in the pre-Reformation era. Protestantism certainly does not merely reflect a theory and practice of church-government. When we set apart this aspect, the old *Celtic Church*, prior to the arrival of Augustine in 597, in some way bore the resemblance to Puritan Protestantism. Of course, it is far fetched to compare a Celtic Bishop to a Presbyterian Elder.[2] Nevertheless, the Church in the Celtic Kingdoms enjoyed considerable freedom and its bishops did not feel responsible to Rome, nor did they play the part of servility to popes and monarchs as under the later Roman and Anglican systems.

After the collapse of the Roman Empire, the heathen Saxons invaded and submerged Celtic Christian culture in most of England. From Rome, the Saxons were christianised. However, surviving Celtic Christian communities found it difficult to accept the Roman religion introduced by Augustine. After the Synod of Whitby in 664, however, they gradually conformed to the acceptance of the Roman Church. This does not mean that the Papal system in its entirety, was introduced in England. The early English Church, before the *Norman Conquest*, was distinctly a national Church. It did not refuse to the pope respect and deference; yet it was largely independent of him. The laws of the land could not be superseded by Roman canons. The Roman separation of clerical and lay jurisdiction did not exist in Anglo-Saxon England.[3]

b. The Normans

A great change was initiated by the Norman Conquest in 1066. William of Normandy and his Archbishop Lanfranc introduced the Roman system and implemented Papal legislation, on e.g. clerical 'immorality', i.e. celibacy of the

---

[2] Thomas Cartwright, the leading Presbyterian-Puritan of the 16th century, 'read Presbyterianism in the constitution of the early Church' and even proclaimed it as a model for all times. He did not doubt that there were elders in Augustine's time and that then the division of preaching and ruling elders was already used. A.F. Scott Pearson, *Thomas Cartwright and Elizabethan Puritanism*, Cambridge University Press, 1925, pp. 26, 42, 89, etc.

[3] G.G. Perry, *A History of the English Church*, London: Murray, 1891, vol. 2, p. 2. 'No legate then attempted to administer the Church affairs of England in defiance of the laws of the land'. The expedition of William of Normandy is described as 'almost a crusade against' this national character of the Church.

clergy, and diocesan administration. Church-courts were separated from secular courts, thus marking the privileges of the clergy, which would cause much disturbance in later periods. The Roman Episcopacy was firmly established in England, The Papal power was to be reckoned with, as is shown by Pope Alexander III's submission of King Henry II Plantagenet, after the latter's murder of Archbishop Thomas Becket in 1170. However, at the same time, the Norman Kings were not inclined to give the pope more authority than was in the interest of their own position. In the feudal system that they instituted, they were largely dependent on the Norman nobility. These barons, eager to safeguard and expand their feudal rights, pressed the kings not to indulge a system that would give the upper hand to the power of foreign popes and bishops. Yet, Pope Innocentius III succeeded in submitting King John.

In 1215, the barons forced the king to sign the *Magna Charta*, thus limiting royal power and curtailing the influence of foreign ecclesiastical princes. The *Magna Charta* checked regal and papal powers. No taxes or arrests were allowed without the laws of the land. It meant that the jurisdiction of Papal Courts and canons was seriously challenged. Apart from this foundation of all later English Constitutions, there was the gradual development of the parliamentary institution. William of Normandy's *Curia Regis* was only an advisory body, limited in membership and strictly dependent on the King. However, under Simon de Montfort (1265) and his successor Edward I, widened councils were formed, which were able to push back subservience to the pope and the selling of benefices to foreign bishops. It became increasingly clear to the Norman Kings that the pope could not help them against the representative body of Parliament. Under Edward III, Parliament and King for the first time discovered that cooperation was in their mutual interest.[4] Edward sided with Parliament against the Avignon-Popes, who were tools of French national policy, and threatened the national interest of England.

The national characteristics of the English Church continued to assert themselves: resistance to the law of celibacy for the clergy, opposition against clerical immunities and special rights, attempts to further the limitation of foreign ecclesiastical rule by various statutes, e.g. to restrain the transfer of lands to the Church (*Mortmain-Statute*), to restrain the giving away of English benefices by the pope (*Provisors-Statute*), and the extremely important *Statute*

---

[4] L. von Ranke, *Maria Stuart in haar tijd* [translation], Borkam, Amsterdam, 1944, pp. 1- 54. A description of the prelude of the Henrician Reformation and its aftermath. The author explains the difficult position of Norman Kings and their policy with regard to Papacy, France and English representative institutions.

of Praemunire, which restrained English clergy from acting under Papal authority.[5]

Reaction against the papal system by kings, feudal lords and parliamentary representatives at this stage does not reveal much of the attitude of the English people itself. Higher and lower classes, though differently motivated, much agreed in their dissatisfaction about the Papal Church. The antagonism of crown, nobility and the new classes of merchants and industrialists was inspired by jealousy of the competing power of Church and clergy. However, the lower classes were more receptive to scriptural and spiritual arguments.

c. John Wycliffe

Often suffering from social and economic misery and oppression, a relatively large group of people felt attracted by the teachings of university Professor John Wycliffe (1330-1384). In the climate of social unrest, his appearance contributed to the preparation of fertile soil for the peasants' revolution led by Watt Tyler. Wycliffe also mouthpieced the religious feelings of pious Christians who felt increasingly unhappy with the alarming condition of the Church. The significance of Wycliffe's views is summarised by Livingstone:

> 'His growing repugnance at the religious institutions of his time, led him to elaborate a concept of the Church, which distinguished its eternal ideal reality from the visible material Church. He denied to the latter any authority, which did not derive from the former. ... He argued that secular and ecclesiastical authority depend on grace, and that therefore, the clergy, if not in a state of grace, could lawfully be deprived of their endowments by the civil power. He later maintained that the Bible was the sole criterion of doctrine, that the authority of the pope was ill-founded in Scripture, and that the monastic life had no biblical foundation'.[6]

These ideas may have been new to many churchmen of the 14th century. However, in later times they would reflect the program of a complete Reformation of the Church. McGinn draws a parallel between Wycliffe and the 16th century Presbyterian-Puritan Thomas Cartwright:

---

[5] Perry, pp. 2, 28, 29: A survey of clerical privileges laid down in Roman canons and their limitation by early English statutes.
[6] E.A. Livingstone, *Concise Oxford Dictionary*, Oxford, 1977, pp 561, 562. Cf. Von Ranke, *Maria Stuart en haar tijd*, 9-13; D.J. McGinn, *The Admonition Controversy*, New Brunswick, 1949, pp. 4. ff.

'Like Cartwright, in place of the doctrines of the Roman Catholic Church, he would substitute the Scriptures as the perfect rule to life and manners to be read by the people'. Like Cartwright, he rejected the government by bishops. 'He would only have two degrees in the sacrament of orders, namely presbyters and deacons. ... In other words, he held that the primitive Church, as he conceived it, must be made the model of the Church of his own time. This demand became the fundamental principle of Puritan reform'.[7]

In the revolutionary turmoil that followed Wycliffe's period an uprising by the lower classes was subdued, but Parliament manned by lower nobility and wealthy citizens, succeeded in expanding its rights at the expense of King Richard II, who had to abdicate (1399).

d. Prelude to Change

The reforms proposed by Wycliffe and his movement of *Lollards*, were far from removing the dissatisfaction with the Papal and Episcopalian hierarchy. The relatively national characteristics of the English Church had not saved it from its share in the corruption in doctrine and discipline, which had gradually overspread the Western Church. Perry catalogues some of the evils:

'The knowledge of Holy Scriptures which was during the earlier Middle Ages remarkably prevalent, had in the beginning of the 16th century almost died out'. The lay-orders of the 'friars, who had been the most effective preachers of the Church for a long period and who had supplied the lack of clerical ministrations in the crowded and neglected towns, had lost the fervour of their first institution and had become the possessors of estates and grand buildings. The monks, once the living conscience of idle church kings, had fallen into a general neglect of their church rules. Therefore, monasticism had fallen into contempt. The leading clergy of the Church had ceased to have any regard for their teaching office and were content merely to govern, and that often by very questionable ways. Most of the clergy in England were completely occupied with secular employments; many of them had accumulated a great number of benefices'.[8]

Such was the situation of the Church by the end of the 15th century.[9] In addition to these ecclesiastical abuses, the social state of England was thoroughly rotten.

---

[7] McGinn, 4 ff, designates 'the followers of John Wycliffe, the Lollards of the 14th century as the direct ancestors of the Puritans of the 16th century'.
[8] Perry, pp. 2 – 6.
[9] Steven Paas, *From Galilee to the Atlantic: A History of the Church in the West*, Zomba: Kachere, 2006^2, 157-163, for a brief survey of the 15th and 16th centuries as an 'era of great change'.

Ministers and Elders

The 'wars of the roses' (1453-1483) had torn the country apart and had brought it on the verge of anarchy. Everything cried for reform.

A new era started with the reign of the Tudor Kings. They were destined to restore law and order in England. Henry VII (1485-1509) brought peace and orderly government. He stimulated education along the lines of the *Renaissance Movement* and made trade and commerce flourish again. However, his reign produced no solution for the basic problems of the Church. He was succeeded by Henry VIII (1509-1547), whose reign meant the end of papal rule in England. The Church, however, needed more than merely a change in the top of its hierarchy. A very important aspect of the early Tudor period is that the system of feudalism was dissolved. With the support of the *House of Commons* in Parliament, the power of the Lords was broken. This cleared the way for a change of the organisation of society, in agreement with the economical, social and religious requirements of the time.

Because of it, the influence of parliament was diminished temporarily. The Tudor rulers were far from promoting the democratisation of political and ecclesiastical institutions. They intended to introduce a highly centralised government, the effectiveness of which was to be safeguarded by severe judicial measures. The Tudors were in favour of reform, but in their minds, this meant that State and Church were to be reorganised in such a way that all power was centralised in the King.

3. Papacy Decapitated and Episcopacy Retained

a. Proto-Puritans Dissatisfied

The political and ecclesiastical measures taken by Henry VIII with regard, led the Church of England into a Protestant direction. That is to say, the *organisational* links with Papacy -not the *spiritual* and *doctrinal* links- were cut off. The *Henrician Reformation* established a national church-type, which became known as the *Anglican Church*. Originally, *Anglicanism* was only intended to meet the demands of English national independency. Save for the top of the hierarchical pyramid, the Roman Catholic doctrines and the Episcopalian structure were to remain unchanged. This structure fitted the Tudor ambitions of a centralised government of State and Church.

However, under the influence of Wycliffe's *Lollards* and particularly by the dissemination of the teachings of Martin Luther, many people were convinced that Henry's measures were not sufficient. Some decades later, these critics were called *Puritans*. It is easy to understand why emerging Puritans collided with Henry VIII and with almost all his Tudor and Stuart successors. They could not be satisfied with a merely political Reformation, not even with an educational or literary Reformation. Henry's eminent educational reformers like Wolsey, More, Colet and Erasmus desired to produce a Reformation without convulsion or organic change, by diffusing intelligence and destroying the grosser forms of abuse and superstition. However, the proto-Puritans wanted much more. Their concern was the authority of Scriptural doctrine. Some even claimed that everything that could not be justified from Holy Scriptures should be excluded. Gradually this brought them to the refutation of the authority of Anglican archbishops and bishops and to the conviction that the Church should be essentially independent of the State. Although during Tudor reign almost all Puritans remained in the national bishops' church, an independent attitude towards the bishops was present from the beginning.

Lloyd Jones, admitting that the term 'Puritan' was not used until 1567, asserts that Puritanism really first began to manifest itself in William Tyndale, as far back as 1524. Lloyd Jones looks upon Puritanism as a type of mind.

> 'It is an attitude, it is a spirit, and it is clear that two of the great characteristics of Puritanism began to show themselves in Tyndale. He had a burning desire that common people should be able to read the Bible. However, there were great obstacles in his way. It is the way, which he met and overcame the obstacles that shows that Tyndale was a Puritan. He issued a translation of the Bible, without the endorsement and sanction of the bishops. That was the first shot fired by Puritanism. It was unthinkable that such a thing should be done without the consent and endorsement of the bishops. But Tyndale did so.
>
> Another action on his part that was again most characteristic of the Puritans, was that he left his country without royal assent. That again was a most unusual act and most reprehensible in the eyes of the authorities. But in his anxiety to translate and print the Scriptures, Tyndale left the country without royal assent and went to Germany, and there, helped by Luther and others, he completed his great work. Those two actions were typical of what continued to be the Puritan attitude towards authority. It means the putting of truth before questions of tradition and authority, and an insistence upon the liberty to serve God in the way which you believe is the true way'.[10]

The authority of the Word of God is prevalent and normative to all other authority. With this conviction, the Puritans challenged the established Church of monarch and bishops until the end of the 17th century. An influential minority

---

[10] D.M. Lloyd Jones, *The Puritans, their Origins and Successors*, Edinburgh: The Banner of Truth, 1987, pp. 141, 142, in an address at the Westminster Conference in 1971. Tyndale is a monumental figure in the history of the English Bible, as we find in e.g. Westcott's *A General view of the history of the English Bible*, London, 1868, 173 ff., and H.W. Hoare, *Our English Bible*, London, 1911, 109 ff.

among them translated this conviction into the aspiration for the replacement of regal and Episcopal power by a Presbyterian system of church-government.

b. Anglicanism Challenged

We do not intend to write an extensive survey of the landmarks of the English Reformation. Our concern is to draw the line of Presbyterian Puritan thought on the government of the Church, as opposed to the Roman Catholic and Anglican ecclesiologies. As far as Roman ecclesiology is concerned, there was at least one aspect of it with which the Presbyterian Puritans had no need to deal. Henry VIII, in his desire to divorce his wife, was led to the decision to end all authority of the pope over the English Church, in order that he himself might be the supreme head of it. In 1534, by a number of acts, he submitted the clergy to the crown and replaced Papal Supremacy by Royal Supremacy. However, the Roman Catholic character of the Church he did not change. The majority of Henry's bishops and priests were essentially Roman Catholics, even if they had ceased to accept orders from Rome. During his reign, the structure and the doctrines of the Church remained thoroughly Roman Catholic. Also later, when most of the clergy came to be deeply influenced by the salvation-doctrines of the continental Reformation, monarch and prelates retained Roman-like ideas on the government of the Church. At least this was the opinion of the Puritans, among them those who were to be designated as Presbyterians.

Henry's attitude is most apparent from the *Ten Articles*, which he authorised in 1536 and the *Six Articles*, which were passed by Act of Parliament in 1539.[11] By these Articles, the king tried to prevent the spread of Reformation doctrines and practices. They maintained the whole fabric that is needed to uphold a Roman Catholic type of episcopacy, e.g. transubstantiation, communion in one kind, enforcement of clerical celibacy, monastic vows, private masses and auricular confession. Especially the maintaining of the Roman mass with its sacrificial character, made clear that Henry did not want to exchange sacerdotal priests for preaching ministers. The proto-Puritans on the other hand stressed the importance of the ministry of the Word of God as the central element of further reforms. In his Articles, Henry also retained the Roman Catholic costumes to be worn by the clergy. This policy with regard to the *vestments*, though these things were seemingly indifferent in themselves, would soon bring about far-reaching consequences.

---

[11] Perry, 14, 15; McGinn, 5-8. The *Six Articles* were put to force in the form of the *Act for Abolishing Diversity of Opinions in certain Articles concerning Christian Religion'*, 1539. Every clergyman had to subscribe. Some, however, refused and, like Latimer, were imprisoned, or like Hooper, fled to the continent.

The king did not hesitate to persecute Lollard and Lutheran preachers. In 1521, he had been so much angered by Luther's view on the sacraments, that he wrote a book against it.[12] The book earned him the title *Defender of the Faith*, solemnly conferred upon him by the pope. Yet before this, Henry and his Chancellor Wolsey had already begun to dissolve the monasteries. The revenues were sometimes used for the establishment and improvement of educational institutions. In this way, the Church was robbed of the source out of which the upkeep of buildings and clergy was paid. This together with the persecution of Lutheran-minded ministers diminished and weakened the already small number of preaching clergy in the Church of England.

The proceedings of Henry's divorce affair soon led to the downfall of Wolsey and the appearance of church-princes who seemed to look further than merely political Reformation. Those who were anxious for change in the spiritual state of the Church were not satisfied. Lutheranism increased daily, also in the universities of Oxford and Cambridge. There a learned clergy was bred who would become the leaders of the emerging *Puritan Movement*. Soon Lutheranism in England would be mingled with the influences of the Swiss Reformers. The day was dawning when Anglicanism had to defend itself against completely different conceptions of Church-government.

---

[12] Henry's book was entitled, *Assertio Septem Sacramentorum, adversus Martinum Lutherum, edita ab invictissimo Angliae et Franciae rege et domino Hiberniae, ejus nominus octavo*. The book was meant as an answer to Luther's writing, *On the Babylonian Captivity of the Church* (1520). Perry describes the doubts that were raised about the king's authorship. Luther replied to the book, and his reply was answered by Thomas Murner, a Franciscan Friar, who was subsequently rewarded by the king. Perry, 33-35.

Chapter 2

Church-Rule: By Whom and How?

1. Authority and church-government

a. Authority of the Scriptures

The movements of *Reformation*, *Renaissance* and *Humanism* brought about a change in the opinions on authority in State and Church. The Tudor Era is the period in which English society turned from medieval feudalism to the structures of modern times. This meant a complete rearrangement of the country's governmental system. Royal power was centralised, but at the same time from low to high, there was a tendency to independency and individual freedom. The king himself set the trend by cutting off authority of the pope in England. In addition, his people followed suit by increasing the demands of Parliament and promoting far-reaching changes in the government of the Church. Since practically all citizens were embraced by the universal membership of the *corpus christianum*, the question of church-government was of paramount importance to the position of the country's government as such.

In State and Church, the king tried to maintain absolute royal power. The Tudor monarchs tried to curtail the influence of Parliament by often dissolving it or by proroguing its sessions. Privy Council and Star Chamber were the royal institutions by which they ruled the State. Ecclesiastical matters were regulated by the monarch's obedient hierarchy of archbishops and bishops. Any other idea of church-government, be it Roman Catholic, Puritan or Anabaptists, was rejected and suppressed. However, these non-conforming groups could not be easily silenced. That is why the question of the order and office of the Church became one of the most important aspects of the English Reformation. In Henry's time, Puritanism had not yet received its name. Those who aspired the continuation of the Reformation often thought in Lutheran terms. Presbyterianism had not yet emerged as a movement, but the Reformer of Wittenberg had lit a fire that could not be contained by the semi-medieval structures of Royal Supremacy and Anglican Episcopalianism. Soon Calvin's *Institutes of the Christian Religion* (1536-1559) would bring back the ideals of old Lollardism, but then in a much more comprehensive form.

All parties in the conflict professed the absolute authority of the Holy Scriptures. However, they differed as to the question in which way the Bible was to be explained and applied. There were different opinions with regard to the authority of tradition and of the early Church. The conflict concentrated on two series of problems.

The first pertained to the question whether, according to Scripture, the office-bearer had to be understood in an Episcopalian or in a Presbyterian sense. Are New Testament terms *episcopos* and *presbyteros* used indiscriminately for the same office-bearer? Is there hierarchy or parity in the relationship between office-bearers? A simple yes or no to these questions is not always sufficient to define the dividing line between Episcopalianism and emerging Presbyterianism. Some Anglican prelates, like the archbishop Grindal, came very near to accepting parity of ministers. Many Puritan Reformers followed Calvin and Bucer in the conditional acceptance of the *episcopos* as a bishop, alongside the *presbyteros* as an elder, although they -like their Swiss teachers- did not agree with the Episcopalian regime of the Tudor church-settlements.

The second series of problems concerned the question of the origin of authority. The authority of Christ in Church and State was generally confessed. Yet how and by whom was this authority to be represented? Did the office-bearer derive his authority from kings and bishops, or was the authority of the office embedded in the local congregation of believers? Election and nomination of preachers, was it to be done by the bishop or by the congregation? Puritans, especially the Presbyterian group among them, adhered to the latter position. However, it must be kept in mind that they were no democrats and certainly no revolutionaries in the modern sense of these words. They wanted to revive the Church of the New Testament in the midst of a world in which the social, economic and political pattern of the Middle Ages was breaking and the need was felt for the remodelling of authority structures, which would leave room for more freedom of thought, initiative and enterprise.

b. Emergence of Presbyterian Thought

The ideas of the continental *Reformation Movement* invaded England and merged with existing internal attitudes in favour of reform. From a 21st century vantage point we can see that there was a tendency of *democratisation* in the Puritan Movement, which would eventually enable the citizens at the grassroots to lay hands on a much greater part of authority in State and Church. However, the Reformers of the 16th century did not work with modern aspirations of . They were not consciously aiming at the *democratisation* of political and ecclesiastical authority in terms of people's sovereignty. These were ideas of later centuries. The conception of a people's democracy was quite incongruent with their line of thought. Authority rests in God and in the King. Even extreme Puritan thinkers would not denounce the divine right of royal authority. Here they differed from the Anabaptists, but not from the Episcopalians. Differences arose on the conclusions drawn from Scripture with regard to the application and organisation of divine and royal authority: The relationship between Church and State and the internal order of the Church were at stake.

The first two phases of this great controversy ended in the 1580's. On the one side there were the Presbyterian Puritans like Thomas Cartwright. They demanded that the Church of England rid itself of all remnants of Roman Catholicism and be reorganised according to 'the order and policy' of 'the most ancient and gospel-like Church that ever was or shall be'. This was to be the Church of the Holy Scripture and the Church of early history. The first step in the rebuilding of it was the substitution of the eldership or Presbytery, for the Episcopacy and civil magistrate. On the other side, there was the Archbishop John Whitgift who maintained that Cartwright's demands were 'false principles and rotten pillars'. According to Whitgift, the Bible did not command a rebuilding of the Apostolic Church. This primitive Church was not suitable for Elizabethan England.[1] Episcopalians like Bancroft and Hooker went further than Whitgift and defended the institution of the Episcopalian structure by Christ and the Apostles and by the *apostolic tradition*.[2] Our Lord really meant the foundation of a national church under the supreme headship of a king, with a hierarchy of archbishops, bishops and parish priests. This was the position of the English Episcopalians. Their ecclesiastical nationalism became known as *Anglicanism*.

The early Puritans did not deny the duties of king and civil magistrate with regard to the Church. They often tolerated the existence of bishops. However, they saw a different church-picture arise from the Bible. The primitive Church of the New Testament was not a hierarchical organisation of dignitaries under an earthly king. God himself planted His Church as a body that is independent of earthly rulers. It is the congregation of believers, instituted by Jesus Christ, through the Holy Spirit. Christ is the King of the world and the King of the Church. In the world He rules through kings and civil magistrates. In the Church He rules through the Holy Spirit. In the Church the biblical rule that all men are equal before God, is to be applied. There is no visible fundamental difference between men, which can lead to a hierarchy. Kings, clergy and lay-people are only divided by the great rift, which runs between believers and unbelievers, between the elect and the reprobate. This rift is often invisible to men and cannot be ground for hierarchical divisions in the Church militant.

How is this Church to be governed? Many Puritans attempted to solve the question of church-government. Often their organisational structures were

---

[1] McGinn, 141
[2] Perry, 339 ff.; J.K. Luoma, 'Who owns the Fathers: Hooker and Cartwright on the authority of the primitive Church', in: *Sixteenth Century Journal*, vol. VIII, 3 (1977), pp. 45 ff.

temporary compromises with the Anglican system, which did not survive when put to the test of suppression. Only the gradually developing core of Presbyterians among them came -at least in theory- to a solid form of church-government; they believed their church order to be as close as possible to the New Testament. However, a full-fledged Presbyterian system was never established in Tudor England. Monarch and Episcopacy did not allow the State-Church to be reformed into this direction, and the time of Separation had not yet really come. Nevertheless, a coherent body of Presbyterian ideas was developed under the surface, ready to be revived at a suitable time.

Through His Holy Spirit Christ gave to His Church various and different talents. In every congregation He provides for men who are gifted for the preaching and teaching of the Word of God, for the administration of the sacraments, for the government, for the exercise of discipline, for the administration of the poor. The Church is there where these elements are present. The central figure is the *elder*. He may be preaching and ruling or only ruling, but he is the office-bearer in whom the nerves of the Presbyterian church-system are joined together. He substituted the bishop and the civil magistrate of the old system, and to him the most vital functions of the Church are entrusted. In the old Church of the Middle Ages the bishop could exist above or even without the congregation. In the New Testament pattern of Presbyterian thought this is impossible. God does not give the offices of preachers and rulers in vain or independent of the congregation. He gives them in and to the congregation. They are not hovering above the congregation but they are part of its organism. They are members with a special office. When bearing this office, they represent the authority, which Christ embodied in the whole congregation. They should be obeyed. Not because they belong to a different or higher class of people, the clergy, but because they are called to represent the power and authority of the Word of God, yes of God Himself, in the midst of His congregation.

When we refer to the Presbyterian theory of *eldership* in Biblical perspective, it must be stressed that an elder fundamentally was considered an ordinary member of the congregation, because in His Church God only knows regular ordinary members. At the same time the elder channels the Word of God to the congregation. He is the mouth of God, he is God's chosen instrument. In this sense, his position is also *opposite* the congregation. Collinson emphasises that in the Presbyterians' exalted vision of the office of preaching, there was a tendency to raise the minister *above* the people. This tendency was most apparent in the operation of regional presbyteries and synods and less in the local *seigniories* or *consistories*. According to Collinson, the early *presbyteries* in this respect already showed the danger of a new *clericalism*.³ Yet, at least in theory, the parity and purely instrumental character of the (preaching) eldership was stressed. It included that this office could never function 'ex opere operato', as an independent and exclusive channel of divine grace. In every aspect the preacher was to be dependent on the Word of God and the power of the Holy Spirit.

Here we have another important difference with the (assumed) functioning of the bishops and priests under the early Anglican system. Elders are not at a higher level of priesthood, than all other believers are. The Anglican Church, though its articles of religion point into a different -more Calvinistic- direction, in practice never completely rooted out of the idea that in the Eucharist its priests are performing something like the Roman Catholic act of sacrificing the Body and Blood of Jesus Christ. The refutation of the idea of sacrificing has characterised the position of a Presbyterian elder more than anything else. He is not a *priest* who is some way indispensably involved in the repetition, actualisation or finalisation of Christ's crucifixion. He is a minister who preaches the message of the great historic and historical event of God redeeming the world through Christ's sacrifice. A minister is only an instrument, not an indispensable element, of the way to salvation; but he is a God-willed instrument.

Eventually a large number of the clergy of the Anglican Church appeared to be receptive for Puritanism. Because of the *ejectments*, there was a growing number of preachers who had no official position in the State-Church. They were open for more radical Puritan ideas and soon accepted some program for a Presbyterian order of the church. Others went further into the direction of the theory and practice of complete independence of local congregations. Although among the bishops the Puritan-minded element was certainly not absent in these early days of the incipient movement, the Episcopacy as such recognised the threat to its own position and tried to check and suppress aspirations for change of church-government.

The Episcopalian system was interrelated with, subservient to, and safeguarded by the king or queen. That is why the original Puritans, especially the Presbyterian-minded among them, began to clash with the monarchy. They did not clash because they were enemies of the monarchy as such. Even the hardships and persecutions in the period of Elizabeth did not prevent most

---

³ P. Collinson, *The Elizabethan Puritan Movement* London: Jonathan Cape, 1967, part III, ch. 1. According to the author, the organisational structures of the first Presbyterians took the shape of an *oligarchy*. This oligarchy, though showing a new form of clericalism, was very subversive to the old clericalism of the monarchical-episcopalian system. It put the Church above the State, whereas the Tudor State had submitted the Church. In the controversy of Anglicanism versus Presbyterianism, the Monarchy acted against the Oligarchy.

Puritans from having warm feelings towards their queen. Her headship of the Church was not openly attacked, until it became clear that a compromise of having presbyteries within the Episcopalian system could not be reached. Even then the Puritans continued to recognise monarchs and civil magistrates in their specific calling to safeguard the Church from political, economic and social evils, which the ruling presbyteries were unable to ward off.

At the same time, the Presbyterian Puritans, the proto-Congregationalists, and those who tended to complete separation from the State-Church, rejected the unity scheme of the Middle Ages. They emphasised the distinction and division of the spheres of Church and State. Both are governed by Christ and in both the king and his magistrates are called to perform certain duties. On the ultra-radical side, the Puritan movement tended to cross the boundaries of Lutheran and Calvinist thought. There the authority of State and civil magistrates in church matters was rejected altogether.

c. Christ Defines the Church-Structure

Most Puritans, including those of more or less Presbyterian shades, never accepted the negative stance of ultra-radicals and Anabaptists with regard to the State. In Tudor times, the majority of them even shrank back from the establishment of independent separated congregations. However, the State should not interfere with the Church in spiritual matters. In the realm of the Church, only the Word of God has authority. God entrusted the Word to the congregations, and their presbyters. Kings and magistrates should bow under the Word of God. They should not try to make the Church an instrument of the crown. They should do their part in safeguarding and promoting the authority of the Word of God in all domains of life. The spiritual field is not domain of State authority. That is what the Presbyterian Puritans wanted to stress. This not only pertained to the doctrines of salvation, but also to the outward and inward order of the Church. The government of the Church is in its essence a spiritual matter.

The structure of the Church is defined by Jesus and the Apostles. Especially at this point, the Presbyterian Puritans clashed with monarchy-based Episcopalian opinion. Originally, the Tudor monarchs and the leaders of the State-Church professed that the organisation and government of the Church in its internal and external aspects was a thing indifferent and certainly not a spiritual or doctrinal matter. The Bible did not prescribe a specific church-structure. People of all times were free to have it their own way, according to the circumstances. In every era, people had to look for a structure, by which the Church was helped best.

The Puritans could not understand this argument. They would answer like this. If you think the church-structure is a thing indifferent, why then don't you leave us our own views and practices? To them the Anglican stance appeared to be weak. It was neither based on Scripture, nor on logics. Therefore, they continued their struggle. Later, the Episcopalian theologians made much effort to link their church-structure with the details of Scripture and to early church history. However, they could not convince the Presbyterians anymore of the rights of Episcopacy.

Although the 16th century Presbyterians consciously belonged and adhered to the national Church of England, gradually they acquired characteristics which separated them from the other Anglicans. In the beginning, they did not differ from many Anglicans in the reformed views on salvation. However, in the end of our period the cleavage was not merely a question of temporal, economic and administrative differences. Anglican fundamental theology began to be gradually mingled with a line of thought that was not born in the Wittenberg, Zürich and Geneva of the original Reformers. Anglican divines like Richard Hooker construed a theological system with more humanism in it than the Calvinistic Puritans could bear. Differences began to arise also in matters of fundamental doctrine, like those of man, Scripture, the sacraments, eschatology. However, in our period the main emphasis was still on the ecclesiology side of the conflict. Lloyd Jones summarises the differences like this:

> 'The Puritan emphasises the spirituality of worship; the Anglican emphasises the formal aspect of worship', has less concern about the pastoral side of the work, is 'more interested in the mechanics of worship. The Puritan is interested in fellowship' and has an 'international outlook'. The Anglican is 'more individualistic' and has a 'national outlook'. 'The gathered Church is at the heart of the Puritan idea', locally but also internationally. 'Puritans also believed in the ferreting out of sin and in a rigid church-discipline. The Anglicans tended to be content with outward conformity'.[4]

d. Three Phases

Long before Puritanism got its name, the struggle for power and authority in matters of the Church began. Roughly three periods are to be distinguished.

First, the pre-Reformation period, in which popes, kings and parliament more or less balanced their power without changing the abusive internal situation of the Church. Then, the period of the Henrician Reformation, in which the pope, as the extreme consequence of Episcopalianism, was excluded from the government of the Church. We dealt with these two periods in the previous

---

[4] Lloyd Jones, 256, 257

chapter. Thirdly, there was the period, in which the supremacy of the monarch in church-matters and the Episcopalian system itself were challenged by a surfacing and growing Puritan movement.

The three periods are three distinct phases in the history of the ideas on church-order and church-government. Who governs the Church?

In the first phase, struggle between the leaders of the universal Roman system and the head of a strengthened national State alternated with cooperation in their mutual interest. As long as pope and king saw their positions served by mutual support, they left to each other part of the authority over the Church. However, when parliament grew stronger the national interests required so, the king tried to win more independency. In the second phase, the national State and its king refused to be hindered anymore by universal papal power, and shed it. The king substituted the pope as head of the Church. The system of archbishops, bishops, priests and the doctrinal state, he left more or less untouched, as they served his royal national power. However, the late Middle Ages had unleashed energies of reform that could not be completely checked by the *Henrican Settlement*. In the third phase, the reforming powers were getting momentum. Inspired by the teachings of both Testaments of the Bible and of the primitive Church, the early Puritans were not satisfied with superficial reforms. They wanted a fundamental resettlement of the Church in nearly all its practices and doctrines. They aspired a reformed Church, in which the parishes together with their regional and national upper structures were to be governed by the Word of God only. Kings, civil magistrates and ecclesiastical prelates must vacate places of power and influence for the living Word of God, as it was to be proclaimed by the congregation-born and divinely called elder or minister.

In this way, the focus point of the struggle shifted from the power of the pope, to the authoritative positions of king and bishops, to the wrestling Puritans for the exclusive authority of the Bible, heralded by preaching and ruling elders. In the reign of Henry VIII, Presbyterianism had not yet been born as a movement. Later, when the *Puritan Movement* emerged, the Presbyterians always were a minority movement among them. The choice for a more radically Puritan or Presbyterian Reformation was made in a climate of repression by the Tudor regimes and of increasing contacts with the Reformers on the European Continent. Both, though in different ways, stimulated reformation of church-government and church-discipline. Eventually, the birth of Presbyterian structures was the most obvious result of it.

2. Continental Models demand Completion

a. The Gap is too Wide

The English Reformation in its different stages, has been continually influenced by the Reformation on the continent. The Lutheran, Zwinglian and Calvinistic aspects and phases of the continental Reformation had their impact in England, on both sides of the deepening rifts between Anglicans and Puritans. Both sides, at times, solicited the support of the German and Swiss Reformers. However, the reception of continental thought was different, as both sides often expected different things.

The policy of Henry VIII divided the partly reformed English Church. There were those, like Chancellor Thomas More, who rejected the king's enterprises, because they did not want to lose the connection with Rome. The majority of the king's dignitaries, however, followed him without heeding the lack of scriptural foundations of his measures. Others took an ambiguous position. To them belonged the newly made archbishop of Canterbury, Thomas Cranmer, who had been instrumental in Henry's divorce proceedings. Cranmer c.s. grew to the conviction that the Reformation of the English Church was in need of completion, and that continental models could be helpful. However, they lacked courage or were simply not prepared to sacrifice their influential positions. They hoped for better times and meanwhile they indulged the king's church-policy.

Real opposition came from those who were not only conscious of the questions at stake, but also drew the conclusions. To these scriptural Reformers, like William Tyndale, John Hooper and Miles Coverdale, the king's policy was intolerable. At this stage, ideas of church-government by elders, seigniories and presbyteries had not been formed yet. Later some of these Reformers even did not agree with the anti-bishop attitude of the Presbyterians. These people, however, realised that between the *Henrican Church Settlement* and the Church of the New Testament, there was a wide gap. They knew that this gap was defined by much more than matters of ceremonies and clerical dress. Henry's Church was still fundamentally a popish Church. That was what they wholeheartedly rejected. That is why they clashed with the king and had to flee to the European continent.

b. Waves of Exiles

This flight of English proto-Puritans to continental Western Europe has been of great importance for the development of the Church-doctrine of the Puritans movement. Lloyd Jones' comment on these Henrican exiles is worth reading:

'They went to the continent and while there they came under the influence of Bullinger, and still more the teaching of Zwingli, who had been teaching at Zürich before Bullinger, and John Calvin at Geneva and others. Now Zwingli was a very radical Reformer. He had made a clean sweep in the matter of ceremonies and dress of the clergy. These Englishmen were greatly influenced by this, with the result that quite soon they were not content merely with being opposed to Roman Catholic doctrine. Until this point that had more or less been their position. They had their eyes opened to the errors of Roman Catholic teachings and were objecting to it. But now, under this continental influence they went a step further and began to object to religious ceremonialism. They now began to feel that the Reformation was incomplete, and that it was not enough merely to change the doctrine and get rid of false Roman Catholic teaching. The Reformation had to be carried through and worked out in terms of practice also. The notion of an incomplete Reformation came on'.[5]

This feeling of an incomplete Reformation, born under the influence of particularly the Swiss Reformers, is called by Lloyd Jones 'the most characteristic note of Puritanism'. The Reformation had not gone far enough. As to this opinion, the *Henrican Exiles* and many Englishmen at home agreed. However, they were not unanimous about what should be done. Tyndale would soon be murdered at Vilvoorde near Antwerp, as a victim of the Roman Catholic *Inquisition*. Henry's regime certainly shared responsibility for his cruel death. Yet, Tyndale was not a revolutionary opponent to the king's church-settlement. He only wanted freedom for the translation and proclamation of the Word of God. He was even prepared to tolerate the Roman-like ceremonies and dresses, as long as they were explained to the people.[6] However, this relative tolerance was not generally accepted. Here we have a prelude of later divisions among the Puritans. There were others -like Hooper- who said that these 'outward' things were intolerable. They were relics of Roman Catholicism and they must be got rid of.

Completion of Reformation! That was the burning desire of all Puritans, even in the time when the designation 'Puritan' was not yet known. Under Henry VIII they were persecuted as 'Lutherans'. After his reign those who had to flee, returned from the continent, filled with the teachings of the Swiss and German Reformers. King Edward's Lords Protector gave room to those who tried to turn the English Church into a more Protestant direction. However, the Roman Catholic regime of Mary and the *via media* policies of

---

[5] Lloyd Jones, 240 ff.
[6] Though independent of Luther, Tyndale was influenced by the Wittenberg Reformer. This is worked out by Westcott, pp. 192-202. Luther was certainly not a radical with regard to vestments and certain old ceremonies. Later Puritans came under the influence of the Swiss Reformers who were more critical towards the old rites and customs.

Ministers and Elders

Elizabeth produced other waves of Puritan refugees and of individual flights. These groups too became deeply influenced by the continental Reformers, and they too channelled the ideas of Zürich and Geneva to England.

In this chapter, we tried to explain the questions that were at stake with regard to the problem of church-government. In defining those questions Anglicans and Puritans were all but isolated from the Reformation Movement on the European continent. The examples of Reformers like Luther, Zwingli, Bullinger, Bucer and Calvin played a very important role in the further development of Puritan ecclesiology and in its conflict with the Anglican Episcopacy and the crown. The Anglicans in general were influenced by the European Reformation. In a wider sense Anglicanism developed as a part of the European Reformation. However, as to the government of the Church the conformist main stream of Anglicans adopted only those theories and practices of the Reformers that suited their own national, Episcopalian and monarchist vision of the Church. Both sides in the Anglican-Puritan conflict used the ideas of the Reformers and at times claimed their support, though in a different way and with different objectives. Therefore, in the next chapter we will summarise the aspect of church-government in the continental Reformation.

Chapter 3

Continental Reformers and the Church

1. The Ideas of the Reformers

a. Break with Rome

Just like the *Henrician Reformation* in England, the *Continental Reformation* abolished the authority of the pope over the Church; and by consequences also over the State. However, the qualifications of this abolishment, were quite different. In England, it was a king, who first cut off the links with the Papacy. He was not motivated by the mood of the Scriptural Reformers, neither by spiritual dissatisfaction of his own subjects. Political and personal motives inspired him in the first place. He retained Roman Catholic doctrine. On the continent, however, the Habsburg Emperor, the national and regional princes, and the independent city magistrates were not first in removing the Papacy from the ecclesiastical and political scene. It is true that the Habsburg Emperor and the French King, though entangled in a competitive mutual struggle, both tried to get the upper hand over the pope, thus making him subservient to their political objectives. However, they did not break the traditional Papal structure of the Church.

This break was initiated by a number of ecclesiastical Reformers. Their ideas not only brushed aside Papal authority, but also swept away almost the entire Episcopalian structure of the Church in large areas of Europe. They developed and introduced alternative forms of church-government at local, regional and national levels. Many territorial princes supported the Protestant reorganisation of the Church. There were those who favoured it as an instrument to reach independence from the Holy Roman Empire of the German Nation and the centralising aspirations of its Habsburg rulers. Some of them, like Stadtholder William of Orange (The Netherlands) and Landgrave Philip of Hessen, were real adherents to the Reformation. An important role was played by the cities, which had acquired a privileged position and were anxious to safeguard their relative independence against the universal claims of the clergy and the Church. The Reformation was in line with essential elements of their aspirations. The city-councils contributed greatly to the destruction of the old system of church-government and to the establishment of new forms. An important instrument was the organisation of religious *disputations* between representatives of the old system and defenders of a reformed church-order. The city-council's judgement at the disputation was almost invariably in favour of those who desired to recognise the Church according to Lutheran, Zwinglian, Bucerian and Calvinist principles.[1]

At empire level, there were also religious disputations. Under the umbrella of Charles V, Roman-Catholic and Reformed theologians and politicians tried to reach a consensus with regard to a great number of doctrinal and organisational bones of contention. Martin Bucer, the Strasbourg Reformer was a central figure in those meetings. However, in Regensburg, 1541, the attempts for a compromise proved to be a failure, because of irreconcilable contradictions concerning church-government and sacraments. As to the doctrine of the Church, Rome refused to accept any alternative structure.[2] Subsequently, at the Council of Trent Rome hardened its claims of exclusive Papal and Episcopalian authority over the Church. These developments meant that the Reformation on the continent distanced itself from the entire Roman Catholic church-structure. Not only the pope was ejected, but also the whole hierarchy of cardinals, archbishops, bishops, priests and deacons were toppled. Unlike England, where the Episcopacy was gradually reshaped in a Protestant sense, continental Protestantism generally did not retain forms of the old Episcopalian system.

b. The Lutheran position

This is not to say that the continental Reformers always agreed to one another in their adoption of new church-orders and alternative forms of church-government. Some of the original Reformers were no contemporaries. They did not all live in the same political situation, and there were shades of difference as to the conclusions to be drawn from Scripture and from the early church fathers. Therefore, they sometimes differed notably in their solutions to the problem of

---

[1] C.f. Hollerbach, *Das Religionsgespräch als Mittel der Konfessionellen und politischen Auseinandersetzung im Deutschland des 16. Jahrhunderts*, Peter: Frankfort am Main, 1982. In the late Middle Ages, academic disputation became a method of scholasticism. It was used as a way of taking decisions as to the question of who is right, when there were conflicting opinions. Civil magistrates in the Reformation era considered the disputation as a suitable means for the silencing of opinions that hindered the introduction of political and ecclesiastical reforms.

[2] Cf. C. Augustijn, *De godsdienstgensprekken tussen rooms-katholieken en protestanten van 1538-1541*, Haarlem: De Erven Bohn, 1967. As to the doctrine of justification, Bucer and Gropper worked out a complicated compromise in the so-called 'Regensburger Buch'. Their description of 'duplex iustificatio' was accepted by the Papal representative, Cardinal Contarini. However, the conferences broke apart on the issues of ecclesiology and sacramental doctrine. Rome could not accept, that the Church is not a communio sacramentorum, but a communio sanctorum. Cf. R. Stupperich, *Der Humanismus und die Wiedervereinigung der Religionen*, Leipzig: Heinsius, 1936, who gives insight in the influence of Erasmian religious humanism in the religious conferences of the 16th century. Cf. Steven Paas, *A Conflict on the Church and the Sacraments: How Rome and the Reformation Differed at Regensburg in 1541*, Zomba: Kachere, 2006.

church-government. The Presbyterian idea of ruling and preaching elders, substituting the bishops and the civil-magistrates, was not generally accepted. The Lutherans even went into a different direction and chose for a system, which retained certain elements of the old Episcopalian structure. This was most apparent in their vision of the congregation. Common church-members were excluded from the procedures of election and nomination of ministers. However, there were also differences among those who adopted the Reformed-Presbyterian line. The Reformation movements, centred in Strasbourg, Zürich and Geneva, are interrelated and bear similar characteristics. At the same time, they reflect important shades of difference with regard to the order of the congregation, and the positions of ministers and ruling elders. However, differences should not be over-accentuated. Actually, the Calvinist type of congregations governed by ruling and preaching elders is the result of a gradual development, which began in Lutheran Wittenberg, proceeded to Bucerian Strasbourg and Zwinglian Zürich, finally culminating in Calvin's Geneva.

Yet the Lutherans could not accept the solutions by Calvinism. They created authority structures above the congregation, which were occupied by regional princes and superintendents, thus leaving the lay-members of the congregation without any say in matters of the Church. Their structure is not an imitation of the old Episcopacy of Rome, as Anglicanism is. However, there are similarities. One could say that the Lutheran opposition to Presbyterianism, like the Anglican objections, came from the right. Lutheran and Anglicanism theories of church-government bore a conservative character. However, they were not the only opponents of Presbyterian church-order.

2. The Reformers and the Radicals

a. No Divine Right for Elders?

Presbyterianism was also attacked from the left side of the Reformation, that is to say from the more progressive and radical quarters of this movement.

Van Ginkel, in his thesis on the *elder*, summarises the Reformers' views on church-government and the origins of their theories. He 'makes an attempt to describe how the Presbyterian church-structure came into being and to value the same structure'. First, he deals with the question whether there was reason for such a high estimation of the office of *elders*. Details of the Old Testament, the New Testament and the early church-history are researched by him. Then he reviews the opinions of the 16th century Reformers Luther, Zwingli, Bullinger, Oecolampadius, Bucer and Calvin. Finally, he draws the conclusion that the office of *elders* 'originated from the need for church-discipline and supervision', and that 'the theological foundation was thought of only later on'. Therefore, in his view Presbyterians were pragmatists. They did not found their views on Scripture, but they were inspired in the first place by contemporary political and social circumstances. The elder fitted the aspirations for political and social change and cannot be derived from the Word of God, at least not in the traditionally Presbyterian sense of the word. In this sense, Van Ginkel rejects the divine right of eldership and therefore of the whole Presbyterian model. So far, his highly critical conclusion more or less coincides with the objections of Lutherans and Anglicans, as we shall see in the dispute between Cartwright and Whitgift. However, Van Ginkel's opinion does not mean to favour Lutheranism and certainly not Anglicanism.

Van Ginkel's critical stance towards the Calvinist type of Presbyterianism 'should not be directed towards the Episcopal tradition, but on the contrary, in the sense of a further democratisation'. In his view, the Presbyterian Reformation is not radical enough. It still contains certain elements of the old hierarchy, especially by elevating the minister above common people. In a way, there is agreement between Van Ginkel and Collinson in the opinion that Presbyterianism in practice often existed as an *oligarchy*, which did not leave sufficient room for the development of various other functions of the Christian congregation.[3]

Although we cannot interpolate Van Ginkel's view in the developments of the 16th century, it is obvious that he reflects an old tradition of opposition, not only against conservative Episcopalian thought, but also against less conservative Presbyterian thought. In 16th century Europe, there were those who not only despised the Roman Catholic, Lutheran and Anglican types of church-government, but also the elder-centred Reformed Presbyterian rule of the Church. They considered the introduction of elders in Strasbourg and Geneva as the establishment of a new form of tyranny. Whereas Presbyterianism professed the government by elders as an instrument for the completion of the Reformation, these more progressive groups thought them stumble blocks on the road to completion and perfection. They did not reject the idea of eldership as such, but they could not stomach the way in which Bucerian, Zwinglian and Calvinist ruling bodies operated and were nominated.

b. Anabaptist Radicalism

On the European continent, radicalism in the Reformation particularly developed under the umbrella of the *Anabaptists*. Friedman describes their ecclesiology as eschatological and covenantal, a suffering brotherhood of voluntary members, an empiric visible community of the Holy Supper; under

---

[3] A. van Ginkel, *De Ouderling*, Amsterdam: Ton Bolland, 1975, 295-312, 323, 324

the rule of independently chosen elders with far reaching authority to discipline and ban members of the congregation. Perfection of sanctity under the authority of the Spirit-given 'inner-light'; that was the ultimate objective of these groups.[4] Luther rejected them right away, because they did not fit his doctrine of justification by faith alone and his conservative idea of church-order. The Reformers of the South-German and Swiss city-states could better understand the radical aspirations of Anabaptist ecclesiology. They even made the Church an instrument for the promotion of discipline and sanctity, partly as an answer to the demands by Anabaptists. However, in the end, Strasbourg became less friendly to the radicals, Zürich persecuted them, and the gates of Geneva were kept shut to them. Apart from objections against their subjective views on salvation, the Reformers distrusted their anti-social behaviour. The radicals refused to recognise the prevailing political and ecclesiastical institutions, even if they were Reformed. Princes and civil-magistrates feared their revolutionary spirit, which at times could inspire to violent uprisings. Political leaders sometimes did not recognise the difference between Anabaptism and the mainstream Reformation. Therefore, political and military measures against Anabaptist 'breakers of the society' could threaten the progress of the Reformation movement as such. This was the political background of the Reformers' rejection of the Anabaptist 'free church' idea. Their fear was closely related to their scriptural and spiritual objections.

In England, the Anabaptists were not numerous. Radical opposition emerged within the *Puritan Movement* itself and differed from Anabaptism because Puritan adhered to general Reformed theology, and they did not demonise the State as a matter of principle. Radical groups were often named after their founders or leaders, Brownists, Harrowists, Barrowists, Greenwoodians, or just Separatists. They propagated the severing of all links between the spheres of the Church and the State, and they separated from the Anglican Church long before Presbyterian Puritans showed signs of secession. The type of elders proposed by the Swiss and Strasbourg Reformers they could not accept, because these elders, as they saw them, again constituted the despised authority link with the State, being as they were *lay-officers* who very often operated as representatives of the civil magistrate i.e. the city-council.

Noticing that the Reformers were no Separatists, we have to realise that they shaped their anti-separatism especially in reaction to *Anabaptism* and much less to extreme radicalism within the mainline Reformation. Let us elaborate a little more on the motives of the Reformers. Their intention was not the foundation of independent sectarian churches. However, they had a vision of the one Church of Jesus Christ, healed and purified. In practice, this meant that they

---

[4] R. Friedman, *The Theology of Anabaptists*, Scottdale: Herald Press, 1975. Part III, E.

often seemed to hold a middle-position, which the Anabaptists condemned as a compromise with the world. Although they distanced themselves rigorously from the Papal hierarchy of the Roman Catholic Church and its practice, they were ready to retain certain old forms and customs and to indulge certain things which they considered to be *adiaphora*, things of lesser importance. In the opinion of the radicals, this moderate attitude hindered the progress of the Reformation. The Reformers, on the other hand, feared that the *Reformation Movement* would be broken apart or at least weakened by the forces of radicalism. Nearly all Reformers, after a period of formulating their opposition against Rome, felt the need of balancing their views, because of the danger of extremism, which appeared on their left.

d. Radical and Magisterial Reformers

Williams in his study, *The Radical Reformation*, pictures the radical movement of Anabaptists, Spiritualists and Evangelical Rationalists and he distinguishes them from the *Magister Reformation* i.e. the Reformation by Luther, Zwingli, Bucer, Calvin, c.s. There was a whole range of fundamental differences between these two movements. Actually, the objective of the Anabaptist Radicals was not Reformation, but Restitution was their adagium. They envisaged a complete break with the old order of Church and State. Restitution of the primitive Church of the New Testament meant to them the doing away of all thinkable characteristics of the medieval Church and the foundation of an absolutely new one. This also included a most rigorous rupture of the Church-unity scheme of the Christian commonwealth, as history from Constantine onwards had developed it. The radicals completely rejected the idea that the civil magistracy would be in anyway involved in ecclesiastical matters.[5]

The *Magisterial Reformers* of Wittenberg, Zürich, Strasbourg and Geneva worked with a much more positive vision of the State. They were men of law and order. Internal and external anarchy was the thing they feared. The Reformation was often realised with the help of princes and civil-magistrates. They saw the orderly government and discipline of the Church threatened by the Radicals. In their opinion, a miscarriage of the whole Reformation would be immanent, if the Radicals got the upper hand. Therefore, they cooperated with the civil-magistrates in taking severe measures against them. At the same time, they left the magistracy a say in the government of the Church. Their comparatively conservative ideas of reform did not envisage revolution, but evolution, not an abrupt break with existing structures, but continuation on a different line of development.

---

[5] G.H. Williams, *The Radical Reformation*, Philadelphia: The Westminster Press, 1962.

Continental Reformers and the Church

This is most clearly reflected in their conceptions of church-government. The Lutherans diminished the significance of hierarchical Episcopacy. However, the congregation was left without authority, and the regional prince emerged as a kind of emergency-bishop. The South-German and Swiss churches absorbed part of the proto-democracy theories of the city republics. Their ruling and preaching elders not only operated as functionaries of the congregation, but they were also dependent on the State. The Radicals interpreted this as unfaithfulness to the Lord who commanded a break with the affairs of the world. A clean break with the world meant to them: restoration of the pre-Constantinian Church to be reconstructed after the model of the New Testament. The classical Reformers also wanted to apply the New Testament model. However, they did not accept the radicals' interpretation of Scripture and tradition. Their organic view of Scripture prevented them from a spiritualist and revolutionary course.

The continental conflict between the *Magisterial Reformation* and the *Radical Reformation* also spread to England. The context was different as English Radicalism was not Anabaptist in the first place. Radicalism found fertile soil in circles of Wycliffe's *Lollards*. In the reign of Edward VI, various radical groups appeared in public. Henry Hart was the first who defended complete separation of Church and State. He was an Anabaptist, but like we said before Anabaptism did not have many followers in England. Radicalism with regard to the question of church-government soon emerged within the *Puritan Movement*. This movement could easily have split into a far greater number of disorderly functions and sections than happened really, if there had not been the moderating and disciplinary influence of the Continental Reformers. Some of the Reformers left more traces in English church-history than others. However, the various shades of their influence can be recognised in the wider spectrum of Anglicans and Independents, of Puritans and Separatists, of conforming Puritans and nonconforming Puritans, of Anglican Puritans and Presbyterian Puritans, of Established Church and Dissent. The questions of church-order, church-government and church-discipline play an important role in these divisions and in the lines of thought that produced them. Here we want to picture the impact of the continental Reformers to the Anglican-Presbyterian conflict on church-government. A review of their theories and practices will be given, before we return to the English scene.

3. Martin Luther

a. Communio Sanctorum

The father of the 16th century Reformation did not choose for a Presbyterian church-order. The question is whether he ever made a choice for any definite form of church-government. According to Lohse, Luther never designed an ecclesiological programme. Only in the course of the conflict certain conceptions were born.[6] He certainly cherished the idea of free self-constituted congregations according to the New Testament pattern. The Church as a *communio sanctorum*, in which all believers were members of the Evangelical priesthood. However, in practice he did not work with this ideal. The offices of the Church are constituted in confluent actions from below and from above. They are derived from the priesthood of all believers and at the same time, they are a divine institution.

b. Princes rule the Church

However, gradually this harmonious balance was broken in Luther's thought. More and more he came to emphasising only the aspect of the office of the minister as a divine institution. Luther did not introduce lay-elders alongside the preachers. He also maintained a kind of ecclesiastical hierarchy, leaving the place of ruling bishops to *regional princes*. It was not the congregations but these princes who nominated the preachers, directly, or later through superintendents. However, Luther rejected the idea of *apostolic succession* through bishops and he defended parity of parish-ministers and bishops in their synods. Lohse therefore designates the Lutheran system as *Synodical-Episcopalian*.[7]

b. Princes Rule the Church

As to the common members of the congregation, in Luther's opinion they were neither able to call, elect and nominate their own preachers, nor to produce elders who could be responsible for the government and the discipline of the Church. Therefore, he needed bishops, no imitations of the Roman prelates, but evangelical pastors who could supervise the parishes and their ministers. Because no bishops joined the Reformation Movement, and because the political and religious situation required leadership, the Reformer of Wittenberg

---

[6] B. Lohse, *Martin Luther, eine Einführung in sein Leben und sein Werk*, München: Beck, 1981, part v, section 1. In medieval theology, the doctrine of ecclesiology was not the central theme. There was no well-defined conception of the Church. Luther was not drawn to his Reformation by the ecclesiology question. He was led to independent views of church-order, only later, when his opponents pressed him. Cf. Paas, *From Galilee to the Atlantic*, 172

[7] Lohse, part v, section 5

called in the princes and civil-magistrates, to whom he left the carrying through of the Reformation as to the order and government of the Church. This led to the establishment of territorial state-churches, in which only those lay-members took part in the government, who belonged to the magistracy. The great mass of believers had no more say in ecclesiastical matters, than in the days of the old Roman system.

This result of Lutheran development was not in accordance with Luther's original vision of the priesthood of all believers. Nor did it fit his doctrine of the two kingdoms, the one of the present and the one of the coming *aion*. He always saw the operation of princes in the church as an emergency solution. In his, *Von der weltlichen Obrigkeit*, he called the civil authorities to their duty of safeguarding the progress of the Reformation. Here Luther definitely did not mean that civil rulers had to take permanent positions of all-embracing authority over church matters.

Much of what Lutheranism soon became, was not meant so by Luther himself. One of the causes of this development is that Luther did not draw the right consequence from his basic belief of church-members as a communion of saints. He dared not accept that the congregation as a spiritual body, built by the Holy Spirit, would provide for all the required functions and offices. Bucer and Calvin were to emphasise this very pneumatological aspect of the congregation. Therefore, more than Luther, they could entrust to the congregation the functions of self-government. However, this does not mean that the Lutheranism adopted a type of episcopacy in which bishops are the exclusive channels of the Spirit to the congregation. Quanbeck, in his study on the authority-question in the Lutheran Church, says: 'Lutherans share with Reformed Christians and with the left wing Reformation a skeptical attitude toward the proposition that God had willed Episcopal orders. Against those who maintain that succession of Episcopal orders, they believe that the perpetuity of the Church is the sovereign work of the Spirit'.[8]

The problem of the office of the church has vertical and horizontal aspects. It is to be deplored that Lutheranism remains vague about the question whether a system of bishops is a legal representation of the vertical aspect. This vagueness could be the result of the lack of attention for the horizontal aspect of the office, i.e. for the office as an integral part of the organic spiritual body of Christ. Vertical and horizontal aspects are confluent in the office-bearer. This is definitely one of Luther's original ideas. In addition, the horizontal and the vertical are also the aspects of the congregation as such. This was too much lost

---

[8] W.A. Quanbeck, 'The Formula of Concord, and Authority in the Church', in: *Sixteenth Century Journal*, , vol. VIII 4, 1977, 56-59

sight of in later Lutheran thought.⁹ Here his incomplete conception of church-government was picked up by the Swiss and Strasbourg Reformers, who developed it further.

4. Huldrych Zwingli

a. A Christian Commonwealth

The political climate in South Germany and Switzerland was much more marked by the rise of independent city-states than that of North-Germany. In those tiny city-republics citizens took part in the election of their magistracies and they also demanded influence in the affairs of the Church. Van Ginkel, in declared agreement with Kühler, thinks that in Zürich we find the origin of the government by *presbyters* or *seniors* in the Reformed churches. However, at the same time he admits that these *seniors* never had any significance as bearers of an independent ecclesiastical office.¹⁰ Zwingli did not introduce *elders* in the later sense of the word. He allowed the citizen-chosen magistracy to govern the Church. His *elders*, or 'älteren in namen der Kilchen' were not much more than the members of a vice-squad, without real authority. It was the civil magistrate who exercised church-discipline, and who had a final say in the government of the Church. Zwingli's vision of the Church is certainly inspired by his great respect for the preaching of the Word of God. His community-idea does not allow a separation of Church and State. When the Word of God is proclaimed, the Holy Spirit moulds a *commonwealth*, in which Church and State are knit together to a unity. All functions of this comprehensive *commonwealth* are to be mobilised in the struggle for sanctification and purification of all spheres of life.¹¹

Zwingli's theories matured under the challenge of Anabaptist Radicals, who wanted free and holy churches. The demand for holiness he tried to meet by the introduction of ecclesiastical discipline. However, the exercise of discipline he did not give in the hands of independent elders, as the Anabaptists desired, but of the city-council. The Anabaptist demand for free churches was rejected by Zwingli. He feared the tendency of anarchy in the radical movement. This was another reason why he needed the civil magistrates. They should defend the Church against the turmoil of Anabaptism. The *presbyteroi* of the New Testament were to be found in the city-council!

In 1525, the magistracy's authority over the Church took shape in the establishment of a court for matrimony-affairs, the *Züricher Ehegericht*, with far

---

⁹ C.f. Van Ginkel, 47-61
¹⁰ Van Ginkel, 74
¹¹ G.W. Locher, *Huldrych Zwingli in neuer Sicht,* Zürich: Zwingli Verlag, 1969, Part VII, section 17

reaching supervisory and disciplinary powers. Although Zwingli offered the magistracy the rights of the Church, during his life the Zürich Church was not a real State Church. His powerful prophetic ideal of an all-embracing political and religious community bound Church and State together in a certain harmony. At the same time the Church, *Kilchören*, organised in disciplined nucleus-congregations, *Kilchören*, remained distinguishable from the State. State and Church formed a unity after the ideal of the Old Testament. However, the Church kept its recognisable identity and a certain degree of independency.[12]

b. Supremacy of the State

After Zwingli's death, under his successor Bullinger, the State gradually acquired a position above the Church. State and Church merged to a kind of unity in which the independent authority of the Church was completely dissolved.[13] Although Bullinger wholeheartedly cooperated with Calvin, his *ceasaro-papist* vision of a Church under the State, differed fundamentally from the Genevan Reformer's ideal of a theocracy in which Church and State cooperated on the same level beside each other.[14]

Zürich's State supremacy over the Church was soon designated with the term *Erastianism*, after the contemporary Swiss theologian Thomas Erastus. In a dispute with Calvin's successor Beza, Erastus professed the ascendancy of the State over the Church. He claimed that the civil authorities had the right and duty to exercise jurisdiction in both civil and ecclesiastical matters. Bullinger sided with Erastus against the Calvinist line of thought, expressed by Beza c.s. According to Van Ginkel he did so, because he feared an emerging clerical oligarchy in churches governed by *presbyteries*.[15] Therefore, he condemned everything that was opposed to the authority of the State over the Church. At the same time Van Ginkel admits that Bullinger's *Erastianism* was more than an incident. It was a consequence of his Zwinglian community-idea, which in its hardened form had no room for *ruling elders* or *presbyteries*.

Zwingli and Bullinger, more than Luther, emphasised the pneumatological character of the congregation, as the Body of Christ built by the Holy Spirit. However, the final result of their thought was not positive for the independent life of this spiritual body. Too many of its vital functions were taken away. Under Lutheranism the State filled up the gap caused by an

---

[12] Locher, Part I, section 6. In Zwingli's thought the Church, though part of the commonwealth, is free. It exercises the office of a guardian, the 'Wächteramt'. Cf. Paas, *From Galilee to the Atlantic*, 176, 177
[13] Locher, 284, 285
[14] Cf. Locher, Part I, section 6, and Van Ginkel, 75
[15] Van Ginkel, 77

assumed lack of capacities in the congregation. Under Zwinglianism, the independent functions of the Church were dispersed by the fiction that the community of the Church could not exist in a balanced bipolarity with the State. In this thought the functions of the Church were taken over by the State. Zwingli's minister was presented as a *Wächter*, a guardian of the Word of God in the *commonwealth* of Church and State. However, the spiritual community of the Church was dissolved in this *commonwealth*, because its functionaries operated too much as the officials of an Erastian State.

5. Martin Bucer

a. Relative Obscurity

Bucer's ideas have been of tremendous impact for the English situation, more than those of the three Reformers mentioned above. The Strasbourg Reformer spent the last period of his active life, as a refugee in England. More than any other continental Reformer, he was quoted by Anglicans and Puritans alike.

Bucer developed his concrete proposals for church-government in cooperation with other Reformers, like Oecolampadius of Basel.[16] Oecolampadius, unlike Zwingli and Bullinger, was convinced of the necessity of an independent church-institute with supervisory powers of the exercise of order and discipline, in which members of the congregation worked together with their ministers. Bucer's ability to work out a comprehensive system of Presbyterian church-government rested in the whole of his theology. More than with Luther, Zwingli and Bullinger, his vision of church-government was in harmony with the rest of his teachings. This emphasises the importance of his ideas. Besides, he was very influential on the main-founder of Presbyterianism, John Calvin.

Remarkably enough, writers of church-history left Bucer in comparative obscurity for a long time. A comprehensive study of his conception of the office of the Church was not available until 1970, when Van 't Spijker published his thesis on the subject. We owe much to him for the following survey of Bucer's thoughts on the internal and external characteristics of church-order.[17]

---

[16] Van Ginkel, 8 ff; Van't Spijker, 205 ff

[17] W. Van 't Spijker, *The Ecclesiastical Offices in the Thought of Martin Bucer*, Leyden: Brill, 1996 [transl. of: *De ambten bij Martin Bucer,* Kok Kampen, 2nd edition, 1987] In this thesis the author describes the development of Bucer's ideas from the beginning of his career in Strasbourg, up to the end of his life in England. As to the comparison of Bucer's conception of church-government with that of Calvin, we used Van Ginkel's *De Ouderling.*

b. Christology and Pneumatology

Interwoven in the whole of Bucer's theology, a new conception arose of the priesthood of all believers. Luther had also stressed the common priesthood of believers. However, contrary to Luther, Bucer fully recognised the pneumatic character of this doctrine. The congregation is a spiritual community, the Body of Christ, bound together by the work of the Holy Spirit. Zwingli also recognised the spiritual character of the congregation but only in the second place. With Zwingli, so Van 't Spijker stresses, christology was the visible side of pneumatology, whereas with Bucer pneumatology was the visible side of christology.

It should be emphasised that Bucer's pneumatology, though playing a very important role, was not worked out independently of other spheres of doctrine, like with some of the Anabaptists and Spiritualists. Stephens emphasises that in Bucer's thought the Holy Spirit works by means of the Word of God, the sacraments and church-discipline.[18] In addition, Van Ginkel is of the opinion that certain bipolarity' in Bucer's ecclesiology prevented him from dispersing the visibility of the Church into sheer spiritualism. His two poles are the work of the Holy Spirit and the incarnation of Christ.[19] The congregation is a pneumatic community, worked by and kept alive by the Holy Spirit. However, this spirituality is not invisible. It is visible as the spiritual Body of Christ. Therefore, it has a visible structure of order and discipline, exercised by the office-bearers. In this pneumatic community of believers an organic place was given to the Word of God. From this central ministry the offices were derived.

Bucer's views got a theological form in his famous pastoral work, *Von der waren Seelsorge* (1538), in various church-orders and in other books. Especially during the time of his involvement in the religious disputations or conferences between Protestants and Roman Catholics, initiated by the Habsburg Emperor Charles V, Bucer emphasised the aspect of the ministry. Although other aspects were dealt with as well, the pastoral side remained the most important characteristic of the Bucerian view of the office of the Church.

When the disputations failed and the emperor imposed the stern measures of the *Interim* on the German Protestants (1549), Bucer's work in Strasbourg came to an end. At the invitation of Archbishop Crammer and with the assent of King Edward VI and Lord Protector Somerset, he left for England. There he was soon appointed Regius Professor of Divinity at the University of Cambridge. Less than two years later he died (1551), after a period of active involvement in English affairs. His relevance to England will be discussed in the

---

[18] W..P. Stephens, *The Holy Spirit in the theology of Martin Bucer'*, London: Cambridge University Press, 1970; sections 7-11
[19] Van Ginkel, 103

next chapter. Now we turn to some of the characteristics of Bucerian ecclesiology.

c. Christ is King through the Spirit

When reading Van 't Spijker's account, we are struck by the comprehensiveness of Bucer's view as compared to his Wittenberg and Zürich contemporaries. First of all, his conception of the ministry – the nucleus of his theory of church-government – was many sided and at the same time a harmonious unity. Preaching and ruling he gave an organic place against the total background of his christology, pneumatology and ecclesiology.

However, actually there was only one conception behind his vision: the christocracy in the Church, through the Holy Spirit. Christ is King of the Church through His Spirit. This means the renouncing of any hierarchically tinged vicariate and at the same time, it emphasises the relation of Christ and His ministers. The minister is a servant of Christ. Christocracy through the Spirit means that Christ and His people constitute a unity, and also that the believers are a unity. This is a unity with vertical and horizontal aspects. In this conception, the congregation is a spiritual community. The existence of unity and community is stressed, not the existence of specific ruling and disciplining offices. Every member of the congregation is an office-bearer under the government by Christ through His Spirit.

Later the emphasis on the common office in the spiritual community faded away a little in Bucer's thought. Lack of cooperation from the side of the city-magistracy in the building of a disciplined Church, the danger of anarchy because of the Anabaptist radicals, a tendency of worldly liberalism among the church-members, belonged to the circumstances that undermined Bucer's original ideal. These things forced him to pay more attention to the organisation of the government and the discipline of the Church and to its independence of the State.[20] Christ rules the congregation through His Spirit. He is present

---

[20] Cf. Stephens, sections 8,9. During his whole life, Bucer has stressed the duties of the State with regard to the Church. He even called the civil-magistrates ministers of the Word of God. However, later, when the city-magistrates appeared to persist in their negligence with regard to the purification of the Church, Bucer was forced to distance himself from State involvement in the discipline of the Church. He began to emphasise the importance of small congregations with independent congregation-chosen office-bearers who could effectively exercise church-discipline. Lloyd Jones, 132-136, points out that this phenomenon of 'ecclesiola in ecclesiae' was first found in medieval monasticism and with the United Brethren and Waldenses. Calvin and Zwingli never considered this idea and seemed to be opposed to it. Obviously, the same was true for the Anabaptists. However, Luther got interested in it, when he saw that Church and State would never realise a true ecclesiastical discipline. He proposed the formation of small groups within the Church. However, he never went further than that, because he could not find the people who were fit to govern these small

through His Spirit. That is one aspect. However, at the same time it should be realised that Christ is also the incarnation of the Word of God. He became flesh. Through His Spirit, He assumes flesh and blood in His people. This is most apparent when He calls people to preach the Word of God. In this way, He uses His ministers. They are His mouth. He speaks and rules through them. With that, there is an indissoluble relationship between Word and Spirit, between the preacher of the Word and the spiritual community of believers. The true words of the minister are inspired by the Holy Ghost and they are in accordance with the Word. This means that the preacher speaks with authority. Through the minister Christ grants His grace and remission of sins within the communion of saints. Here, the minister's task is not only declaratory, but also effective. His words are the Words of Christ.

d. No Absolute Office – Equality of Believers

Bucer certainly did not want the office to become something absolute in a Roman Catholic sense. He also wanted to avoid that the words of grace spoken by the minister should become something independent and unreliable. He warded off the extremism of Rome, which gave clergy an independent position above the congregation. However, he also warded off the extremism of the Radicals, which drowned the independent authority of the ministry of the Word of God in the wild waves of spiritualism. In his ideas of church-order and government, Bucer seemed to take a middle-position in between Roman Catholics and Anabaptists. He described the office in terms of *via media* or *via media et stricta*. That the Anglicans felt attracted by these qualifications, although they did not grasp Bucer's intentions, we shall see later.

Roman Catholicism and Anabaptism constituted the two main opponents of Bucer's teachings. In the conflict with Rome, he denounced the sacrificial character of mass and the automatic character of liturgical acts as such. Besides, he refused to accept the Roman view of the keys. The ministry he dissociated from altar and confessional box and he connected it with pulpit and communion table. Bucer put an end to the division of clericals and laymen into different classes of men.

The ordination of clergy only refers to the difference in commission. Many of his later Anglican admirers lost sight of these Bucerian principles. They would find it hard to accept that all believers are essentially equal, though different in talents. Especially after the failure of the religious disputations with representatives of Roman Catholicism, Bucer again began to proclaim these views in all their sharpness. Abolition of celibacy was underlined again by him,

---

churches, and in the end, he laid the government of the church into the hands of the leaders of the territorial States.

as well as the rejection of robes of office. As to the vestments and some other *adiaphora*, he adopted a more moderate position later in England. If only the preaching of the true Word of God was restored in the Anglican parishes, the 'popish rests' would disappear gradually, so he tried to conciliate the quarrelling parties. Both then and now he stressed the unity of office and congregation. In a way the office emerges from the congregation, can be considered as a representative function of the congregation. Apostolic succession, the pet of the Anglican hierarchy, was rejected by Bucer long before he came to England. The presence of Christ through His Spirit and Word, is the only guarantee for a reliable succession of the truth. This is the way Bucer defended his ideas on the Church against Roman Catholicism in general, and against Episcopalianism in particular. Bucer's defence against Anabaptism bore a more conciliatory character.

In his contacts with Anabaptists, he was challenged to refine his conceptions of church-order, church-discipline and church-government. Contrary to the Anabaptists' church ideas, Bucer's church-order embraced the whole *commonwealth* of the city in the membership of the Church, thus rejecting their idea of a congregation with only visibly converted members.[21] However, he tried to meet the Anabaptists' demand for sanctification and holiness, by promoting the training for the ministry and by the attempt to introduce a system of church-discipline. He made the congregation choose the functionaries for the disciplinary bodies. In addition, he tried to constitute a ministry independent of the State. The result was not satisfactory, at least not for the Anabaptists. The Church of Strasbourg remained under the direct influence of the magistrate. Bucer had to accept compromises. This, together with the whole conception of State and Church as cooperating elements in a Christian commonwealth, the Anabaptists could not bear. Bucer's expectations with regard to the spiritual government of the Church were not fulfilled. When it became clear to him that his institution of *Kirchenpfleger* [church-attendants] would never succeed in establishing a real church-discipline, Bucer began to form nucleus-congregations, *Christliche Gemeinschaften* [Christian Communities], in which members voluntarily accepted the exercise of discipline by congregation-chosen elders. However, this did not suffice to satisfy the Anabaptists either.

---

[21] According to VanderSchaaf, Bucer's conception of Church-State relationship 'remained thoroughly attached to the Constantinian model of society' ('Archbishop Parker's efforts towards a Bucerian discipline in the Church of England', pp. 88, 89, 102). This would mean that Bucer propagated absolute royal authority over the Church. However, the author seems to forget that in his *Christliche Gemeinschaften* Bucer distanced himself from Constantinian and Erastian authority of the State over the Church. Cf. Van 't Spijker, 286-313.

By then he was not only suspected as a compromiser because of his acceptance of Church-State cooperation, but also because of his conception of the office. In Bucer's description of the relation of charisma and office, the challenge is felt of those who are opposed to all compromise with earthly and worldly powers. Here the formulations were being refined to the utmost. Charismata are gifts of grace granted by Christ through His Spirit in order to build up His Church. The office bearer finds his place organically in the centre of the congregation. He can only function well, if every member takes his place within the body. The minister's charisma is not better, higher or worthier than the charismata of other elders or of other members. Every believer is called to his own duty. This is also true for the minister. He receives his own vocation, according to division of clergy and laity. The Church is Christ's Body in which the differently talented members are equal. No member is in a position opposite to other members. The only 'opposite' is the 'opposite of the Word of God'. Both, office bearers and congregations bow humbly under the one Head: Christ. The relationship of office bearers and congregation was not explained in terms of people's sovereignty. Bucer did not see the office bearers as executors of the will of the people, but as servants of Christ. They are servants, just like the other members, but with a special assignment. Their power and authority is no other than Christ's. Christ's authority is conferred to the congregation, in which certain talented members are called to represent it.

e. Presbytership, the Basic Office

How many offices are there and what is the difference? Bucer accepted a great plurality of functions and departments with a special emphasis on the diaconial and pastoral services. However, fundamentally -as Van 't Spijker and Van Ginkel both conclude- he recognised only one basic office: the *presbytership*.[22] He distinguished the governmental and ministerial sides of it, but essentially to him there was one office, that of the presbyter. Bucer's conception was definitely Presbyterian. The New Testament *episcopos* and *presbyteros* were used by him as synonyms. They constitute aspects of the one office of the Church. However, these aspects may be exercised by different people. Bucer, just like Calvin, worked out a system of preaching and ruling elders, of ministers and lay-elders, but more than Calvin he stressed their essential unity. In his English period, Bucer was forced to emphasise differently and to make greater distinctions, but also then, he did not abandon his ideal of lay-elders. This idea was not worked out by the Anglicans, but in circles like à Lasco's congregation of refugees in London.

---

[22] Van Ginkel, 110; Van 't Spijker, 360 ff, 399; cf. Paas, *From Galilee to the Atlantic*, 182, 183

The Anglicans were only receptive for the application of his distinction to the ministry of the Church. Even here, they misunderstood him. *Presbyteroi* and *episcopoi* are ruling and ministering the Church. The terms are synonymous. Yet there is a difference in order. The *episcopos* leads the way before the other presbyters. Some Anglicans thought that Bucer was their man, assuming that he laid a basis for Episcopalian hierarchy. However, they ignored the context of Bucer's distinction of *presbyters* and *bishops*. The church is governed by presbyteries. In the presbytery all presbyters, that is all ministers, elders and bishops, function in complete parity. The *episcopos*, the bishop, is the head of the presbytery. However, he is essentially a *presbyter* among the *presbyters*. This is what Bucer said in his *De Regno Christi*, which was written in the English situation. [23] These formulations were part of his attempt to introduce Presbyterianism into the Episcopalian situation of the English Church. He only accepted bishops as a part of a Presbyterian church-order. Essentially, the *episcopoi* to him were elders. The ideal of church-government by the one office of preaching and ruling elders was to become one of the main characteristics of the Presbyterian movement.

Although the Strasbourg Reformer was its architect, his attempts to put it to practice in a lasting system, were not successful. The role of introducing a Presbyterian form of church-government, which would endure the storms of the time, was designated to the Reformer of Geneva. In general John Calvin used the ideas of his Strasbourg friend and teacher. He not only worked them out to greater consequence, but also added different notions.

6. John Calvin

a. Comparison with Bucer

Generally, Calvin is regarded as the founder of the Presbyterian form of church-government as it came to existence in the Reformed Churches. However, we have already noticed that Presbyterianism also originates in the Strasbourg Reformer Martin Bucer. There is an obvious connection between Bucer and Calvin. Calvin's stay in Strasbourg in the years 1538-1541 contributed to the similarities in their views on the Church and its order. In many respects Bucer was the initiator of the theories, which Calvin in his own way developed further. One could say that Calvin 'stands on Bucer's shoulders'.[24] This also led to differences.

---

[23] Van Ginkel, 112-115; Van 't Spijker, 389 ff. Bucer's bishop is a *primus inter pares*. Other presbyters take part in his ordination. He cannot function without the congregation and without the other presbyters.

[24] Cf. Paas, *From Galilee to the Atlantic*, 187, 188

Van Ginkel compares the two Reformers: 'Calvin adopted Bucer's ideas of church-discipline in nucleus-congregations or *Christliche Gemeinschaften* [Christian Communities]. He only made a clearer distinction between the office of minister (pastor and teacher) and that of elder. More important is that Calvin succeeded in realising the idea of Presbyterianism, in Geneva. After a long struggle, an ecclesiastical collège for supervision and discipline functioned there, independently of the city-council'.[25] As to the practical application of their systems, Calvin succeeded whereas Bucer's experiment in Strasbourg failed. However, the latter's ideas were applied elsewhere, not through Calvin, but also through à Lasco's London congregation, in the Reformed Church of The Netherlands. Here the difference between Calvin and Bucer was smaller than Van Ginkel seems to suggest, although he does not fail to mention the à Lasco-line. When Van Ginkel says that Calvin as compared to Bucer 'made a clearer distinction' between the offices of minister and elder, he confuses an important point of difference between the two Reformers. One can wonder whether in Calvin's view ministers and elders are not only distinguished, but also separated from one another.

Another question is whether Calvin's theory at this point is really clearer and more comprehensive than Bucer's. Niesel points to it that concerning the government and discipline of the Church, with Calvin, the doctrine of the common priesthood of all believers does not play a role.[26] If that is true, then here we have a deviation from the Bucerian line of thought. Bucer, as we have seen, derived the governmental and ministerial offices from the priesthood of all believers. Calvin did not follow him at this point, because he had a different vision of the Church as the Body of Christ and the work of the Holy Spirit in it. Whereas Bucer in the first place recognises the Kingship of Christ over the Church, Calvin emphasizes the rule of the Holy Spirit. Bucer stresses *christocracy* and Calvin stresses *pneumatocracy*. Both see the Church as the Body of Christ, built by the Holy Spirit, but they emphasise different aspects.

This requires some further explanation. Krusche, in his book on Calvin's pneumatology, describes the Reformer's view on the work of Christ and the Spirit in the Church. Christ is present through His Spirit. At this point, there is total agreement with Bucer. Then a specific Calvinist emphasis follows, a so-called *extra calvinisticum*.[27] Christ is not only present as the Holy Spirit. According to His humanity His Body is in heaven. On earth it is represented by the Holy Spirit and directed to the specific functions of the Church. However,

---

[25] Van Ginkel, 321
[26] W. Niesel, *Die Theologie Calvin's*, München: Kaiser Verlag, 1957, chapter XIII, section 7,8
[27] W. Krusche, *Das Wirken des Heiligen Geistes nach Calvin*, Göttingen: Vandenhoeck und Ruprecht, 1957; pp 145-151

according to His divinity He is present everywhere; He is *ubiquitous* in the Person of the Mediator. His bodily presence through the Spirit is not sufficient for salvation. He also needs to be made present as the Mediator in the heart of believers. His works, His sacrificed Body and Blood must be represented in His children. Christ uses the Holy Spirit to perform this. In this way He binds the work of the Holy Spirit to Himself, to His works. The Spirit does not replace Christ on earth, but He represents Him, and in His work He applies the redeeming acts of Christ to man.

This Calvinist notion is a refinement of Bucerian thought. It bars the way to a false spirituality without Christ and His Word, in accordance with Bucer's intention. However, it also leads to a difference with Bucer. In fact, Calvin distinguishes, if not separates, two spheres of the working by the Holy Spirit, the one to Christ's divinity and the other to Christ's humanity. There is a distinction of charismatic gifts. First the gifts which convert people to members of the Body of Christ and apply to them Christ's work of redemption. All believers need them. They pertain to the common priesthood of all believers. Then there are the special gifts for those who are the office-bearers of the church. Apart from the charisma of the priesthood of all believers, they receive gifts for the exercise of the government, discipline and ministry of the Church.[28] These office-gifts are not derived from the charisma of the common priesthood. They are of a different gender. Therefore, there is an essential difference between office-bearers and other common church-members. The Holy Spirit bestows charismata on both the office and the common priesthood. However, the two spheres of pneumatic activity are not connected in such a way that the charismata of the office flow from charismata of the common priesthood. Like Bucer, Calvin recognises the Church as an organic spiritual community of office bearers and other members. However, unlike Bucer he divides the charismata into two kinds. The office-bearer is called by the Holy Spirit and not by the congregation. When the congregation elects and nominates, through its presbyters, the ministers and elders, it affirms the choice by the Holy Spirit. It recognises the specific call by the Spirit. Essentially, there is no call by the congregation out of its common priesthood.

Bucer saw this differently. He fully recognised the charismata of the congregation as a fundamental unity. In this unity there is a range of various gifts. The common priesthood contains a wide variety of gifts, according to the needs of the congregation. Every believer has his own gifts, his own place in the organism, his own office. In the specific office of *presbyters*, the Holy Spirit works in the same way as in the *common office of all believers*. Presbyters are called through the Spirit, and this call is represented and realised through the

---

[28] Krusche, 320 - 322

call by the community of believers, i.e. by the Body of Christ. Christ is King. Through the Holy Spirit He is embodied in His congregation. Through His presbyters He rules and ministers the Church. Bucer's *christocracy* recognises the fundamental unity of charismata and community of all offices. Calvin's *pneumatocracy* stresses the essential difference of offices.

This distinction between Bucer and Calvin not only concerns the common and special offices. Calvin after his initial period in Geneva and his stay in Strasbourg, also began to deviate from Bucer's conception of the one special office of the Church. Bucer's *presbyterate* was the only and fundamental office from which all other special offices had been derived. The ministry of the Word, the government of the Church and the exercise of discipline are functions of the *presbyterate*. Ministers and elders are bearers of essentially the same office. Calvin, however took a different course. In his conception, the representation of the common priesthood in the government of the Church, had no natural place. The ministry of the Word was central in his system, as it was in Bucer's. However, unlike Bucer, he did not connect this special office to the operation of 'lay' elders. He needed the 'lay' element of the elders for the discipline of the Church and for the creation of a governmental structure, independent of the State. However, as Van Ginkel points out, this does not mean that Calvin wanted to introduce a Roman like difference between clergy and laity. He did not want to draw sharp lines between ministers and elders. Yet there is certain vulnerability into that direction. The Body of Christ is a spiritual community in an invisible and visible sense. It is ruled through the Holy Spirit by the ministry of the Word of God, i.e. by the proclamation of the Gospel. All governmental and disciplinary functions are derived from this. The elder comes after the minister. Here the relationship of ministers and elders easily can get a tinge of hierarchy. At least, Calvin's concept is more open to this danger than Bucer's. This does not necessarily mean that Calvin's system leads to disconnection or disharmony of ministry and eldership. Nevertheless, there is a danger of loosening the eldership from the proclamation of the Gospel, as Van Ginkel underlines.[29] When elders don't preach, when they are only concentrated on the government and the discipline of the Church, the office of the Church is in danger of disintegration, then the eldership can degenerate to an unscriptural and unspiritual judicial office. In this way, also the ministry can degenerate. When ministries are loosened from their organic place in the *presbyterate*, the they can develop hierarchical and even tyrannical tendencies, which are most detrimental to the functioning of a Presbyterian system of church-government. Here Van Ginkel recognises that Presbyterianism, from the beginning was threatened by a kind of *oligarchism*, the rule by a self-maintaining elite, which

---

[29] Van Ginkel, 147-150

has not served the well-being of the Body of Christ. He mentions this problem in connection with the emergence of *lay-elders*. However, we want to suggest that *oligarchism* can threaten the elder-side as well as the minister-side of the Calvinist type of Presbyterianism.

The problem originates in Calvin's division of the charismata for the common priesthood and the special offices on the one hand, and the emphasised distinction of ministers and elders on the other. In his comparison of Calvin and Bucer, Van Ginkel does not mention this important reason. It could have served his pleading for a further democratisation of the Presbyterian church-order. It could have supported his explanation of the gradually diminishing significance of *lay-elders* and the increasing dominance of ministers in the history of Presbyterian churches.[30] Therefore, Van Ginkel's claim that Calvin made 'a clearer distinction between ministers and elders' than Bucer, is not very helpful. It seems to neglect the great value of Bucer's unity-conception. Unity in the harmonious many-sided and much gifted community, built by the Holy Spirit and governed by Christ and His Word. Unity of congregation and presbyters; unity of preaching presbyters and ruling presbyters. One great vision, which held the work of the Holy Spirit in one grasp, the spiritual community of believers with the varied aspects of the pneumatic charisma.

b. Elders and Ministers

Calvin's idea of Presbyterian church-government was the result of a development. It was moulded, partly by his theocratic ideals, partly by the political circumstances. His definitions of the office of the Church are not only directed towards the internal order of congregation. In his later struggle with the Genevan magistrate he also defined the office in terms of State-Church-relationship. More than Bucer, he succeeded in designing a type of Presbyterian church-government that was able to resist the usurping powers of the State. He needed ministers and elders with the capacity and competence to uphold the independence of the Church with regard to the State. At the same time, he recognised the State as an organism, which embraces spiritual and civil authority.

The opinion as if Calvin envisaged a theocratic State, governed by the Church, is called by Bohatec 'a wide spread and deeply rooted error'. State and Church are both entitled to independency in their own matters. They are elements of equal value. They can serve each other without sacrificing their own independence and authority. Both, the subjection of the State by the Church and of the Church by the State, end in tyranny. The supremacy of the State over the

---

[30] Van Ginkel, 311

Church, like in Anglican England and Lutheran Germany, was rejected by Calvin. He distanced himself from the Erastian commonwealth, which originated in the Zwinglian Zürich. Calvin did not want a State-Church. At the same time, he did not favour a Church-state either.[31] State and Church are like the focus-points of an ellipse. They help each other in mutual assistance. The State is called to maintain the peace of the land, to safeguard the true worship of God. Yet it is not allowed to weaken the independence of the Church and it cannot govern in spiritual matters.[32] The Church in its visible aspect is still imperfect. It needs the ministry of the Word of God and the Sacraments, and the maintenance of a system of government and discipline.[33] Government and discipline, these two notions are the main elements of Calvin's vision of the Church's independency. He needed them because they were scriptural notions and helped him to meet the dangers, which threatened the independency of the Church. Without a scriptural system of government and discipline, the Church of the Reformation would not be able to ward off the pressures by Roman Catholicism and radical Anabaptism.

Parallel to this Calvin saw the dangers of *tyranny* and *anarchy*. These dangers are interrelated. Tyranny refers to the way in which the Church is governed. Anarchy refers to the way in which the church lives. The first is an issue of government, the second of discipline. Tyranny is apparent in the relationship of the congregation and the ecclesiastical and civil authorities. It pertains to the Church's *external order*. Anarchy shows in the lack of love and other sins of the members of the congregation. It is a question of the *internal order* of the Church. The external and internal order of the Church, government and discipline, were the spheres of activity for Calvin's ruling elders. However, we have seen that originally the *lay-elder* had no natural place in Calvin's thought. The idea of involving lay-elements in the ruling and disciplining of the congregation, only grew after his experiences in Bucerian Strasbourg, in his struggle with the civil magistracy of Geneva, under the challenge of Anabaptist radicals and faced with the persecutions of his followers in France. Van Ginkel points out that Calvin, before his return to Geneva in 1541, did not yet recognise the office of elders. Apart from the deacon -whom we do not consider in this study- he only knew the minister of the Word. To the minister he gave the complete care of the congregation, including the government and the exercise of discipline.[34] Moreover, originally Calvin much more stressed the importance of discipline than the need for an independent church-government. In the first editions of the *Institutes of the Christian Religion*, he dealt with church-order

---

[31] J. Bohatec, *Calvin Lehre von Staat und Kirche*, Breslau: Marcus, 1937 pp 611-625
[32] Cf. Niesel, chapter XV
[33] W.F. *Dankbaar, Calvijn, zijn weg en werk*, Nijkerk: Callenbach, 1982; chapter VIII
[34] Van Ginkel, 115-118

under the aspect of internal-anarchy. Public sinners offend the Lord and spoil the congregation. They must be banned in order to bring them to penance and to set an example for the rest of the congregation. In theory, the minister of the Word was responsible for the exercise of discipline. However, in practice the minister was completely dependent on the civil magistrate. A number of supervisors were chosen to assist the minister, but they acted as officials of the city-council. They handed over persistent sinners to the court of the city, leaving the minister and the rest of the congregation without real influence. Such was the situation during Calvin's first stay in Geneva. Apparently in those years he did not approach the question of church-order from the angle of external tyranny. The problem of independent government was not stressed, nor the need for elders. Even in Strasbourg, Calvin's congregation of French refugees did not use elders for the government and the exercise of discipline. Originally, Calvin did not expect much danger from the side of external tyranny. We can understand this, because the civil and ecclesiastical government of the city-states in Switzerland and South-Germany were, generally, in a reforming mood. The Lutheran, Bucerian and Zwinglian Reformation had swept away almost the entire infrastructure of the Church of Rome, thus clearing the field for other types of church-order. Regional princes and city-councils were anxious to defend their political independency against the claims of the Habsburg *Holy Roman Empire*. They granted their churches room for the furthering of reformed conceptions of church-order, as long and as far as these conceptions would be in agreement with their own desires for supremacy and independency.

In this congenial situation, the call for church-order was not in the first place inspired by the danger of tyrannical civil and ecclesiastical rulers. These regional and urban magistrates did not threaten the Reformation. On the contrary, they protected the early Reformed churches from the tyrannical forces of the Counter-Reformation, which invaded vast regions of Europe under the umbrella of the Habsburg Empire. Neither was Calvinist church-order in the first place meant for the neutralisation of ecclesiastical rulers of the old Episcopalian type. These church-princes, like cardinals, archbishops and bishops, simply had ceased to exist in the Protestant areas of Switzerland and Germany.

c. Calvin's Context

We elaborate on this in order to make clear that Calvin's ideas were born in a situation that was different from the English one. Therefore, his conceptions of church-order must have landed in England in another way than on the continent. In England, the Reformation did not take away the hierarchical, Episcopalian structure of the Church. The Swiss and South-German Reformers did not have to defend themselves against a semi-Roman, *via media* structure, as the Puritans had. They did not work under monarchs whose sole desire was to replace the pope as the supreme head of the Church, and who did not leave much room for Protestant doctrine. They did not develop their ideas under the threat of an ecclesiastical hierarchy of bishops who rejected any principle of church-government that did not conform to the Episcopalian theories.

Originally, Calvin, therefore, did not emphasise the problem of church-government, nor the functioning of elders. We shall see that the English Presbyterian Puritans worked out a Calvinist church-order with different accents. Calvin was led to a conception of eldership when he had to hold up the independency of the Church in the context of the Reformed Genevan city-state. The idea as if Calvin had nothing to fear from the Genevan magistrate, is denounced by the fact that his first stay in the city was forcefully terminated in 1538. The city-council banned him as a result of a conflict about ecclesiastical ceremonies and about the very question of the exercise of church-discipline. Who is responsible for the discipline of the Church? Behind this there was the other question: who governs the Church? Calvin had no elders yet. The minister was his only office-bearer. However, the ministry of the Word was not able to balance the power of the State. When Strasbourg received him as an honorable guest and gave him the position of leading minister of the French-speaking congregation of refugees, Calvin had ample opportunity to communicate with Bucer and to study the latter's church-order in which the eldership already had taken shape. However, this did not lead him immediately to nominating elders himself. The second edition of his *Institutes,* in 1539, though dealing extensively with the demand of discipline, did not proceed to the institution of elders.

Only after his return to Geneva in 1541, he wrote a church-order, the *Ordonnances Ecclesiastiques,* in which the Presbyterian example of Strasbourg, can be recognised. Like in Strasbourg, the eldership was introduced. However, we have seen that there was a striking difference. Calvin instituted *four offices*: pastors, doctors, elders, and deacons. Bucer also knew several offices, but with him they were all forms of the one *presbyterate.* Calvin differentiated more emphatically. The Genevan Reformer dealt with eldership as a separate office with separate duties. This does not mean, however, that in Geneva ministry and eldership worked independently of each other. In the matters of government and discipline there was a close cooperation of ministers and elders. Gradually the minister would acquire a position of authority over the elder. However, this was not yet a fact in Calvin's Geneva. Like the Strasbourg *Kirchenpfleger* [church-attendant], the Genevan *elder* was chosen from and nominated by the civil magistracy, and in both cases the city-council held the ultimate say in conflicts on doctrine between ministers.

According to Van Ginkel, the Genevan eldership acquired more the characteristics of an ecclesiastical office, than the Strasbourg *Kirchenpfleger*. In Strasbourg the *Kirchenpfleger* was practically a civil-officer who could easily bypass the minister. However, Geneva had its *Consistoire*, in which ministries and elders closely cooperated. This meant that the independent government of the Church and the exercise of discipline were better realised than in Strasbourg, so Van Ginkel concludes.[35]

Although Van Ginkel is right when he says that in Strasbourg the introduction of a Presbyterian church-order eventually failed, it should be stressed that Bucer's vision
of church-discipline was not less promising than Calvin's. Apart from his institution of *Kirchenpfleger*, who worked in the official city churches, which embraced practically all citizens, Bucer's ideal of eldership was much more realised in the *Christliche Gemeinschaften*, the small communities of believers who voluntarily submitted themselves to the exercise of discipline by congregation-chosen office bearers. Bucer did not succeed in creating a Church independent of the State, but he made an attempt through these 'little churches in the church'.

Calvin did not reach full ecclesiastical independency either. The *Consistoire* could operate quite autonomously, but at the end of Calvin's life the government of the Genevan Church was still connected with the civil magistracy. Yet, in the later editions of his *Institutes* and in his commentaries, Calvin had never abandoned the vision of complete independency of the Church. Van Ginkel comments: 'At least there now existed in theory as well as in practice a form of church-government, which could be taken over by other churches. ... The office of elders developed simultaneously with the ecclesiastical discipline'. He concludes: 'From a purely civil functionary, the elder became through various mixed forms, a full church functionary[36]'; we would like to add: a church functionary, who at the same still was not independent from the State.

---

[35] Van Ginkel, 119-124
[36] Van Ginkel, 321

Chapter 4

Reception of Continental Thought

1. Original interest in Luther

a. Early Influence

The English Reformation was influenced deeply by the continental Reformers. Traces of Luther, Zwingli, Bullinger, Bucer, Calvin and Beza can be found on the Anglican side as well as on the Puritan side of the historical developments. Generally, all Reformers were acknowledged as authoritative sources by Anglicans and Puritans for a very long time. This is certainly true for questions of salvation-doctrine. However, as the continental Reformation progressed and differentiated along the lines from Wittenberg to Zürich, Basel, Strasbourg and Geneva, the English Reformers began to show certain preferences. These preferences gradually grew to emphasised distinctions and divisions. After our period, these differences would characterise the phenomena of Separation, Establishment and Dissent. Even then, there was not a strict separation of the loyalties. As to the question of church-order, church-government and church-discipline a varied interest began to show at an early time.

Prior to the *Henrician Reformation*, Luther already had a tremendous influence in England. As early as 1518, Luther's writings found their way to England. In 1521 Archbishop Warham wrote to cardinal Wolsey: 'I am informed that ... divers be infected with the heresies of Luther and ... having among them a great number of books of the said perverse doctrine ...'. Wolsey issued a proclamation, ordering all books of Luther to be brought to the bishop of the diocese and afterwards to be sent to himself. The cardinal determined to make a solemn holocaust. The condemned books were ranged before him in baskets, which then were emptied into the flames.[1] However, the spread of Lutheranism could not be combated by repression, nor by Wolsey's educational measures, nor by King Henry's written attack at the Wittenberg Reformer.[2] During Henry's life, his prelates remained more or less faithful to his Romish doctrinal stance. However, gradually even Henry himself understood that he needed the support of foreign Reformers. After all, the pope had excommunicated him and he experienced the pressures of the Habsburg Empire. An alliance with the Protestant German princes would be welcome. However, negotiations with Lutheran divines failed, because the king refused to adopt

---

[1] Perry, 31-34
[2] Cf. chapter 1.3.b, footnote 12

their views, the Lutherans openly condemning the abuses in the English Church.³

b. Cranmer and Luther

That the top of the Anglican was receptive for the ideas of continental Reformers is apparent from the attitude of Archbishop Cranmer. In the question of the eucharist he shifted from the Roman Catholic doctrine of transubstantiation to the Lutheran formula of consubstantiation, but he did not stop at this point. Dyer describes that after the death of Henry in 1547, Cranmer began to turn attention to Switzerland. The English primate attempted to realise a union of all the Protestant Churches. In the end of his life he even included the Church of Geneva in his project.⁴ Cranmer's view of the Lord's Supper may have changed from Lutheranism into the direction of Zwinglianism, as Dyer suggests. Perhaps a more important shift of attention concerned the question of church-order. The Anglican episcopate was interested in Lutheranism, because it left room for existence of bishops and other 'indifferent' rests of the old system.

However, the bishops gradually discovered that Lutherans only wanted to communicate on the basis of acceptance of the *Augsburg Confession*, and that Lutheranism was far from supporting a full-rate Roman-like Episcopacy with a king hovering above its hierarchical structure and that Luther did not see the State and the Church as a comprehensive unity. Disappointed by these things, the Anglican leaders more or less turned their back on Wittenberg. Besides, the Lutherans, accusing the English Church of all kinds of evils, were not in an ecumenical mood.

2. The Bishops Focus on Zwingli and Erastus

a. Congenial Climate

A much better climate existed in the Reformed regions of South-Germany and Switzerland. In their correspondence with the Anglican divines, the Reformers of Zürich, Strasbourg and Geneva were much more cooperative and ecumenical than the Lutherans. Moreover, the commonwealth-doctrine of the independent city-states seemed to fit the situation of Tudor England in a way. In both cases, State and Church were held together in one political and religious conception, functioning under the civil magistrate. However, there were also tendencies in those free city republics, which were abhorred by the representatives of the

---

³ Perry, 155, 156
⁴ Th. H. Dyer, *Life of John Calvin'*, London, 1850, 288-291

Tudor establishment in England. The city-councils were *oligarchies*, but there was also an increasing *democratic* element in them. The Reformed churches, though partly governed through council-dignitaries, struggled for independence of the State and -as in the case of Geneva- they reached a considerable degree of autonomy. These aspects were not attractive for the English Episcopate. Yet, this tendency of freedom and independence was attractive to its opponents, the proto-Puritan friends of a completer Reformation.

Many proto-Puritan activists had to flee from Henrician England. They went to the centres of Reformation on the continent. Here we see another shift from Lutheranism to the Reformation movement in the South. Though the first English refugees, like Tyndale, were warmly welcomed in Wittenberg, later waves of proto-Puritans felt restrained by the Lutherans and directed their ways southwards. Naturally they were drawn by Zürich, the city where Zwingli did away with 'the popish rests' and instituted the authority of Scripture over Church and State. There with Zwingli's successor Bullinger, the Henrician refugees met with a more congenial climate.

b. Church and State in Unity

It is the irony of history that Zürich never became the great example for the English Puritans, but that it did for their opponents, the Anglicans. Locher draws our attention to the fact that there is a line from post-Zwinglian Zürich to the Tudor Church settlement in England. As we have seen, the Zürich Church, after Zwingli, degenerated to a position of servitude to the State, i.e. to a system of Erastianism. The idea of Erastianism was attractive to Henry VIII and his bishops, and under Edward VI it would be coined as Anglican doctrine. However, the Zürich Erastians as well as the Anglican Erastians thoroughly misunderstood the conception of Zwingli. Zwingli's vision was the realisation of the Kingdom of God and of a Christian magistracy working for this. However, the ultimate objectives of royal supremacy over the Anglican Church were not religious, but judicial and political. Locher calls the Christianity of this type of church-government 'a farce'.[5]

Apart from this misuse of Zwinglianism, the English Reformation also underwent positive influence of the Zürich Reformers. The guidance of the Holy Spirit is not restricted to the Church, but is also to be acknowledged in the public affairs of the State. State and Church are both dependent on the guidance of the Holy Spirit. Faithful to this principle, the English Puritans have never rejected the specific authority of the State, even in certain ecclesiastical matters. The State has its domain apart from the Church, and has also an obligation

---

[5] Locher, 285

towards the Church. The deeply felt community of both, as represented in the *commonwealth*, has its foundation in the work of the Holy Spirit. Both spheres are governed by the Word through the Spirit. Not only the ecclesiastical office is an instrument of the Word through the Spirit, but also the civil-magistrate is such an instrument. Church and State need the Spirit of the Word of God, just like the human body needs the soul.

Especially the Anglicans adopted this line of Zwinglian thought. The Puritans too were touched by it. The Puritans, however, stressed the independence of the Church within the *commonwealth*. Under the direct influence of Calvin, they recognised the existence of an organism embracing Church and State, in line with the organic unity in medieval conception. However, they also distinguished the spheres of State and Church. Calvin's ideal was independence of the Church and of the State. In his own at times rather congenial Genevan climate he more or less acquiesced to a role by the State in the affairs of the Church. For the exercise of church-discipline he even needed the powerful backing of the city-council. But in his writings he made clear that the Church, in its government and discipline, should be absolutely free of interference by the State.[6] This was especially true for those Reformed churches that lived under hostile regimes, like in The Netherlands and France. There the Church should take a form and structure that could survive the attacks by the State. Calvin even developed a theory of resistance for situations in which the authorities try to eliminate the Church and the proclamation of the Word.[7]

The English Puritans learnt these lessons and they tried to apply them. But their situation was different from those in Geneva, France, The Netherlands and even neighbouring Scotland, where Calvinism soon became rooted. On the one hand, as English nationals, they were attracted by the Old Testament-like community-idea of a *commonwealth* of Church and State, liberated from medieval Papal tyranny and rephrased in a Reformed sense according to Zwinglians thought. Although Calvin taught them to see the negative aspects of a political and ecclesiastical *commonwealth*, they could not abandon this ideal. This is why the Presbyterian Puritans did not separate. They tried to change the *commonwealth* from within, trying to realise a Presbyterian church-order in an Anglican community. On the other hand, there was the Anglican establishment, who refused to accept any experiments as to an alternative church-order. The Anglicans even retained 'the popish rags' and other rests of popery in ceremonial and doctrine. This was very hard to accept for the Puritans who on the continent had experienced the blessings of the purified Church. They

---

[6] Cf. Bohatec, 611 ff
[7] Bohatec, 75 ff

succeeded in introducing the Swiss model of *prophesyings* into the State-church. More they could not reach. The later Swiss example of a presbyterianised Erastian Church was only attractive to certain noblemen and dignitaries at Court. Its realisation would produce a result that would not be much different from the prevailing Anglican Erastian Church. The idea of an independent Presbyterian Church instead of the Anglican Church could not be realised without revolution against the *commonwealth*. However, revolutionaries were only to be found in the most radical sections of the early Puritan Movement. At the time of Henry's death, in 1547, Calvin's views were probably not yet well known in England.[8] That is why the thoughts of Presbyterianism were not yet consciously shaped.

c. New Influx of Ideas

Under Edward VI, Erastianism mixed with the Henrician ideas of supremacy and episcopacy. The Anglican system hardened. At the same time, however, the barriers against the influence by the continental Reformation were taken away. The arrival of a large number of foreign Protestant divines in England has been of paramount importance. They marked the end of the old Henrician regime and the beginning of a more Puritan-minded era in the history of English Episcopalianism. It should be stressed again that the days of Edward VI the Puritans were not yet known by that name. Sometimes they were called *Gospellers*, a reference to their allegiance to the New Testament. Presbyterian ideas were not yet much apparent among them. This was soon to change.

The new influx of ideas from the continent made them more conscious and strengthened their position. In the days of Edward, the incipient Puritan movement was still hidden in the cadres of the Anglican Church. When fleeing foreign divines appeared on the English shore, the great division into different church parties had not yet taken shape. That is one of the reasons why these foreign divines later could be quoted as authoritative sources by both sides of the conflict. Another reason is that most foreign guests were anxious to support the Reformation of the English Church without dividing it. Most of them promoted Presbyterian reforms, but at the same time they kept close and friendly contacts with their Anglican hosts.

---

[8] VanderSchaaf, 93, 94, is probably right when he puts forward this opinion. He thinks that Calvin's disciplinary ideas 'were not even well-known in England until after the Marian Exile' Here the author seems to underestimate the influence of important Calvinistic refugees in England during the reign of Edward VI. To us it would seem that Calvin's ideas at that time were well known with Cranmer and other Anglican leaders. However, proto-Puritans like Knox and Hooper did not yet feel the direct need of putting them to practice. During and after the Marian Exile Calvinistic convictions were strengthened.

3. Bucer: a Sympathetic Refugee

a. Claimed by all

To the influential foreign church leaders who fled to England, belonged the Strasbourg Reformer Martin Bucer. In Edwards's time, Bucer contributed to a more Reformed tendency of the Anglican Church. Later, when Puritanism had emerged as a movement, he was claimed by both conflicting parties, the Anglican and the Puritan. During his short stay in England, from 1549 till his death in 1551, the Strasbourg Reformer was able to summarise his thoughts on church-order. Moreover, he tried to apply them to the English situation. Were his many-sided but comprehensive answers to the problem of church-government and church-discipline, really understood? The Anglicans accepted Bucer's *via media* theology, because they looked upon it as in accordance with their own 'middle of the road' theology. It remains to be seen, however, whether Bucer and the Anglicans really were in agreement. Bucer's conception of a *commonwealth* of State and Church may have favoured the Anglicans for a time, but that did not mark him as an Anglican.[9] His defence of a Presbyterian church-order, independent of the State, left room for the existence of bishops, but not for the Episcopalianism nor for the Erastianism of the Anglican Church. VanderSchaaf points out, that during Bucer's stay in England one theme dominated all others: the necessity for the internal discipline in the Church. It was 'the proper organisation of church-worship and government for the twofold purpose of glorifying God and sanctifying the members of the Christian community'. At Cambridge Bucer befriended a number of coming men in the Anglican church, among whom two future archbishops Matthew Parker and Edmund Grindal. They were influenced by Bucer's ideal of discipline, and they certainly used his ideas to a certain extent. However, these Elizabethan prelates found the Anglican and Tudor reality too stubborn for their Bucerian sympathies.

VanderSchaaf sums up the bottlenecks. In his, *De Regno Christi*, Bucer proposed limiting the prevailing clerical authority. Although not favouring a dismantling of the ecclesiastical hierarchy, he proposed a *democratising* of it. Bishops should remain, but should decide 'nothing without the consultation of other presbyters'. In *De Regno Christi* he described the basic ways in which discipline within the Church of England should be improved. He recommended that discipline be extended to cover life and manner of all Christians, including ecclesiastical prelates and civil magistrates, and that *laymen* should exercise a

---

[9] Like Zwingli, Bucer was closer to the medieval unity-conception of State and Church than Calvin was. However, he never agreed with the political and ecclesiastical absolutism in the *Tudor Settlement*.

great role in caring for the spiritual and temporal well-being of the Church. In particular pastors and lay-elders should supervise the lives of Christians.

Bucer's book not only contained practical rules for the realisation of his conception in England, but also an analysis of the English Church and its various offices, which was not really flattering.[10] However, King Edward to whom the book was presented, was impressed. In an essay, he recognised Bucer's disappointment with the lack of progress in the English Reformation and with the low level of preaching and catechising. Bucer's direct influence in Edwards reign was considerable. This was apparent from the *Book of Common Prayer* 1552, which will be the subject of our next chapter. It contains numerous alterations amenable to Bucer's views. Those changes generally relate to liturgy and doctrine, and not to the government and discipline of the Church.

The question of church-order was regulated in a new set of ecclesiastical laws, which meant a complete overhauling of the canon law inherited from the Roman Church, the *Reformatio legum Ecclesiasticarum* of 1552. 'The new code was along Bucerian lines in its endeavour to institute a godly discipline', so VanderSchaaf comments. However, these Reformed laws never got an official status. When two years after Bucer's death, Edward VI also died, in 1553, the direct Bucerian influence was cut off. With that, Bucerian tendencies in the incipient *Puritan Movement* lost much of their significance.

b. Articles and Canons

In the Marian interlude of Roman Catholic repression, many English proto-Puritans fled abroad to the Reformation capital of the time, Geneva. That is why Calvin would take the lead in Puritan thought. On the Anglican side, however the Bucerian line of thought re-emerged after Mary's death. A Bucerian discipline continued to be of interest to members of the Elizabethan Episcopate. The policies of Edmund Grindal, Archbishop of Canterbury from 1576 to 1583, reflected Bucer's disciplinary thought. In chapter 9 he will appear in our story, just like his predecessor Matthew Parker. According to VanderSchaaf, Parker was even more familiar with Bucer's thought than Grindal.[11] He was co-executive of Bucer's estate and orator at his funeral. The Anglican confession of *39 Articles*, drafted by him in 1563, was of a Reformed character. Being Queen Elizabeth's first archbishop, Parker was the man behind the ecclesiastical canons of 1571. The canons set forth rules of discipline affecting both clergy and laity. Concern was expressed over improving the education and the performance of the clergy. Somewhat similar to Bucer's institution of lay-elders who would administer discipline along with the preaching elders, Parker's

---

[10] Cf. VanderSchaaf, 89-91; Van 't Spijker, 338-341
[11] VanderSchaaf, 93 ff

canons mentioned the function of *churchwardens*. In each individual parish these churchwardens were to be responsible for examining the credentials of ministers and for overseeing the moral behaviour of the parson, vicar or curate. They were laymen, chosen by the consent of the parish and its minister for a term normally not to exceed one year. There were strong parallels with Bucer. However, as VanderSchaaf concludes, 'The biggest difference between Bucer's *elders* and Parker's *churchwardens*, was their place within the Church as a whole. Bucer's ideal Church was founded on the grassroots of piety, with the government deriving its consent from the government. ... In Parker's system the lines of ecclesiastical authority still originate with the English monarch and flow down through the Episcopal structure to the laity'.[12] In fact, Parker's canons, though moderating strict Episcopalian rule, did not envisage a Presbyterian form of church-government. Moreover, in practice they did not play an important role. Unlike the Reformed church laws of 1552, the canons of 1571 were officially adopted by *Convocation*. However, Elizabeth did allow them to be put to practice. Therefore, they were not enforced. The Bucerian experiment within the English State-Church had got a severe blow.

Parker's successor Grindal made a new attempt, by allowing and promoting the working of *prophesyings*. We shall see that his conflict with the monarch over the issue, ended all hope for a change of the Anglican system from within, into the direction of Presbyterian forms of church-government. Bucer's ideals of church-order appeared to be largely incompatible with the Anglican order.

c. Bucer Misunderstood

Bucer's view of the ministry and his rejection of the division of clergy and laity, should make Anglicans very careful calling him their 'father'. Bucer allowed the existence of bishops, but this did not entail the acceptance of a hierarchy of Presbytery under Episcopacy. Bucer was a Presbyterian. He did not tend to Episcopalianism. Pastoral concern made him accept the prevailing Anglican system as a starting point for his reformative work. In this way, he tried to introduce his Presbyterian views into a Church with a completely Episcopalian past. This subtle position did not prevent him from exercising severe criticism on the English Episcopate. As van 't Spijker concludes, 'the very criteria of Anglicanism are not to be found in Bucer'.[13]

The Anglicans who felt attracted by Bucer's *via media* lost sight of his accent on the unity between presbyter and congregation, and between the presbyters themselves. They did not see that this unity conception excludes the

---

[12] VanderSchaaf, 99
[13] Van 't Spijker, 445-455, cf. 437-431

sacrificial character of the parish priesthood, the difference in ordination of clergy, and the operation of a hierarchy. Bucerian views could not become productive in Anglicanism as such. That they became productive within the Anglican Church at the time, is due to the changing climate because of the emerging Puritan Movement. VanderSchaaf says that Parker's canons were perhaps most successful in bringing about a 'godly discipline', when they were used illegally. In certain regions where Puritanism got strong, 'churchwardens functioned as shadow-elders' in later Elizabethan times. Preaching and sanctification was a Puritans' primary concern. This was gradually worked out to ideas of organisation and government of the Church. 'Discipline functioned at the local level, while bishops either overlooked or were unaware of such subversive activity'.[14] In an *indirect* way the foundations were laid for the conscious Presbyterianism of later days.

There was also a *direct* line from Bucer and other Edwardian foreign guests to Presbyterian Puritanism. Apart from men like Bucer and Peter Martyr Vermigli, who received important posts at the universities of Cambridge and Oxford, Archbishop Cranmer also invited Bernard Ochino, Paul Fagius, John Uttenhovius, Peter Alexander, Francis Dryander, and others. John Knox was among them. Blunt describes their impact.[15]

To these refugee-guests also belong to Polish Reformer John à Lasco, who became superintendent of the 'Stranger's Church' in London. Directly inspired by Bucer, à Lasco organised his congregation of refugees in a Presbyterian way. This example was taken over by other congregations of foreigners, e.g. in Canterbury and Glastonbury, and it contributed to the consciousness of the English Puritan Movement. À Lasco's Bucerian church-order also served as an example for the formulation of church-orders for the situation in The Netherlands.

In the reign of Edward VI, the proto-Puritans in the English Church were true Bucerians. However, some question the Bucerianism of the Elizabethan Puritans. To them it is indicative that Bucer's friend, the Archbishop Parker, was not a Puritan himself. VanderSchaaf explains more, he thinks that at least two facets of Bucer's thought are opposed to that of the Puritans. First, he is of the opinion that Bucer would have allowed a model for the English Church that was not to be found in the New Testament, his ideal would have been 'a Constantinian Church with a definite Episcopal hierarchy'. Secondly, Bucer 'never suggested that the Church should actively resist

---

[14] VanderSchaaf, 100
[15] J.H. Blunt, *The Reformation of the Church of England*, London: Riving tons, 1882, 162-170. Van 't Spijker, 425 –427, describes Bucer's influence on à Lasco's church-order, and he mentions the use of it which was made by the Dutch.

monarchs who fail to go along with the Church's every desire'.[16] We think that VanderSchaaf here is very far from hitting the mark. If he were right, Bucer would have been an Episcopalian Anglican. However, Van 't Spijker concludes that 'the very criteria' of Bucerian thought are incompatible with hierarchical Episcopalianism in general and with Anglicanism in particular. It is true that Bucer never preached revolution against the monarchs, but he was not an admirer of the Henrician supremacy and his commonwealth-ideal certainly did not fit the rigid Erastianism of the Tudor church-settlement. Bucer's concern was pastoral, and his method pragmatic. As a foreign guest, he adapted his Reformation program to the prevailing situation, without abandoning his ideal of a Presbyterian Church. He cannot be absorbed by Anglican tradition. The emphasis definitely lies on his contribution to the Presbyterian way of ruling ad disciplining the Church. In this he was inspired by pastoral concerns and by the desire for sanctification. The Puritans have certainly taken over this important Bucerian notion. Like Bucer, they wanted a church-structure, which was in accordance with these concerns and desires. That Bucer, to a certain degree, lost his significance for the Puritan movement, was not because the Puritans did not acknowledge his basic principles. The Elizabethan Puritans were not Bucer's contemporaries. During the Marian Exile they experienced that the momentum of the Reformation had shifted to Geneva. There Bucerian thought was being developed in an independently and free from Anglican interference.

4. Shift to Calvin

a. Varied Reception

In Geneva, the Puritan refugees found fresh answers to old questions. Calvin's approach appealed to the English Protestants in their actual situation. This is not to deny that radical Puritans sometimes found questions to which the Genevan Reformer did not always give the desired answers. Radical separation of Church and State, revolutionary approach of monarchs, and mechanical use of Scripture, were not supported by Calvin. However, generally the Puritans recognised Calvin as their teacher.

A fertile soil was prepared by Calvinist foreigners in Edward's reign, especially during the protectorate of Lord Northumberland. Mary's reign provided for direct contact between English divines and Geneva. The Marian Exiles contributed greatly to the establishment of a Presbyterian State-Church in Scotland and to the emergence of Presbyterian Puritanism, i.e. to the acceptance of Calvinism in England. John Knox was probably the most prominent Genevan

---

[16] VanderSchaaf, 101-103

agent to disseminate -in his own way- Calvin's views in Britain. However, Calvinism was not only propagated by men like Knox, and it was not only accepted by declared Puritans. There was also a differentiated reception, a varied degree of loyalty to Calvin's thought. The Presbyterian minority in the *Puritan Movement* were the only group who professed to adopt the whole of Calvin's teachings, including his conception of church-order. This is not to deny that there are shades of difference, or perhaps even deviations. Other early Puritans were more radical than the Presbyterians. They did not accept Calvin's vision of ultimate state-involvement in ecclesiastical matters, and they also did not follow him with regard to the institution of authoritative regional presbyteries and synods. They favoured the absolute independence of the local congregation. They wanted the Church to be independent of the State, independent of the Anglican hierarchy, and also independent of extra-congregational Presbyterian bodies. A third group of Puritans was less radical than the Presbyterians. They were the Conforming Puritans, or the 'Anglican Puritans', as Lloyd Jones calls them. They accepted the salvation doctrines of Calvinism, and agreed to his desire for church-discipline. However, concerning the question of church-government, they conformed to royal supremacy and Anglican Episcopacy. In the reign of Elizabeth this was perhaps the largest and most influential group within the English *Puritan Movement*.

Even among the Church-prelates sympathisers of Calvinism were found. Archbishop Grindal, whom Collinson calls a Bucerian because of his interest in the introduction of church-discipline,[17] is presented by Cremeans as a friend of Calvinism.[18] These designations do not contradict each other. It is a matter of course that old Bucerians would turn to Calvinism in the time of Elizabeth. Grindal, though loyal to the authority of the State Church, recommended the works of Calvin. He sympathised with the cause of the Scottish Calvinists and tried 'to work out a compromise between his obligations to the Church of England and the Calvinistic ideas'. When Elizabeth proposed to limit the number of preachers and to abolish the *prophesyings*, he took a firm stand against the queen. This cost him dearly, for Elizabeth practically suspended him from office. Grindal's successor was John Whitgift. He too, was a man of Calvinistic ideas, though less than his predecessor. We shall see how the *Admonition Controversy* of the 1570's revealed the great difference between conforming Calvinistic Anglicans like Whitgift and nonconforming Presbyterian Puritans like Thomas Cartwright.

---

[17] Through VanderSchaaf, 86, who quotes Collinson's 'The Reformer and the Archbishop; Martin Bucer and an English Bucerian', in: *The Journal of Religious History*, 6 (1970/71)
[18] C.D. Cremeans, *The reception of Calvinistic Thought in England*, University of Illinois Press, Urbana 1949, 70, 71

Calvinism can also be traced in the Anglican Confession. The *42 Articles* of 1552, were a product of the Edwardian reign. They appeared before the period of the greatest Calvinistic influence in England. It was the time when Bucerian views still were of direct interest. But Bucer's influence had greater bearing on the worship and the discipline of the Anglican Church, than on its Articles of religion. More than in the question of church-order here Bucer was outweighed by the Swiss. Bullinger was the recognised leader of the Reformed Church at the time. However, his influence on the *42 Articles* was not incompatible with Calvinism. When the *39 Articles* were formulated, in 1563, Geneva was on the way of replacing Zürich's doctrinal influence in the Anglican Church, and this is reflected in the Elizabethan Articles.[19] The *39 Articles* show numerous points of doctrine which are compatible with Calvinism and in which a Calvinist might see much of his own doctrine.

However, Anglican Calvinism was by no means Presbyterian Calvinism. Although Calvinism by the end of the 16th century was the ruling theology in England among conformists and nonconformists alike, the Episcopalian Anglicans would only accept Calvinistic doctrines of predestination, justification, sanctification, etc. They did not follow Calvin in his ecclesiology, certainly not in his conception of church-government. This attitude of Anglican ambiguity was already showing in the reign of Edward VI. It became strikingly apparent after the Marian period, in the reign of Elizabeth. The nonconformist Puritans, especially the conscious Presbyterians among them, came to a much fuller acceptance of Calvinism. They not only absorbed Calvin's doctrines on the salvation of individual man, but they also followed his views on the government and the discipline of the local, regional and national Church, as well as his theories of Church and State.

b. Different Situations

This does not mean, however, that English Presbyterianism was an exact copy of Genevan Calvinism. The *Puritan Movement* as such collided with a 'halfly Reformed' system, in which they found a lack of preaching of discipline. The Presbyterian Puritans, i.e. the real Calvinists among them, looked further than that. In their conception, Anglican Episcopalianism and Erastian royal supremacy constituted the root of the lacking church-order. When they endeavored to criticise the 'popish elements' of this system, they began to

---

[19] Cremeans, 74-76. The author points to the Calvinistic character of the articles, 9 on original sin, 10 on free will, 25 on the sacraments, 26 on the possibility of falling away from grace, 27 on predestination and election. He also mentioned the *Lambeth Articles* of 1595, which contain a clear statement of Calvinistic theology in the England toward the end of the 16th century and of the acceptance which it received in the highest circles of the Anglican Church'.

experience its repressive force. In other words, they found themselves in a situation, which was different from Calvin's circumstances.

In the Reformed areas of Germany and Switzerland the civil magistrate favoured a Calvinistic type of church-government. No 'halfly' Reformed church systems, in the sense of the Anglican settlement, existed there. Therefore, Calvin could apply his church-order in the first place to the internal situation of the Church. His ways of church-government and church-discipline were in the first place meant for the regulation of the *internal* affairs of the church. The *external* aspects of government and discipline refer to the Church's independence as to the State. They did not play an important role with Calvin, because of the congenial political climate and the absence of old type of church-princes. The external independence was stressed as being important. Yet at the same time, Calvin's ruling elders, the exercisers of discipline, could be agents of the civil magistrate, without blocking the Church's progress to independence. Church and State in Geneva had similar interests. Finally, the Geneva city-state allowed the Church a considerable degree of autonomy, although the State remained to be represented in the Church's *consistories*.

External government in view of external independence was not Calvin's main concern, because the circumstances made it possible for him to win it. Church-discipline was not only exercised internally in the Church, but the circumstances made it also possible to exercise it in the public life of the State's citizens. All this left Calvin free to concentrate on the *internal*, less political aspects, of church-order. He was involved in Genevan politics. He had to struggle for the independence of the Church, but these things were not the real problem for Calvin. His followers in France, however, had to build up a church-order under hostile political and ecclesiastical regimes. They accepted Calvin's church-order, but they directed its use against the repressive powers of State and Church. A similar situation existed in The Netherlands. The *consistories* and *presbyteries* of the Reformed Church served as instruments in the struggle for ecclesiastical independence and for religious and political freedom. The situation in England was different from France, and from The Netherlands in its early stages, but also from Geneva. It was somewhere in between. There was no intolerant and powerful Roman Catholic church-system and no feudal monarchy. Contrary to Geneva, in England the political and ecclesiastical authorities were not on the side of Presbyterianism. The Puritans like the French Huguenots, constituted an illegal movement. They had to fight the powers of Church and State. In France, repression was much heavier than in England. This led to a violent revolution in the Huguenot wars. In 16th century England, the danger of revolution was prevented by the -after all- Protestant character of the State Church. The community-sentiment of the English *commonwealth*, strengthened by Zwinglian and Bucerian conceptions, tempered the fire of revolution. Like Calvin, the mainstream Puritans, including the Presbyterians, were no revolutionaries, but evolutionists. Their desire for church-order, however, was more inspired by extra-ecclesiastical factors than in Calvin's situation in Geneva. The Puritans, not less than Calvin, were interested in keeping up internal order of discipline. In fact, they waged a ferocious war against the moral iniquities with which the late Middle Ages had infected the life of the community. However, their concern was greater than that. They feared that the Reformation would halt and that they would be eventually strangled by the Anglican system of royal supremacy and Episcopalianism. Therefore, the Presbyterians wanted a church-order, which would not only check sin and incipient anarchy in the individual parishes. Their church-order should be able to maintain itself against the usurping powers of monarch and prelates. The books of discipline that they drew up, bore this tone and accent. The ruling and preaching elders they nominated, were no mouthpieces of the official ecclesiastical and political authorities. They looked for protection and defence, and even more for ways along which their church-order was to take over the prevailing one. Only a militant, though non-violent, system of Presbyterian characteristics would provide for that. Calvin's conception of church-government and discipline formed the basis of their thought.

The Presbyterian Puritans did not merely initiate their Presbyterianism, but they adapted the existing Presbyterianism to their own situation. In doing so, they contributed to an importance nuance of the history of Presbyterian eldership. According to Van Ginkel, 'the origin of the office of elders lies in the practical needs to have a college of people with supervisory powers, when it concerns the sanctification of life'.[20] In this thought, the origin of Presbyterian eldership is derived merely from the internal aspect of church-discipline. Looking at Presbyterian practice in England, Van Ginkel's definition is incomplete. It lacks the indication that the Presbyterian institution of elders also originates from the need for church-rulers and preachers, who were a match for the Anglican prelates and for the supremacy of the civil magistrate and the monarch in ecclesiastical matters. The ruling and preaching elders and ministers of proto-Presbyterianism were much more than safeguardians of internal discipline. They were influential people with definite ecclesiastical and political views, which they defended in the bishops' palaces, in parliament, at the law-courts and at the royal court. Their vision was religious and political at the same time, embracing the whole existence of the English *commonwealth*.

This vision produced an outward looking, independent type of church-government that was more aggressive than in Calvin's original design. In this the nonconformists differed as much from original Calvinism as the Scottish,

---

[20] Van Ginkel, 321

Dutch and French Presbyterians. However, there was at least one point in which they were closer to Calvin than their fellow-Calvinists in Scotland, The Netherlands and France. Although aggressive, they did not profess revolution. To the ecclesiastical and political establishment their ruling and preaching presbyters, elders and ministers, prophesyings and conferences, consistories and presbyteries, looked subversive enough. However, these institutions were not meant as the expressions of a revolutionary mood. At first, the English Calvinists trusted that they did not need to overthrow the Anglican Church, but that they could simply introduce their church-order in the already existing structure. This distinctive development of English Calvinism began about 1570 when Thomas Cartwright and Walter Travers started to emphasise Calvinistic church-government and discipline. Their adaptation of Calvinistic discipline was formulated in Travers' books on ecclesiastical discipline. Cremeans points to it that the difference with original Calvinism especially lay in an 'expanded and perfected system of church-government'. The functions and duties of office-bearers were clarified and emphasised, because English Calvinism depended entirely on its presbyters for leadership and direction.[21]

Church-government was closely connected to the ministry of the Word. This could explain why in the English Presbyterian tradition, the distinction of preaching/ruling elders and merely ruling elders as to the office of preaching was sometimes less rigid than elsewhere. In the 1580's the English Presbyterians began to realise that their project of introducing the Presbytery into the Episcopacy, could not be carried out as long as they did not have a Presbyterian monarch, who would accept the Calvinistic system of thought. They then developed the concept of the Christian magistrate who would admit and protect the Church's right to independence. They waited for better times and in the meantime, underground and illegally, the Presbyterian network expanded; in the next century it would surface in a Puritan Movement that was strong enough to temporary submit Episcopate and Monarchy. In Presbyterian church-orders the importance of independent church-governments was stressed. Again, this does not mean that they were revolutionaries, ready to violently force the civil magistrate the allow independence to the Church. That would not fit their ideal of a Presbyterian State Church. This does not mean either, that they ignored the internal aspects of the Church. On the contrary, internal and external aspects were interwoven. Church-government was the instrument of exercise of discipline.

The deeper motive of the Presbyterians for their opposition against the *Anglican Settlement* was their concern for the *sanctity* of the congregation. The purity (hence Puritans!) of the community of believers, they saw not at all

---

[21] Cremeans, 120-122

guaranteed in the Episcopalian system headed by the monarch and the bishops. In their opinion the negligence and the tyranny of the Episcopate were causes of the poor moral state of the Church. Internal disorder was caused by a lacking system of government. This they wanted to change. They were inspired by the holiness demands in the Gospel. Their desire to combat internal anarchy and lewdness, led them to fighting the worldly rule of princes and bishops. In this, they were less moderate than Calvin himself, but more moderate than contemporary Calvinists in Scotland, The Netherlands and France.

However, we should not exaggerate these differences. Calvin allowed resistance against the civil magistrate. Even more so this was done by the successor, Beza. Moreover, the Scottish Reformer, John Knox, provided for a more radical strain in the English Puritan movement. Knox, the great protagonist of Calvinism in British, did not hesitate to speak against the views advanced by Calvin, in cases where he thought this necessary. He disagreed with Calvin about the duty of Christian people with regard to their princes and rulers. He advocated opposition to rulers in certain circumstances, and even revolution. He was not completely governed by Calvin in this matter, but he thought things out for himself, according to the special needs of England and his homeland Scotland. Knox's view of State-Church relationship was definitely Calvinistic, but he followed a more radical course. He allowed the subjects of the State to overthrow their Roman Catholic sovereign by armed revolution. Calvin was more careful. Under no circumstances were private persons entitled to resist their authorities in a violent way. He rejected the people's sovereignty conception of the *monarchomachs*. The right of resistance is not based on the will of the people. It is not a matter of natural law. The best weapon against bad rulers is patience and suffering.[22] Only when the sovereign forces his people to wickedness and to disobedience against God, resistance can be allowed. Even then, private persons are not entitled to armed revolution. It is the duty of the lower magistrates to take the initiative of any form of violent resistance. Knox went further than that. Not only the lower magistrates, but also private persons have the right to resist. He had in mind those people who were called to govern the congregation, the elders in the consistories and presbyteries. Therefore, the right of resistance was not laid in the hands of the general public, but in the hands of rulers of the Church. Calvin objected to this idea. Knox tried to follow him closely, yet at this point, he worked out in his own conception.

However, Knox was not the most radical representative of English Puritanism. On his left operated Christopher Goodman, the man who, according to Danner, 'first argued for a biblical mandate of resistance by elements in English society, in the event that lesser magistrates failed in their responsibility'.

---

[22] Bohatec, 76-91

In Goodman's revolutionary theory, in the last resort, when political and ecclesiastical rulers have failed, the initiative to armed resistance can be taken by common people.[23] With Calvin and Knox, the right of resistance is motivated by the interests of the Reformed Church only. With Goodman, a much wider and more political conception emerged. Calvin did not support the radical ideas of Goodman. Neither did he favour Knox' radicalism. Calvin's successor, Beza, was more congenial to Knox. However, he too would not condone Goodman's revolution of common people. In the 16th century Puritan radicalism did not take the shape of violent resistance. Upon the accession of Elizabeth, radicals like Goodman acquiesced to the system and sought a legal, parliamentary revolution. Violent revolution lost its significance in Elizabeth's *via media*.[24]

c. Not Violent but Adamant

Therefore, when comparing Calvin's conception of church-government and State-Church relationship on the one hand, and the reception of it by the Presbyterian Puritans on the other, one can conclude that there were shades of difference. In England the external aspect of church-government and the question of resistance were taken more seriously than in Calvin's conception. However, as already has been said, these differences should not be exaggerated. Like Calvin, the English Puritans enjoyed the support of certain magistrates. Many noblemen and influential politicians, even in court circles, belonged to their party. At least one of the Tudor kings was as much on their side, as they could have wished. Besides, the Puritans were as much touched by the wave of nationalist enthusiasm as anyone else in the 16th century. This bound them in affection to their monarchs. The Tudor monarchs were by no means similar to the continental Habsburg rulers. The English *commonwealth* was more like the political structure of the continental city-states. Like the continental free citizens loved their cities, the English Puritans were patriots. In general, they respected

---

[23] G.D., 'Christopher Goodman and the English Protestant tradition of civil disobedience', in: *Sixteenth Century Journal*, Vol/ VIII, 3 (1977) pp 70 – 73. According to the author, Goodman probably wrote the second Admonition to Parliament of 1572. He calls him 'a typical representative of Elizabethan revolutionaries, more revolutionary than contemporary Puritan revolutionaries'. Exiled in the reign of Mary, together with Knox, Goodman went to Geneva in 1555. Prior to his exile, he was involved in plans to murder the queen. In 1572, he retracted his ideas of violent revolution.
[24] Cremeans, 117 ff, says that Puritan patience was by no means inactive. 'The aims of English Calvinists were primarily religious, but their chief aim, a true theocratic state, bore tremendous political implications which were to make themselves felt in English history'. Thomas Cartwright, the leader of Elizabethan Calvinism, expressed the Calvinist theocratic ideas like this: 'Civil magistrates must govern according to the rules of God ...'. The State should be modelled to fit the Church'. This was almost the complete opposite of the Anglican Erastian conception of the State above the Church.

their monarch and loved their country, although they resisted the authority of monarch and bishops in ecclesiastical matters. However, monarchy and episcopate were no foreign powers to them. The political and spiritual danger from abroad was represented by the Papacy and by Spain. Against this, Puritans and Anglicans formed a united front. This moderated the antagonism from both sides. Further, the Puritans exercised a considerable influence in Parliament. This institution, though often silenced and submitted by the Tudor-monarchs, was eventually able to restrict the more obnoxious characteristics of royal power. Another moderating fact was the Puritan-mindedness of a large number of the Anglican clergy, even among bishops and archbishops. These conformist Puritans did not walk the path of conscious Presbyterians, but in many aspects they were Calvinistic Puritans.

All these factors influenced the Puritan movement of those years into a Calvin-like non-violent direction, though not making it less adamant. However, at the grass roots and underground the movement contained the germs of a later revolution. It was restrained non-violent resistance. That was how the underground Puritan movement operated by the end of the century. In this climate the Presbyterians tried to form their bodies of church-government. Calvin's example of church-government was closer to the Puritan practice than one would assume on first sight. Though living in a more congenial situation, Calvin was absolutely not free of worries about the authoritative position of the civil magistrate. In fact he had to fight for the relative independence of his Genevan Church for a long time. Moreover, he had to consider the hostile attitude of kings and magistrates in countries where his followers were persecuted. Of course, these circumstances also influenced his conception of the office and the government of the Church. Although Church and State were never completely separated in Geneva, Calvin's ruling elders gradually became less of city-council-officials and more of ecclesiastical office-bearers who safeguarded the independence of the Church. It is not accidental that churches with a Calvinistic order of elders, consistories and classes, were best equipped to survive periods of a severe oppression by the State.

d. Differentiated Approach

The position of Calvin in Geneva and the position of his followers in England were not fundamentally different. Shades of difference produced a differentiated approach of the issue of church-government and discipline. Calvin's followers in England were also inspired by Zwinglian and Bucerian thoughts. In the end of the 16th century, the Puritans were essentially Calvinists. However, their Calvinism was not uniform. Those who advocated a complete break with the State in ecclesiastical matters had already left the Anglican Church. The issue of

State-Church relationship was also a cause of division among those who stayed in the established Church. A large group of Puritans, including many in leading positions, although generally influenced by continental Calvinism, conformed to the Anglican monarchical system of church-government. Others continued to hope for a more qualified State-Church relationship. They rejected the attitude of the *Conforming Puritans*, but they also denounced the *Separatist Puritans*. This was the position of those who gradually took Presbyterian views of church-government. First, they tried to introduce their Presbyterianism into the structure of the Episcopalian Church. When they discovered the impossibility of their enterprise under the given circumstances, they waited for another chance. In the 17th century, their new attempt to establish a Presbyterian State-Church almost succeeded, and finally they were led or forced out of the Anglican Church. The gradual development to conscious Presbyterianism in the second half of the 16th century originated in the desire to introduce stricter forms of church-discipline and it progressed to the formulation of a church-order with elders, consistories, presbyteries, and general synods or national assemblies.

In these days of Reformation enthusiasm, church-discipline was the household word with all groups. Even the Roman-Catholics had their Council of Trent, 1545-1563, which contributed to the setting right of some of the medieval abuses in the old Church. All groups within the English Reformation stressed the importance of discipline, monarchical Anglicans, conforming Puritans, nonconforming Presbyterian Puritans, radical separatist Puritans, and Anabaptists. They all had theories that emphasised the necessity of church-discipline. However, they came to different conclusions. With the exception of the Anabaptists – who had their own continental examples – all groups looked to Wittenberg, Zürich, Strasbourg, and Geneva for advice and guidance. In the end Calvin's Geneva became the focus point of Anglican and Puritan attention. However, Calvinism could not prevent the English Church from dividing into different sections. Church-order became the central issue. The next chapter deals with certain historical events, which led to these divisions, and to the emergence of Presbyterianism as a movement.

Chapter 5

The Edwardian Prayer Book

1. Hooper and the Vestments

a. Changing Climate

When Henry VIII died in 1547, he was succeeded by his son, Edward VI. The king was only ten years old at the time. He had to delegate his royal power to the Privy Council in which successively two Lords Protector seized the reins of government. Direct royal supremacy over the Church had practically ended. However, this did not mean at all that the road was free for the introduction of alternative forms of church-government. Lord Protector Somerset, and even more his successor Northumberland, swayed all political and ecclesiastical matters.[1] Under them functioned Archbishop Cranmer and his bishops, like Nicholas Ridley, the bishop of London.

Nevertheless, the climate was changing. The Edwardian period proved to be very favourable to the progress of the Reformation in England. The Edwardian rulers of Church and State were ready to go much further than their Henrician predecessors. The Reformation on the Continent served them as an example. Cranmer c.s. first went into the direction of Lutheranism, but soon they were attracted by the Zürich Reformation, especially in its Erastian version, and even by Genevan Calvinism. Returning refugees, like John Hooper, who had undergone the influence of the continent, were nominated to high posts. In addition, a number of Reformers from the Habsburg Empire, who were forced to leave their countries by the Interim measures of 1549, were invited to settle in England. They were given influential positions. In the previous chapter, we described their impact in the English Church.

Most important was the adoption and enforcement by the government of a number of ecclesiastical statements. They were two *Acts of Uniformity*, together with two *Books of Common Prayer*, in 1549 and 1552, the confession of the *42 Articles* in 1553, and new regulations for the ordination of priests. The

---

[1] Both Lords Protector ruled in a centralistic way. However, there was a difference. D.E. Hoak, *The king's council in the reign of Edward VI*, Cambridge University Press, 1976, says that in the years of Somerset's rule the activities of the royal council probably ceased, because the Lord Protector conducted the business of State through his own household. After Somerset's fall, his successor Northumberland, restored the council to its previous position at the centre of Tudor government. He used the council to carry out his will and was able to control it. In this manner he, though a Puritan-minded Protestant, paved the way for Queen Mary to restore a more solid government by royal council, directed against the progress of the Reformation.

The Edwardian Prayer Book

Prayer Book was meant as a prescribed liturgy for public Anglican worship. Its enforcement angered the incipient *Puritan Movement* and gave a strong impetus to it. It kindled the desire for new disciplinary structures and ultimately for new forms of church-government. Although the Prayer Book was a further step away from the old medieval system of ceremonies and rituals, its version in 1549 was essentially still a Roman Catholic liturgy. It was rejected by a large number of believers. The second version in 1552, though essentially Protestant, could not satisfy the proto-Puritan opponents either. They wanted to complete the Reformation by changing the Church from within. The first step would be the removal of all popish ceremonies and rituals. Marsden says: 'They were anxious for improvement, sometimes fretful for change'. However, thoughts of conscious division and separation had not yet emerged. Marsden: 'They revered the great principle of an established Church and did not entertain a thought of a separating from its communion'.[2]

b. Church-robes rejected

The real conflict, which was soon to produce a more organised movement of nonconformism, started with a controversy on the wearing of *church-robes*. John Hooper, who on the continent had been influenced by Bullinger and Zwingli's son in law Gualter, was offered a bishopric in 1550. He was prepared to accept it. This is significant. The earliest Puritans like Hooper, -Van 't Spijker even calls him 'this father of Puritanism'- still felt free in matters of church-government. Even authorities like Calvin and Bucer were not opposed to the office of bishops as such. According to Van 't Spijker, Hooper was guided by the proposals for diocesan reform, put forward in Bucer's *De Regno Christi*.[3] Hooper did not reject the bishopric. However, he did not want to be put into office in the way that was being dictated by Cranmer, Ridley and others. His superiors told him that he had to wear the customary Roman-like vestments. He would not consent to this and withstood them. Lloyd Jones looks upon this controversy as the very indication of the difference between Anglicanism and Puritanism. It shows the origin of dividing visions of church-order, and of later separation.[4] We quote his comment:

> 'In the question of church-robes Hooper was on the one side, Cranmer and Ridley on the other side. The difference about these things was that they were described as indifferent. The Anglican view was, that these things are unimportant; it is the Gospel alone that matters. Also, we should be supremely

---
[2] J.B. Marsden, *History of the early Puritans*, London, 1850; p.6
[3] Van 't Spijker, 428
[4] Lloyd Jones, 244, 245

concerned about the preservation of the Church. That was the typical Anglican attitude. ... To which the Puritans replied: if they are indifferent, why then do you force them? That is the essence of the Puritan argument: if they are indifferent why do you compel us to submit to them. ... Thus at the time of Edwards reign, we see beginning to emerge two basically different views of ecclesiasticism. The Anglican's is a progressive view, a developing view, the typically Catholic view. Whereas the Puritan's is a static view, which says that these things are determined by the New Testament, and that, once for all'.

In the wake of Hooper's conflict, the clash of opinions on matters of ceremonies and vestments would inevitably lead to a difference in views of the church-government in general and of bishops in particular. The qualifications by Lloyd Jones throw light on the birth of the *Puritan Movement.* They also explain why certain proto-Puritans began to move into the direction of Presbyterianism. Picturing their way of thinking, Lloyd Jones continued:

'What is a bishop? Is he to be described as a Lord? Has he the right to dictate in the way that he has hitherto done? The Puritans began to query this, and preferred the continental pattern of government that many of them had seen at first hand, and of which they were hearing constantly in their correspondence with some of the great continental teachers'.

Lloyd Jones is probably right when he says that almost a determining factor in the Edwardian period seemed to the whether or not a person had been on the continent:

'What explains much of the trouble was the fact that by the time of Edward, Cranmer had not been out of England for fifteen years. Ridley had never been abroad at all. Latimer, the great preacher, was primarily concerned about morality and not with these matters. The men, who had been on the continent, and had seen the way things were being done in Geneva and other places, were so influenced by that, that it changed their thinking. Cranmer, Ridley c.s., who had not come under this influence, saw things in a different way, in a more insular way'.

On the other hand, Lloyd Jones should have admitted that some continental Reformers were less persistent in matters like these, than Hooper was. Bucer wrote to Cranmer and Hooper on the subject. He said that the ecclesiastical *habits* might be used without offence to God. At the same time expressed a wish that they should be abolished, as affording to some an occasion of superstition and to others of bickering and contention. Bucer maintained that the fault lies not in the *vestments* as such, but in the minds of the ministers and congregations. Notwithstanding his personal antipathy toward vestments, Bucer considered them indifferent things. He implored Hooper for the sake of the Church of Christ to dismiss his scruples and to accept the office.[5] A similar opinion was held by Peter Martyr. Also, Calvin himself thought that Hooper carried his scruples too far. In a letter to Bullinger he said:

> 'Though I approve of his constancy in refusing to be anointed, yet I should have preferred that he had not contended so pertinaciously respecting the cap and surplice, although I do not approve of them, and so I lately endeavoured to persuade him'.

Calvin also wrote a letter to Lord Protector Somerset, in which he recommended Hooper to his protection.[6] In the end, Hooper gave in, after a period in prison. He was consecrated in Episcopal vestments, thus he became a bishop of the Anglican Church.[7]

Apparently, on the side of the continental Reformers there was more leniency respecting certain 'popish dregs', than the earliest Puritans would indulge. Bucer, Bullinger, Melanchthon and even Calvin and Beza were prepared to suffer a number of 'indifferent things', if this could prevent the Church from breaking apart. However, these *adiaphora* were sometimes 'popish rests', which they would not have allowed to exist in the cities and regions where they themselves had designed and introduced the Reformation. Therefore, many Puritans looked upon their advices in these matters with some scepticism. At the same time, the moderating counsel of continental Reformers with regard to *adiaphora* helped the earliest Puritans in rethinking their problems to the roots. And this contributed to the consolidation of their position.

c. Puritanism leads to Presbyterianism

From the final result of this *First Vestments' Controversy*, Lloyd Jones draws the conclusion, that Hooper cannot be considered as the founder of Puritanism and certainly not of Presbyterian Puritanism. He accepted to be a bishop in the Anglican hierarchy, and at his ordination he agreed to the wearing of robes reminiscent to the popish *vestments*. Of course, he did so with a good purpose. Of course, he was a Puritan at heart, which is shown by nearly all his subsequent

---

[5] Bucer's writings, quoted in 'Wether it be mortall sinne', point out that in the Scripture the Lord has prescribed 'The substance only of the holy ministries of His Word and Sacraments', but has left the Church 'the ordinaunce of all other things which belong to the comely and profitable administration of his sacraments' McGinn, 22; Marsden, 12; Dyer, 286, 287. Later Anglicans, like Whitgift, would use Bucer's words against Presbyterians like Cartwright, who were convinced that Scripture contains a model for church-government, valid for all times.
[6] Dyer, 288
[7] C.f. Blunt, 98, 99, 285 etc.

activities. However, the very act of accepting a bishopric makes it impossible to call him the founder of Puritanism. Anglicanism and Puritanism are incompatible essentially. Lloyd Jones does not stress this, in order to condemn Hooper, but just to define the ultimate difference between Anglicanism and Puritanism, as he sees it. He does not even call Tyndale the founder of English Puritanism, though he admits that the origins of the movement could be traced back to his spirit and action.

Is Lloyd Jones justified in drawing the line like this? Are Anglicanism and Puritanism really incompatible? The answer to these questions depends on the vision one has of the *Puritan Movement*. The crucial point in these questions is whether or not one assumes that Presbyterianism was the natural culmination of the Puritan emphasis. The Anglican church-government and the Presbyterian church-government have proved to be incompatible indeed. If Presbyterianism was the logical and spiritual consequence of Puritanism, then it is correct to conclude that Puritanism and Anglicanism are essentially incompatible.

In our opinion, the Bucerian and Calvinistic emphasis on the nature and independence of the Church, on discipline, on sanctification, on the involvement of the 'lay-element', must lead to the desire for a kind of church-government that cannot be in harmony with the Anglican hierarchical and monarchical structure. In this sense Puritanism produced Presbyterianism. It is true that many early Puritans did not become conscious adherents of Presbyterianism. Presbyterianism was always a minority movement among Puritans. However, this does not denounce the fact that Puritanism came to its head in Presbyterianism. Puritanism in itself was a loose movement of ill-coordinated thought. In Presbyterianism it took shape as an organised body of discipline and doctrine. In the second half of the 16th century, it tried to change Anglicanism in the way of evolution. Finally, both systems collided. The question of incompatibility was answered by the events of history.

In Edward's time, Presbyterian Puritanism had not yet emerged as a movement. Many questions were still open-ended. This explains the Reformers' patience with the leaders of the Anglican Church. Calvin, in his correspondence with Cranmer and Somerset, particularly stressed the importance of lively preaching, the extirpation of old abuses and the punishment of vice. He trusted that preaching and discipline would form the basis for a change of church-government. His commentaries on *Isaiah* and the *Canonical Epistles* he dedicated to the King Edward. Cranmer's proposal of an international religious conference was greeted by Calvin congenially:

> 'As to myself, if I should be of any use, I would not, if need were, object to cross ten seas for such a purpose'.

At the same time, the Genevan Reformer was well informed about the abuses of the English Church. In a letter to Cranmer he said:

> 'I am told that such a mass of popish corruption has been left, as not only to obscure, but almost to overwhelm the pure and genuine worship of God. Meanwhile, that is the soul of all ecclesiastical order, I mean preaching, lives not, or at least is not as vigorous as it ought to be'.[8]

Popish corruption and lack of preaching were the main evils of Edwardian Anglicanism, according to the Reformer of Geneva. The challenge of a strong movement with an essentially different system of government and discipline would be required to remove them. Its emergence was prepared by the events in the Henrician period and by the influence of foreign Reformers. But the very foundations of English Presbyterianism were still to be laid.

2. John Knox and the *Black Rubric*

a. Kneeling at the Eucharist

According to Lloyd Jones, the Scottish Reformer was not only the founder of Presbyterianism in his homeland, but also the founder of British Puritanism and Presbyterianism as such. He mentions Knox's originality and independence of thought, his ability to bring out clearly the principles of Puritanism, and the faithful way in which he applied his principles. These things made him the founder of a movement, which would restrict the powers of episcopacy and monarchy in an attempt to substitute them by a really Reformed church-order.

> 'Knox stood out in his conscientious application of what he believed to be the New Testament pattern of the nature of the Church, and the ordinances and the ceremonies, and the exercise of discipline'.[9]

The ministry of Knox in England coincides with the most crucial years of Edward's reign. After his conversion, his preaching activities in St. Andrews, his two years as a slave in a French galley, Knox settled in England in 1549. The king's council appointed him as a minister of the Word in Berwick-on-Tweed and New Castle. Afterwards we find him as 'one of the king's six itinerant chaplains who were employed to propagate Reformed tenets through

---

[8] Dyer, 283, 285, 292-295. The downfall of preaching was also caused by the spoliation of the Church, begun under Henry VIII and intensified in Edward's reign. Because its chantries etc. were confiscated, the Church could not adequately pay its ministries. This supported the idea of a necessary change of church-organisation and government.

[9] Lloyd Jones, 267-269

Ministers and Elders

the country by preaching'.[10] Contrary to most preachers, who conformed, Knox refused to follow the instructions of the first *Book of Common Prayer*, 1549. He rejected the reception of the sacrament in a kneeling posture, the baptism of children whose parents had been excommunicated and other regulations. The main topic of his opposition became the kneeling when receiving the bread of the Eucharist. The kneeling was not explicitly prescribed in the first Prayer Book, but it was in the second Prayer Book in 1552. This brought about a furious protest by Knox in a sermon before the young king. Edward was so much impressed that he signed a declaration, which said that the kneeling was not to mean adoration to the sacramental bread and wine and not to any real and essential presence there being of Christ's natural flesh and blood. Kneeling only meant a signification of the humble and grateful acknowledging of the benefits of Christ given unto the worthy receiver.[11] The declaration became known as the *Black Rubric* and was inserted in the second *Book of Common Prayer*. It was a safeguard against the danger of superstition and idolatry. It indicated the Puritan conviction that the minister of Word and sacraments is not a priest who sacrifices Christ. Although Cranmer – probably the designer of the second Prayer Book – had abandoned the Roman Catholic idea of mass, it was felt that Anglican practice left room for the idea that grace is dependent on the sacraments and on the acts of the priest, in other words on the hierarchy of the Church of England.[12]

b. Refusal of Bishopric

The prominence of Knox as founder and leader of the emerging *Puritan Movement* was not only apparent in his opposition against some doctrinal aspects of the Prayer Book. His objections also concerned the system of church-government. When the bishopric of Rochester was offered to him, he refused as a consequence of his Puritan principles. Right from the beginning, Knox rejected Episcopacy, even if the bishops were Puritan-minded. This is the most fundamental difference between Puritanism and Anglicanism. Puritans did not

---

[10] Dyer, 284
[11] The text of this post-communion-rubric runs as follows: 'It is hereby declared that there thereby [by kneeling – S.P.] no adoration is intended, or ought to be done, either unto the sacramental bread or wine, there bodily received, or unto any corporal presence of Christ's natural flesh and blood. For the sacramental bread and wine remain still in their very natural substances, and therefore may not be adored (for that were idolatry, to be abhorred of all faithful Christians). And the natural body and blood of our Saviour Christ are in heaven, ad not here; it being against the truth of Christ's natural body, to be at one time in more places than one'; cf. Hague, 56,57
[12] Hague points to it that there is in the communion of the communion service of the Prayer Book a distinct repudiation of the whole idea of 'sacrifice', that is, in the sense of its being a re-enactment of the offering of Christ on Calvary. Hague, 62. Article 31of the Confession speaks of 'the one oblation of Christ finished upon the cross'.

turn against most of the regulations and doctrines in Prayer Book and Articles of Religion as such. Their main objection was the Episcopacy itself. This should be kept in mind when reviewing Puritan criticism against Edward's second *Book of Common Prayer*.

3. Puritans and the *Prayer Book*

a. Protestant Direction

The Edwardian Prayer Books must be understood in a Protestant context. This is true even though the first version, in 1549, bore the characteristics of a Roman Catholic liturgy. Ecclesiastical thought was orientated on the *Reformation Movement*. Gradually this took shape in the formulation of doctrine. There was also an increasing interest of accommodating the regulations of public worship to new conceptions, in which preaching and discipline played a central role. The general public was deeply moved by the question of liturgy and ceremony; much more than by the formulation of Reformed doctrines. Liturgy is a practical thing that pertains to everyone. In the practical regulations of ceremony and worship it would be clear to all citizens which course the Church of England would take. How did people consider these things? Liturgy is a reflection of salvation-doctrine in the daily operations of the church. Conscious Protestants, like the proto-Puritans, tended to be highly critical against those ceremonies and rituals, which reminded of the Roman Catholic conception of salvation. Liturgy is also a reflection of the organised order of the Church, its form of church-government. As such, the *Book of Common Prayer* and the Anglican confession of faith, the *Articles of Religion*, do not deal with the subject of church-government. But it is clear that they got their place in the context of the Tudor church-settlement. They presupposed the government by monarch and bishops, royal supremacy and episcopacy. The Prayer Book was consciously adapted to the prevailing system of church-government. That is why Puritans found 'popish rests' in the formulations of the Prayer Book. Soon their main objections were directed against the monarchical and Episcopalian foundation of the Church's liturgical system.

It was generally felt -also by the Episcopate- that the first version of the Book was inadequate. So, proceedings started to produce a second one. This was largely done by the Archbishop Cranmer. He also involved a number of foreign Reformers. The result was a Book of Protestant character. Hague writes on it in exalted terms:

> 'Not only the men and the times, but the very influences that were at work upon the Reformers, were all of them set in the strongest possible degree in a Protestant direction'.

Hague does not know how far the influence of foreign divines like Martin Bucer and Peter Martyr extended, but he is sure 'that these masterminds moulded in no small measure the English Reformers in the changes introduced by them in the second Book of Edward VI', which according to him 'is substantially the Prayer Book as we now (1912-S.P.) possess it'. Hague concludes:

> 'The consequence was that the Prayer Book was so thoroughly purged on its second revision, that Martyr, in a letter written to Bullinger, ... declared that all things are removed which could nourish superstition'.[13]

Hague belongs to the tradition of those Puritan-minded conforming Anglicans, who have always reproached nonconforming Puritans for not recognising the strongly Protestant character of the second Prayer Book and of the Anglican confession and canons. Nonconformists, on the other hand, have never failed to notice that Anglican liturgy stuck half way the road from Rome to the Reformation. This was why the early Puritans, partly of wholly, rejected the *Book of Common Prayer*, even in its second version. When Hague defends the Protestantism of the second Prayer Book as compared to the previous one, we can be sure that the early Puritans were also aware of the positive differences. Hague's book, *Protestantism of the Prayer Book*, is prefaced by John Charles Ryle, the great evangelical Anglican bishop of Liverpool in the 19th century. No doubt the early Puritans, just like Hague and Ryle rejoiced at the considerable progress, when comparing these two versions. Let us mention some of the most striking examples. The word 'mass' was omitted and substituted by 'Lord's Supper of Holy Communion'. The word 'altar' was not to be found anymore. The mixing of the wine and water and the use of the wafer were done away with. The direction that the communicants should receive the sacrament in their mouths was left out and substituted. The vocation of the Holy Ghost on the elements was not mentioned. The sign of the cross in marriage service and in the consecration of water for baptism was left out. Prayers for the dead were swept away. The permission as to auricular confession was omitted.[14] McGinn calls the most decisive of these changes 'the removal of all reference to the

---

[13] Hague mentions this letter on pp 14, 15. He found it in 'Bradford's letters', Parker Society, p. 403, and in Gorham's 'Reformation Gleanings', p. 280. Calvin who read the Prayer Book in Mary's period, was not very satisfied with its contents. In 'a brieff discourse of the troubles begonne at Frankfort in Germany, 1554', p XXXV, Calvin is quoted like this: Edward's second Book does not possess 'that puritie which was to be desired'. McGinn, 10; Cf. Dyer, 422.
[14] Hague 161-165.

communion as a sacrifice and the emphasis, whenever possible, to its aspects as a commemoration'.[15]

Of course, these points indicate an increasing departure from the ritualism and sacerdotalism of Rome. However, the Puritans did not feel safe with the Book. They were not convinced that the formulations of the Prayer Book would prevent the Church from developing again into a Rome-ward direction. They feared the possible revival of auricular confession, sacramental absolution, a sacrificial conception of the Lord's Supper, denial of justification by faith alone. They also feared that the reading of Prayer Book homilies would substitute lively preaching Hague rejects the idea as if these marks of Romanism could be founded on the faith of the Anglican Church. However, he admits that Anglicanism has been endangered by Romanism along these lines. Indirectly he admits that the fears of the early Puritans were justified.

b. Bucer's *Censura*

No doubt, the Protestantism of the second Prayer Book got shape under the influence of Martin Bucer and other foreign divines, some of whom were disciples of Calvin. Bucer belongs to those who, at the request of Cranmer, wrote comments, which in some way or another have influenced this directory for the Anglican church-service. Bucer's comments became known under the name, *Censura*.[16] Whitaker re-edited the text as it got into the hands of Cranmer.[17] The last main section of the *Censura* is entitled 'De ordinatione legitima'. Here Bucer wrote 'about finding suitable ministers for the sacred ceremonies'. Calling, examination and ordination are described in agreement with his earlier writings. Ordination is accompanied by 'the imposition of hands, before a solemn gathering of the Church'. 'It signifies and represents guidance, strength and protection of the hand of Almighty God'.[18] Whitgift, in his dispute with Cartwright, would later use Bucer's formulation of the imposition of hands in support of the Anglican doctrines of *apostolic succession* and *episcopacy*.[19] However, in chapter 4.3.c we have seen that this is misuse or misunderstanding of Bucer's conception. Bucer did not describe the ordination as a sacramental act that confers ministerial grace. In his view, bishops were to impose hands on

---

[15] McGinn, 7-9
[16] 'Censura Martin Buceri super libro sacrorum seu ordinationis Ecclesiae atque ministerii ecclesiastici in regno Angliae'.
[17] E.C. Whitaker, *Martin Bucer and the Book of Common Prayer*, Great Wakering, 1974; Bucer's *Censura* was sent to the bishop of Ely, who presented it to Cranmer. This does not exclude the traditional view that Cranmer himself asked for Bucer's comments. Cf. C. Hope, *Martin Bucer and the English Reformation*, Oxford: Blackwell, 1946, 58
[18] Whitaker, 176 ff
[19] Hope, 63; Cf. McGinn, 80

the ordained. The bishop's own ordination was not essentially different from the ordination of other presbyters. The bishop just functioned as a *primus inter-pares*.

Bucer's comments found their way to the designers of the Prayer Book. Whitaker's comparison of the *Ordinals* in the Edwardian Prayer Books, leads him to the conclusion that the 'compilers of the Ordinal of 1552 made use of Bucer's treatise'. They included much of his formula for the questioning of *ordinandi*.[20] However, the use of Bucerian words did not go with the adoption of the Bucerian conception of church-order. In the context of the Prayer Book, Bucerian elements sound out of place.

c. Form and Government are Essential

The Puritans were most suspicious with regard to those phrases, which affected the position of clergy and church-rulers. The word 'priest', reminiscent of the old order, is frequently used in the revised *Ordinal* of 1552. The liturgy for the ordination of parish presupposes the existence of different orders: laity and clergy, higher and lower clerical orders.

> 'The bishop with the priests (or presbyters) present, lay their hands severally upon the head of everyone that receives the order of priesthood, thus carrying out...the apostolic practice in ordination, the conjunction of the hands of the presbytery with that of the bishop, the representative of the higher order, in manual imposition'.

In this massive formulation of manual reception and manual imposition by lower and higher orders, the simple meaning of Bucer's laying on of hands cannot be recognised anymore. The conjunction of hands by bishop and priests was a slight indication to Bucer's idea of parity. However, it could not take away the early Puritans' objections against the hierarchical implications of the ordination service.[21] Neither did the Puritans trust the Anglican assurance that the ordination was not meant as a sacrament. In the words of the ordaining bishop, they felt hierarchical implication and sacramental meaning.

> [While the hands are laid on the hands of the candidates,] 'humbly beseeching on their knees, the bishop says the word which convey the committal of the

---

[20] Whitaker, 4-6.
[21] Certain Puritan objections were met in the *Ordinal*. In the directions for the ordering of deacons, priests and bishops all references to vestments were deleted. At the ordination, the presentation of the chalice at the solemn moment, was omitted, likewise the presentation of the pastoral staff at the ordering of bishops. In addition, Parliament declared the marriages of the clergy good and valid. McGinn, 9.

formal authority of the office [to the minister]: Receive the Holy Ghost for the office and work of a priest in the Church of God, now committed unto thee by the imposition of our hands. Whose sins thou dost forgive, they are forgiven: and whose sins thou dost restrain, they are restrained. And be thou a faithful dispenser of the Word of God and of His holy sacraments. In the name of the Father, the Son, and the Holy Ghost. Amen'.[22]

The Puritans were aware of the fact that this Anglican ordination-phrase differed from the Roman Catholic Ordinal, which does not make the priest 'a dispenser of the Word'. However, they found enough elements to which they objected. The word 'priest' in itself might be a harmless etymological contraction of the word 'presbyteros'. In the opinion of the Puritans, however this term was too much open for the meaning of 'sacerdos', sacrificing priest.[23] As long as there was a possibility of understanding the priest as a sacramentally ordained sacrificer in a hierarchical context, the bishop's words 'Receive the Holy Ghost ...' must have sounded to them as most damaging to the Protestantism of the Church.

The established Church had abolished many elements of popery. However, it retained a system of priests and bishops. This again opened the door for popery. This was how the early Puritans gradually came to look upon the situation within the Anglican Church. They attacked the Anglican idea of *apostolic succession*, which was the very foundation of the ordination of the priests and bishops. According to the Anglican theologians, Holy Scripture and the facts of primitive church history indicate that

> 'there has been a succession of carefully ordained Episcopal ministers from the Apostles' time to the present [and] ... that the ordaining power is exercised by bishops and not by mere presbyters [and also] ... that ordinations by others are irregular'.

Thus is taught by the *Ordinal* of 1552 and by the 36th of the *Articles* of Anglican religion. Hague's reaction to these phrases is characteristic for a conforming Anglican Puritan. First, he admits that there is a difficulty here, and that he cannot agree with this conception of *apostolic succession*. He is quick to add that these Anglican phrases should not be explained in a Roman Catholic sense. Apostolic succession, contrary to the Roman conception, is only 'a matter which

---

[22] Hague, 154
[23] In the *Admonition Controversy* during Elizabethan's reign, Whitgift and Cartwright, the protagonists of respectively Anglicanism and Presbyterianism, quarrelled about the word 'priest'. Whitgift supposed it comes from 'presbyteros'; but Cartwright thought it is derived from 'sacerdos', the sacrificing priesthood of the Old Testament. The term should not be used for a minister. McGinn, 165-168.

concerns the form and ecclesiastical government of the Church, but it is not to be considered as touching the very nature and essence of the Church'.[24] The form and the government of the Church do not touch its essence. They are indifferent things.

    This is the argument of conforming Anglican Puritans in order to justify their allegiance to the Anglican Church. It began to be used in the Elizabethan era and it would be applied ever since. This argument was to mark the crisis within Puritanism. Is the question of church-allegiance really important? Are the organisation and the government of the church essentially indifferent things, or do they belong to the heart of doctrine? In Scripture and in primitive church history the nonconforming Puritans found that these things cannot be loosened from the central doctrines of Christianity. They are doctrines themselves. The severe enforcements of the Anglican system on them, made the early Puritans increasingly aware of the vital importance of the doctrine of church-government. The persecutions by Tudor monarchs and prelates made it easy for them to discover that monarchy and episcopacy themselves by no means considered the question of church-government as being unimportant or indifferent. In practice, the Tudor Church proved to be a tyrannical institution. This made the Puritans distrust its official liturgies, confessions, and canons, whatever their Reformed qualities might be.

d. No Compromise

In this way a Puritan view of Anglicanism could grow, which was not in the first place founded on rejection of the *Book of Common Prayer*, the *Articles* and other regulations, but on the practical attitude of the bishops and their monarch. A tyrannical Church cannot have good doctrines. A church, which lays so much weight on royal supremacy, Episcopalian church-government and apostolic succession, must also have perverted the other doctrines. Along this line of thought, the following Puritan picture of Anglican opinion developed:

> 'apostolic succession implies that without bishops there are no presbyters; without bishops and presbyters there is no legitimate certainty of sacraments; without sacraments there is no certain union with the Mystical Body of Christ, that is His Church; without this union there is no union with Christ; and without that union there is no salvation'.[25]

Hague uses these words, in order to make clear what Anglicanism is not. He is certainly right when he suggests that Prayer Book, Articles and canons leave

---

[24] Hague, 237-245
[25] Hague, 245

room for a different picture, even for a Calvinistic picture in certain aspects. However, too many have used the Anglican doctrinal and liturgical formula for the re-introduction of romanising tendencies. However, too often the practical attitude of Anglican leaders has supported these tendencies. The early Puritans, who were daily reminded of the internal and foreign dangers of Roman Catholicism, felt that Anglican theory and practice were based on *compromise*. Hague's words would have reflected their fear of what Anglicanism could become again, i.e. a Catholic Church in the hands of papacy. This inspired them in their forceful attempts to drive out the 'popish rests'[26], and to build a Presbyterian network.

In the Edwardian period, the climate was favourable to those who wanted to further the cause of the Reformation. The soil was prepared for a *Puritan Movement* that -in its Presbyterian form- would take the consequences of the Reformation for the way in which the Church is to be governed. However, first the hardships of Mary's reign were to create a more conscious group of Reformers. The old representatives of Henry VIII's church-regime, like the bishops Bonner and Gardiner, suffered in prison during the reign of Edward VI. After the accession of Mary, they were liberated. Then they could take revenge and contribute to the restoration of Roman Catholicism in England, thus re-instituting a system with more ability to produce the tyrannical consequences of Episcopacy than Anglicanism ever had.

---

[26] According to Marsden, 20, this explains the fierceness of the dispute on vestments, which was to be continued in the reign of Elizabeth.

Chapter 6

Restoration of the Papacy and Exile

1. The old Henricians resume Power

a. Pragmatists

When Henry VIII's Roman Catholic daughter Mary succeeded her half-brother Edward to the English throne in 1553, she immediately restored to power the protagonists of the *Henrician Church Settlement*, who had been in prison or merely put out of office. These people were no Roman Catholics as far as the Papal supremacy over the Church was concerned. They had consciously submitted to Henry's severing of the links with Papacy. However, the substitution of Papal authority by royal supremacy did not fundamentally change their adherence to medieval. They perfectly conformed to Henry's *Articles of Faith*, which were essentially Roman Catholic. In a sense, they were pragmatists. Some of them even conformed to the initial measures taken in the reign of Edward. Gardiner, a former Henrician diplomat of repute, was a friend of Somerset, and he got a bishopric. Bonner also agreed to the first changes under Edward. However, together with church-princes like Tunstall, Health and Day, they soon came to regard the Privy Council's takeover of royal supremacy over the Church as unconstitutional. Subsequently, they rejected all changes, even those minor ones in the Prayer Book of 1549. In this, they differed with other former Henricians, like the archbishop Cranmer, who had orientated themselves on the continental Reformation. As the English Church moved further away from Rome, these conservatives fell back on their previous loyalty to a romanised line of thought. Gardiner was perhaps the most characteristic representative of the old Henrician church-party. In a sermon before the Privy Council, he explained his view on the position of the pope. We quote part of it, because his idea -though extremely unpopular to 16th century Anglicans and Puritans alike- was thought attractive by sections of Anglicanism in later times. Being a loyal Henrician divine, Gardiner denounced papal supremacy over the Church. At the same time, he identified the office of Peter and the office of the pope. This led him to acceptance of papal authority from another angle:

> 'The name of Peter is no foundation for supremacy but ... he might be called the head of the Church, as the head of the river is called the head, ... and in some case the king of England might send to Rome; and if the bishop of Rome were a man of such wisdom, virtue and learning, that he were able in matters of

controversy concerning religion to set a unity in the Church of England, the king might well enough send unto him for his counsel and help'.[1]

Apparently, Gardiner defended a form of Papacy that would be restricted to the realm of religious guidance. However, his differentiated approach of the Papacy did not fit the political and ecclesiastical leaders of Edward's time. They identified Papacy and Antichrist, and gradually removed the remaining religious links with Roman Catholicism.

b. Persecutions

Queen Mary and her foreign advisers were opposed to the halfly loyal attitude of the old Henricians. They demanded the acceptance of papal authority in its classical form, though Mary never completely surrendered her royal prerogatives to the desires of the pope. The old Henricians had no choice, but to conform to papal rule and to cooperate in the persecution of Protestant opponents.

The first period of Mary's reign was still characterised by a certain tolerance. Royal supremacy over the Church was entirely abolished only in a later stage. Then, Cardinal Pole and his ultra-montanist party, inspired by numerous Spanish and Italian advisers, started the oppression of all 'naughty opinions'. Mary's marriage to King Philip II of Spain, England's political and religious archenemy, gave a foreign impetus to the persecutions. Medieval statutes against heretics were revived. Thousands perished in prisons. During the five years of her reign, at least 277 people were burnt. The majority of the victims belonged to the labouring classes. The incipient Puritans were hit most, together with the Anabaptists and other Separatists. Persecution ran hottest in the wider London area. Among the martyrs who were burnt, there were 26

---

[1] Blunt, pp. 136 –150, quotes Gardiner's sermon in order to show the 'different principles of that old Anglican party from those of the Ultramontanes, who subsequently sprang up under the influence of the Spanish advisers of Queen Mary and the Jesuit mission of Queen Elizabeth's time'. Gardiner was an adherent of royal supremacy, and he repudiated papal supremacy. However, this did not take away the fact that in his opinion the pope might be useful for England. As to doctrinal questions, like the character of mass, Gardiner does not seem to have differed much from Cranmer's view at the time. He recognised the Eucharist as a remembrance of Christ's passion, and not as another redemption or satisfaction or sacrifice. However, he believed 'the very true presence of Christ's Body and Blood in the sacrament of the altar'. Gardiner was put in prison in 1548 and he remained there until August 1553. Then he became an adviser of Queen Mary. Blunt, 299, 300, claims that he was not guilty of the bloody persecutions that followed.), but it remains a fact 'that he sat on the trial of Hooper, Rogers and several others who were brought before a commission of which he as Lord Chancellor was head'.

clergymen.[2] To them belonged those Henricians, who under Edward had been in leading positions. They had grown to a Puritan-minded attitude, though they were no Puritans in a narrow sense. We mention some of them, Bishop Taylor, Bishop Ferrar, Bradford, Bishop Ridley, Bishop Latimer, Archdeacon Philpot, and Archbishop Cranmer. Another victim, Bishop Hooper, had been closer to the cradle of the Puritan Movement. This was even truer for yet another victim, John Rogers, a leader of the nonconformists against Cranmer and Ridley.

A large number of future Anglican and nonconformist leaders escaped persecution and execution. Cartwright was still a student, and had not yet appeared as a leader of nonconformist thought. Parker, the future archbishop, went into hiding. Many other potential victims managed to escape to the continent in time, sometimes with silent assent of the Marian government.

2. The Marian exile

a. Refuge on the Continent

The number of burnings would have been much greater, had not many of the conformists left the country in time. The fierce persecution, which followed after the short period of comparative tolerance, drove thousands of English refugees to The Netherlands and the city-states of the Rhine and Switzerland. They left together with those foreigners, like Knox, Martyr and à Lasco, who had held important positions in the reign of Edward. According to Dyer, at the occasion of à Lasco's flight, some '800 Protestants left the shores of England for the continent, in the hope to find asylum either in Germany or in Switzerland'.[3] Bucer escaped persecution because he had died two years earlier. However, the *Inquisition* did not leave his body untouched. It was exhumed and burnt in Cambridge marketplace.[4]

In the Lutheran towns of Northern Germany, the English refugees were repulsed. Cranmer's original desire of friendly relations with the Lutherans does not appear to have been reciprocated. In the southern parts of Germany, and especially in Switzerland, however, the exiles were kindly received and allowed to establish churches. Frankfort, Strasbourg, Basel, Zürich and Geneva were the towns of their chief resort. The Northern German cities of Wesel and Embden -being under the influence of Calvinism- also received them. In these foreign

---

[2] Blunt, 213-226, says that during the first nineteen months of Mary's reign (July 1553- February 1555) 'there was no execution on account of religion'. The burnings took place during the subsequent part of her reign, extending over three years and nine months. In Foxe's account of the persecutions, 277 executions are mentioned.
[3] Dyer, 418, 419.
[4] Cf. A.F. Scott Pearson, *Thomas Cartwright*, 4.

cities conformists like Aylmer, Bale, Turner, Jewell, Parkhurst, Cox, Horn, Pilkington, mingled with nonconformists like Whittingham, Coverdale, Foxe, and with the non-English refugees like Knox, Martyr, and of course with the leaders of the continental Reformation. Marsden says that among the English exiles, there were five bishops and fifty doctors of divinity. Many of them would become bishops in the reign of Elizabeth, e.g. Jewel, Parkhurst, Cox and Pilkington, and there were even two future archbishops, Sandys and Grindal, among them.

The conforming Anglicans felt attracted by the ideas of Church-State relationship of Zwingli's son-in-law Gualter. However, above all, they were close to Zwingli's main successor Bullinger. Marsden calls this leader of the Zürich Reformation 'the sponsor' of the later English Church-settlement under Elizabeth. The future Anglican prelates belonged to Bullinger's circle of close friends. They were among his most affectionate correspondents.[5]

b. More than Vestments

In general, during the Marian Exile, conforming and nonconforming English divines, agreed much in their detestation of the Papacy and in their views of Evangelical truth. Here only few differences existed. In the *diaspora*, conformists and nonconformists seemed to find each other in many aspects of formed doctrine. However, this 'pleasing picture of brotherly unity' was soon to be blotted. Because, with regard to questions of ceremony and church-government, things were different. Here the temporary fusion of the two infant parties -Episcopalians and Presbyterian Puritans- produced no coalescence. In the case of Hooper we have seen, that there was a party that wished to carry the Reformation in England to a greater extent than Cranmer c.s. had done. It is certain that a large party of English Protestants was desirous for further changes. The unsettled question of the church robes, as part of the much broader issue of the *Book of Common Prayer*, would become a main problem in the conflicts of the Elizabethan period. Marsden thinks that the dispute with regard to the *vestments* 'lay at the root of many controversies, and was the root from which they sprang'.[6] This explanation of the conflict may be too superficial. It is true that the contending parties supposed the vestments 'to represent principles of which, it was said, they formed an integral part' and that the Puritans began to despise these Roman-like robes.

---

[5] Marsden, 15
[6] Marsden, 20 ff, represents the Anglican view that 'vestments are decent and becoming, and in themselves indifferent'. The surplice 'was used in the Church of Christ long before the introduction of popery'. He reproaches the nonconformists for not acknowledging this, and seems scarcely to recognise the more fundamental causes of the Vestments' Controversy.

> The Puritans 'identified the vestments with all the superstitions of popery' and looked upon them as 'the badge of antichrist', and they who wore them 'were regarded with suspicion as men either indifferent to the cause of the Reformation, or not yet sufficiently enlightened as to the danger and sinfulness of a system which ought to be avoided with alarm and horror'.

The conflict was much deeper rooted than in the question of vestments. The Presbyterian principle of church-government was not born out of certain ideas about the dress of a clergyman! At the bottom of the conflict, there were divided opinions of the character of the Church itself. They pertained to the question of church-order with regard to church-government, and discipline with regard to royal supremacy and episcopacy. Other issues were the question of the offices of ministers and the common priesthood, the questions of liturgy and confession in view of the Prayer Book and the Articles. Essentially, those were the causes of contention. New conceptions were born, and among the Marian Exiles, they were developed further. The establishment of new churches in foreign lands offered them a favourable opportunity for carrying their views into effect.[7]

c. The Puritans in Frankfort

The episode of the Marian Exile has contributed much to the birth of Presbyterian Puritanism. Lloyd Jones suggests that what happened on the continent was perhaps more important for it than the events at home in Marian England itself.[8] He particularly refers to the 'most visible and conspicuous congregation of the English Church beyond the sea'. By this, he meant the congregation of refugees in Frankfort, and the activities of John Knox in this German city. A description of the events in Frankfort is to be found in a tract, entitled 'A brieff discourse of the troubles begonne at Frankfort in Germany in the year 1554'. According to Dyer, the author of this account was probably William Whittingham, the minister of the congregation.[9] We follow Dyer's summary of the tract. Under the guidance of Whittingham it was determined that the Frankfort-congregation should only adopt a part of the *Book of Common Prayer*. By general consent, it was agreed that the surplice, and many other things in the church-service, as well as in the ministration of the sacraments,

---

[7] Cf. Dyer, 421
[8] Lloyd Jones, 273 ff
[9] Dyer, 422 ff

should be laid aside.[10] The congregation set up a church-government modelled upon that of Calvin at Geneva, consisting of a pastor, a preacher, elders and deacons.

Then they wrote a letter to other congregations of English exiles, with the intention of bringing them over to Calvinistic tenets. The letter in a somewhat disguised manner was directed against the hierarchical organisation of the Church in an Episcopalian system.[11] The Frankfort-exiles also invited John

Knox -who was in Geneva at the time- to come over and be their minister. The congregations of Zürich and Strasbourg answered to the Frankfort circular and sent representatives. From Strasbourg came Edmund Grindal, the future archbishop. He admonished his brethren to keep to 'the substance' of the Prayer Book. However, Frankfort persisted in its objections against the Anglican liturgy and church-order. Calvin in a letter lamented the division that had arisen among the English exiles, but at the same time, he expressed his dissatisfaction with the Prayer Book. Finally, Knox, together with Whittingham and other ministers drew up a new service-book after the fashion of Geneva, which was to replace the *Book of Common Prayer*.

This new order was accepted by the congregation, until the arrival of Richard Cox, a staunch defender of the Anglican system. Cox has been one of Cranmer's chief coadjutors in preparing the Prayer Book. When he arrived in Frankfort, he took immediate measures to restore its use. In the subsequent conflict, the civil magistrate sided with Cox, and Knox was banished from the city.[12] Conciliatory efforts by Calvin did not prevent the Frankfort congregation from being torn with intestine dissension. Cox and his friends felt that Calvin

---

[10] McGinn, 10, reads the *Brieff Discourse* differently, when he states that 'in the administration of the sacraments alone the second Edwardian *Book of Common Prayer* was followed'. To us this seems to be a misinterpretation.

[11] Dyer, 424, quotes this letter of the Frankfort exiles: 'You remember that before we have reasoned together, in hope to obtain a Church, and shall we now draw back as unmindful of God's providence, which hath procured us one free from all dregs of superstitious ceremonies? ... As touching the point of preferment [= appointment to an office, S.P.] we are persuaded thoroughly that it hath this meaning, that every man thought of himself modesty, humbly submitting himself to all men, unabling no man; for so much as you know that he which seeketh ambition, glory, advantage, or such like, is not moved with God's spirit, as witness the instructions, that Christ our master gave to his disciples, who labouring of like disease, were admonished that he which did excel among them should abase himself to his inferior: which malady St. Paul perceiving to infect like a cancer, most diligently frameth his style, that he might not seem to prefer himself to others in the course of his ministry'.

[12] Dyer, 430. Cox and his followers procured the banishment of Knox from Frankfort, by denouncing him to the magistrate of the city as the author of a book, entitled 'An admonition to England', in which he had dissuaded the marriage of Queen Mary with the emperor's son Philip, and compared Charles V himself to Nero, for his cruelties towards Protestants.

had sided with their opponents. Dyer thinks that from this time many Anglicans began to feel less respect than formerly for the Genevan Reformer.

d. Knox and Geneva

Knox's followers left the city and joined their teacher in Geneva, where they formed the nucleus of a Presbyterian congregation of English exiles. The events in Frankfort were of great importance. Lloyd Jones is probably right when he says that this 'was the first attempt at a Puritan Church amongst English people'. In Geneva, Knox introduced the order of service, which had been tried and rejected in Frankfort. It became known as the *Geneva Book*, and it was published in 1556 under the title: 'The Form of prayers and ministration of the sacraments, used in the English congregation at Geneva'. Lloyd Jones stresses its independence of Calvin. The 'first truly Puritan Church amongst English people' was oriented on Calvinism, but it was not a mere imitation of Calvin's structure. While at Geneva, Knox formulated his view with regard to princes and the attitude of the Christian towards 'the power that be'. Here he was ahead of Calvin. Lloyd Jones maintains 'that one cannot truly understand the revolution that took place in England in the next century, except in the light of Knox's teaching'.[13] Indicative of his independence of thought is the courageous treatise against Marian tyranny, 'The first blast of the trumpet against the monstrous regiment of women'. The negative result of it on the attitude of Mary's successor Elizabeth is well known. Elizabeth felt offended and never forgave Knox. It contributed to the queen's distaste for Presbyterians.

When Mary died in 1558, most refugees flocked home. However, several of those at Geneva, among them Knox and Whittingham, remained for another year or two, in order to finish a translation of the Bible which they had begun. Knox's Genevan example had a tremendous impact in England. It gave impetus to those groups who in Marian London, outside the influence of the clergy, had begun to form the little independent churches, which the Pilgrim Fathers would call their predecessors. Knox's example also contributed greatly to the formation of a *Puritan Movement* with adherents in the majority of the Anglican parishes, led by an abundance of Anglican clergymen. Of special importance was Knox's programme of ecclesiastical and educational reform, which he sent from Geneva to England in 1559.[14] In this document, he

---

[13] Lloyd Jones, 275, ff; More revolutionary than Knox sounded the writings of Christopher Goodman, Knox's co-minister in Geneva. His treatise 'How superior powers ought to be obeyed', according to Danner, 70, 'reflects a different and unique thrust in revolutionary political theory'.

[14] John Knox, 'A brief exhortation to England for the speedy embracing of Christ's Gospel, heretofore by the tyranny of Mary suppressed and banished'. Lloyd Jones, 276, calls it 'the first printed statement of Puritan principles with regard to the Church and her management'.

suggested the abolishment of the prevailing system of bishops and dioceses. Large dioceses should be divided into ten parts, and godly, learned men should be instructed to preach and to give instruction to the people in every city and town.

Here Knox emphasised the central ambition of Elizabethan Puritans: the preaching of the Word of God. However, preaching was not one of Elizabeth's favourite subjects. On the contrary, she considered it as quite unimportant. She was not prepared to tolerate any attempt to reorganise the Church in favour of preaching and preachers. This was the most apparent aspect of the new queen's long struggle with her Puritan subjects.

Chapter 7

The Vestments' Controversy

1. The Precisians Disappointed

a. Erastian and Theocratic Views

The reign of Elizabeth, 1558-1603, brought into the open the long brooding conflict of conformists and nonconformists in the English Church. Soon the breach was to open between Anglicans and Puritans. But with Collinson we can say that the terms 'Anglican' and 'Puritan' were not very useful at the time, because the era of Elizabeth did not yet see a definite Separation and 'a clear cut pattern of denominations'. Collinson, in his study of the Elizabethan Puritan Movement, points to the commonwealth idea of State and Church, which -as we have seen in chapter 3- contributed to a certain national solidarity.[1] However, this conception of unity, which was adhered to by Anglicans as well as by Puritans, did not produce similar expectations of the State and the Church. This is most apparent when we compare Anglicanism to Puritanism, especially in its Presbyterian form.

The Presbyterians believed in a State Church, quite as much as the Anglicans did. However, the contents of their beliefs were very different. Whereas the Anglicans thought in hierarchical patterns, this was much less so with the Presbyterians. The Anglicans believed in a hierarchy of bishops, including lower clergy. They also adopted a hierarchy of State and Church. Their Erastian view made the State govern the Church. The Presbyterians completely rejected the idea of rule by bishops under the monarch, dubbed as Episcopalianism. However, like the Anglicans, and unlike the Anabaptists, they acknowledged the important duties of the State in matters of the promotion of true religion. Lloyd Jones states that the Presbyterians also were essentially Erastian, accepting the State to rule the Church, although he thinks they followed 'Erastianism with a difference'.[2] This may be true for the Presbyterians of the 17th century, who with their short-lived political successes, were Erastians in a way, but not so for the 16th century Presbyterians during Elizabeth's reign. They were closer to Calvin's original theocratic ideas, which they adapted to

---

[1] Collinson, part I, chapter 1. In William Ramsey's *Epistle to the Moltonians*, the Church of God is constituted by the whole of society, by all members of the commonwealth. In the reign of Elizabeth, this idea strengthened. The whole nation as the people of the Lord, the godly commonwealth of Israel. The Puritan attacks on the *Elizabethan Settlement* were based on this conception, and led to the demand of enforcement of true Reformation by the public authorities.
[2] Lloyd Jones, 63

their own needs. Cremeans points to this.³ Calvin's theological views included a vision of both the Church and the State. Calvin's emphasis on order and discipline implied strictly regulated regulations of the relationship between the Church and the State. 'His conception of the obligation of the magistrate to serve the Church implied a close cooperation of Church and State'. In this, there was a tendency, which was just the opposite of Erastianism, not the State above the Church, but the Church above the State. Cremeans says that 'the idea of the supremacy of God leads to the theocratic assertion that the Church is the superior of the State'. He adds, however, that the Presbyterian Puritans 'never said so in plain words'. Calvin himself rejected the authority of the Church over the State as a popish tyranny. State and Church serve one another in mutual independence.⁴ Against this background, Calvin developed a very moderate theory of the right of misgoverned subjects to rebel. This theory, however, offered room for various interpretations of Calvin's view. Beza, Calvin's successor in Geneva, tended to a more radical version. We noticed before that in the tradition of Knox and the Scottish Reformation, the right to rebel was not only given to the lesser magistrates -Calvin's idea- but also to the governing bodies of the Church itself. This implies a tendency to a Church, which has authority over the affairs of the State. This apparent tendency in Knox and the Scottish Reformation influenced the English Reformation, especially the Puritan Movement, notably English Presbyterianism. English Presbyterians tended to look upon the State as an instrument for the enforcement of their ecclesiastical ideas. Lloyd Jones criticises the State-Church vision of English Presbyterianism. He wonders whether 'they were not too much influenced by the analogy of the Old Testament, applying it to England', whereas 'in the New Testament nowhere a direct connection between the Church and the State is taught'.⁵ Lloyd Jones' doubt may be justified, but again this does not point to the danger of a subservient Church in the Erastian model, but it points to the danger of a clerical system in which the Church has final authority over the State. In the experience of ordinary citizens, the result of an Erastian State in the Anglican model and of a clerical State in the Presbyterian model would be quite similarly negative. Did not Calvin reject both types because of their ultimate tyranny? Both conceptions were based on a mixture of religious and political interests, and would not

---

³ Cremeans, 111, 118-120
⁴ Bohatec, 614. In certain respects, the Church can be the servant of the State, and the State the servant of the Church, without abandoning their original independence and authority.
⁵ Lloyd Jones, 64-66; cf. McGinn, 103, 126, 313, 298, 522. In his dispute with Cartwright, Whitgift accused the Presbyterians of Judaism, because they identified the Old Testament chief of the synagogue with the elders in the Reformed Churches. However, Cartwright derived his elders and ministers in the first place from the New Testament, e.g. 1 Cor.12: 38, and Eph.4:11 (cf. McGinn, 78).

tolerate religious freedom to dissenting groups. Lloyd Jones finds that Presbyterian Puritanism became an 'alliance between those who were essentially religious and those who were purely political in their motives'. He deplores this, 'because the motives became mixed, as they always will become mixed, if we begin to confuse and admix politics with our religion'.[6] However, again we should stress that Lloyd Jones' qualification might be characteristic for the 17th century only. The aims of the early Puritans, including Presbyterians, in the Elizabethan age were primarily religious, although their theocratic view of the State bore political implications, they did not consciously mix religion and politics.[7]

b. Via Media

Puritans recognised only the authority of Scripture, even in those matters that were characterised as 'adiaphora' (issues of minor importance) by their opponents. Conforming Anglicans, on the other hand, tended to be guided by distinctions between essentials and non-essentials. In their view, they trod the middle road, i.e. the *via media*. The new queen herself was much inspired by a via-media-policy. Being a daughter of Henry VIII's second wife, Anne Boleyn, she was certainly not sympathetic with Roman Catholicism or with the decreasing party of Anglicans that wanted to re-institute obsolete forms and structures. The pope had already denounced her claims to the throne. According to Marsden, Elizabeth 'was deeply attached to the Reformation when she began her reign'.[8] Probably she was attracted by Lutheranism. However, in general she

---

[6] Lloyd Jones, 60

[7] Cremeans, 117, quotes Thomas Cartwright, the leader of English Calvinism in the time of Elizabeth: 'It is true that we ought to be obedient to the civil magistrate, who governeth the Church of God in that office , which is committed unto him, according to that calling. But it must be remembered that civil magistrates must govern it according to the rules of God, prescribed in His Word, and that as they are nourishers, so they be servants unto the Church, and as they rule the Church, so they must remember to subject themselves unto the Church, to submit their sceptres, to throw down their crowns before the Church, yea, as the prophet speaketh, to lick the dust of the feet of the Church'. Cf. McGinn, 114-117, who gives another Cartwrightian nuance: 'The State is less important than the Church. It has its own duties, which in certain occasions may touch the government and discipline of the Church'.

[8] Marsden, 29, 30, describes the day of Elizabeth's coronation, probably in exaggerated words: 'When she kissed the Bible presented to her at St. Paul's Cross on the day of her magnificent procession through London, and then pressed it to her heart, it is possible that no bosom in that vast enthusiastic crowd beat with more fervent loyalty to the Protestant cause'. Marsden also points to it that only 'with great difficulty she could be prevailed to assume the title of head of the Church', and he comments: 'It has been urged, indeed, that lingering reverence for the papal claim of universal supremacy had some share in this unwillingness'. Johnson, in his biography of Elizabeth (London: Futura, 1974), describes her protestant upbringing 'based on a spirit of inquiry, a repudiation of ecclesiastical authority as the sole guide of truth, and the personal study and interpretation of the

The Vestments' Controversy

did not appear to be interested in religion very much. Her personal antagonism against Calvinism was obvious; although this feeling was not shared by many of the members of her Privy Council and occupants of other high offices of the State. Elizabeth may have been a true Protestant, but above all her attitude was governed by the art of statesmanship. In order to safeguard her country's independence, she tried not to offend the impressive Roman Catholic powers on the continent. For her this meant the necessity of a strongly disciplined monarchical Anglo-Catholic Church, governed by obedient bishops. It also meant the oppression of all nonconformism, on the right and on the left. The Roman Catholics she left in peace during the first years of her reign, because not until 1568 did the English ultra-montanist party constitute a danger for her settlement.[9] This did not blind her for the foreign threats by Spain, and France, and by the pope, who had his Counter Reformation policy phrased by the Council of Trent. Invasion plans did not escape her eye; neither did the danger of rebellion by her Roman Catholic subjects.

2. The Elizabethan Settlement

a. Act of Uniformity

However, in Elizabeth's conception the dangers from the right were less serious than those from the left. The emerging *Puritan Movement* with its Old Testament vision of the State was to her feeling an important undermining threat of her settlement. The battle with the Puritans was joined in 1559, by the adoption of an *Act of Uniformity* and a revised *Book of Common Prayer*. Although Hague is convinced that the Elizabethan Book 'was essentially the same as Edward's Prayer Book of 1552'[10], it should be emphasised that some important changes were made. The 'Black Rubric' was removed. Consequently, kneeling at communion again could be made to imply the adoration to a certain corporeal presence of Christ and a weakening of the rejection of the doctrine of

---

Bible'. He says: 'She was not and never became a religious woman. ... She saw Christianity more as an outward and secular instrument to preserve society from disorder, than as a set of immutable truths to be inwardly believed' (p.17). Perry, 238, states that the queen abandoned the title 'supreme head of the Church on earth', and adopted instead of that the title 'supreme governor'.

[9] Blunt, 427-462, pictures the origin and development of *Anglo-Romanism* in the Elizabethan period. The attempt of Pope Pius IV to convert his 'dear daughter in Christ' to 'obedience to our fatherly persuasion and wholesome counsel', failed, and then the pope started his endeavours 'to recover papal authority by force and fraud'. The founding abroad of missions for the education of Jesuit missionaries of English birth, support to the Northern rebellion, invasion plans, the plotting with the Scottish refugee, queen Mary Stuart. The anathemata of the Council of Trent and the formal excommunication of Elizabeth directly caused the Roman party to be driven out of the Church and to be seen as a subversive element of society.

[10] Hague, 206ff

transubstantiation. McGinn confirms that the doctrine of transubstantiation is not denied in the Elizabethan Prayer Book (p.15). The revised Book also returned to 'the ornaments of the Church and the ministers thereof'. This meant that the use of popish clerical dress, which was restricted in the second Edwardian Prayer Book, was introduced again. The queen was extremely anxious that no offence should be given to the Romish party. The removal of the surplice would, she feared, afford a pretext for some new outrage.[11] The queen tried to enforce the Prayer Book by a set of regulations, known as the *Elizabethan Injunctions*, and by the establishment of a commission for church visitation. Later, Archbishop Parker followed with a number of directions, known as the *Advertisements*.[12]

The Elizabethan settlement of church affairs, though cautiously formulated, was a severe blow to the ultra-montanists, who were still represented in the *House of Lords* and in the *Higher House of Convocation*.[13] At the same time, the hopeful nonconformists, represented in the *House of Commons* and in the *Lower House of Convocation*, felt that the queen would not concede to their demands with regard to church-order. It was increasingly clear that Elizabeth fully rejected the line of thought, begun among the 'Known Men' of her father's reign, and continued by the 'Gospellers' of Edward's time, and

---

[11] Hague, 122, 201ff; cf. McGinn, 9,13; Marsden, 30. Hague, defending the protestant character of the *Prayer Book* and the Anglican canons, is convinced that they 'illegalised the chasuble, alb and other sacrificial vestments, and on the other hand legalised, and exclusively legalised, the wearing of the surplice' (122). Alb and chasuble are the garments worn at mass. The surplice is, according to Livingstone (p.494) 'the distinctive dress of the lower clergy used by priests outside mass ... a loose white liturgical garment with wide sleeves ... now worn by all Anglican clerics, and used by laymen, e.g. in choir'. The Puritans rejected the wearing of all clerical vestments that reminded of the Roman priesthood, including the surplice and the square cap.

[12] Hague, 209. The *Advertisements*, unlike the *Elizabethan Injunctions*, 'expressly ordered that the ministers without any exception ... should wear as the ecclesiastical garment, the surplice. In cathedrals and college churches only, the cope was permitted in the ministration of the Holy Communion'. So, in certain cases mass garments remained in use. The cope is a semicircular cloak, still worn at liturgical functions. Cf. Livingstone, 130. Perry, 288-290, compares *Injunctions* and *Advertisements*, and finds that surplice and cope were only expressly prescribed in the latter.

[13] Blunt, 374-380. In the beginning of Elizabeth's reign, there was considerable difference between the attitudes of *Parliament* and *Convocation*. By Cecil's management, the colour of *Parliament* had been changed in favour of the new queen. However, *Convocation* could not be thus manipulated, and in 1559, it still had the same colour as in the latter days of Queen Mary. The Marian divines in *Convocation* demanded the acceptance of transubstantiation in its extremest form, and the supremacy of the pope. At Westminster, they had a conference with some Elizabethan divines. However, the attempt to reach a compromise failed and was brought to an end by a number of arrests. Consequently, the *Convocation*, which met in 1562 was of a very different colour. Fifteen of the original twenty-three Marian bishops had died, and the remaining eight were either living as private gentlemen or abroad, and Protestants had replaced them. Now the division in *Convocation* was of a different character. The struggle had shifted to the dispute between Puritans and conforming Anglicans.

by the Genevan exile-church and the independent "Privy churches' of Mary's period. The Elizabethan successors in this line of proto-Puritans were sometimes called 'Precisians'. They realised that completion of the Reformation was not to be the topic of the new regime. They felt disappointed because of the attitude of the Crown and the Church. They were also painfully struck by the ambivalence of many Marian exiles. Lloyd Jones comments: 'The queen's policy brought out the same division again, which we have seen in the days of Henry VIII. What were these returning refugees to do with the situation? They were all Protestants; and a number of them had been together on the continent. But now they were face-to-face with a real dilemma. The old cleavage reappeared. Some said: We must not desert our churches for the sake of a few ceremonies, ... What then did they do? They protested. All honour to them. They protested to the queen, to her main counsellor Cecil, and afterwards to Leicester. They protested, but having protested, they accepted official positions in the Church, archbishoprics, bishoprics, and others. ... That was the position taken by Cox, Grindal, Jewel, etc. That was the typical Anglican reaction'.[14]

b. Provoking a Breach

Here comes to the surface a crucial difference in fundamental attitude between the parties. The Puritan view was opposed to the Anglican one. The Puritans just defied the queen. They did not adopt a policy of 'join them if you cannot beat them', and they did not indulge in passive protests. Men like Sampson, Coverdale, Foxe, Humphrey and Lever knew that behind the question of ceremonies and clerical robes, there were more important things at stake. The fight continued, against the surplice, but also against the Monarchical and Episcopalian structure, which enforced these things. The Puritans realised that the old Anglican church-discipline, still laid down in medieval papal laws, would never bring discipline according to he rules of Scripture. Sanctification of the lives of church members would never be helped by a system in which the bishops themselves had assumed popish glamour and power. They fought for the restoration of real preaching. Absenteeism, pluralism, simony and the deplorable state of church finances, had caused a great lack of qualified reformed preachers. In the congregations, there was a desire for change.

    A minority of repatriated Marian exiles did not accept positions in the Elizabethan system. Together with others they became active as travelling preachers, and gradually formed the nucleus of the Puritan party. With the help of the increasingly anti-Anglican nobility and gentry, these itinerant preachers began to settle as ministers and lecturers of the local parishes. Based on their

---

[14] Lloyd Jones, 248

experiences in Geneva and elsewhere, they introduced a church-discipline, which they meant as a means to lead sinners to Christ.

Taught by Bullinger and Calvin, they began to organise *prophesyings* among themselves. These were proto-structures of later Presbyterian classes. In this way, organised forms of nonconformism were beginning to take shape. In general, the *Puritan Movement* never became an organised body. However, it was very influential, and even at royal Court the number of its adherents was growing.

Elizabeth's measures against Puritanism helped to make the movement grow faster. Royal Injunctions, the visitation of churches, a High Commission for ecclesiastical matters, the Episcopal Advertisements and other measures were meant to enforce the *Elizabethan Settlement*. In practice, they contributed much to the mood of resistance. The enforcement of subscription and the subsequent ejectment of Puritan preachers created a breach, which widened with every stage of the conflict.

3. The Ejectment of Nonconforming Ministers

a. Birth of the name 'Puritan'

In 1562 the *Convocation*, the Church's representative body, met on the question of the enforcement of the *Prayer Book*. The *Precisians* or proto-Puritans, who were present in larger numbers now, demanded changes in it. They asked for the abolition of the strict rules concerning the wearing of the surplice and for the restoration of preaching. Most bishops out of the Marian exile, like Grindal, agreed with them that the *Prayer Book* did not leave room enough for preaching. These bishops were prepared to allow the proto-Puritans freedom concerning the use of this liturgy formula, and even would grant them a certain degree of autonomy in the government of local parishes. However, the demands of the *Precisians* were rejected by a narrow majority.[15] Then a bitter struggle began, which became known as the *Second Vestments' Controversy*. It lasted from 1563 to 1567, and was highly reminiscent of its first stage with Hooper in 1550.[16] All 'vestiges of popery' should be done away with, especially 'popish rags', like the surplice. During this period, about 1564, the name 'Puritan' came into use for the designation of the party of nonconformists.[17]

---

[15] Blunt, 382ff, 111, 112. The *Convocation* of 1562 rejected the Puritan demands concerning the surplice. The *42 Articles* were revised, seven articles were omitted and four new ones added. The remaining *39 Articles* got their final form in 1571.
[16] See chapter 5.1.b
[17] Blunt, 391; McGinn, 370-372. The word 'Puritan' was originally meant as an abusive term for those who desired a 'purer' system of doctrine and discipline. Derogatory comparisons were made, e.g. by Whitgift, with the *Novatians* of the early Church and with the *Cathari* of the Middle Ages. In

The Vestments' Controversy

Those bishops who were secretly sympathetic with the Puritans, were forced to take measures against them, when in 1565 Elizabeth issued a letter in which she reproached Archbishop Parker and the whole hierarchy for neglect, because they had not put down sedition and disobedience. This royal ultimatum, together with Parker's subsequent Advertisements, led to the literal enforcement on the clergy of Elizabethan liturgy and ceremonial. All had to sign statements, by which they complied with the 'common order' of the Elizabethan Church. Those who refused, were immediately ejected and deprived of their means of existence. Many ministers lost their livings and became travelling preachers again, but much more independent now of the Anglican structure. To those who were deprived of their benefices belonged Puritan leaders, like Coverdale, Sampson, Barlett, Withers.

b. Continental Reformers Displeased

These proceedings greatly distressed the friends of the English Reformation abroad. Bullinger, Zwingli's successor in Zürich, who was initially on the side of the bishops, many of whom were his disciples and affectionate correspondents, changed his mind. He wrote them a letter: 'We exhort you, reverend sirs and very dear brethren, to have respect to faithful ministers and learned men. They have their own feelings: whence the great apostle has instructed us to bear one another's burdens. Your authority can effect much with her serene highness, the queen. Prevail on her majesty that these worthy brethren may be reconciled and restored'.[18] Bullinger could see now how his English friends worked out the Erastian example of Reformation in Zürich, and he shrank from it.

Neither did Beza, Calvin's successor in Geneva, admire the activities of his former friends. He sent a letter to bishop Grindal -the future archbishop- expressing his astonishment regarding the abuses in the State Church. At the same time he asked the Puritans to be patient and not to establish an independent sect: 'We do not think the matter of so great moment, that therefore the pastors should leave their ministry, rather than take up these garments, or that the flocks should omit the public food, rather than hear pastors so clothed'.[19]

---

a later stage of the *Admonition Controversy*, the Presbyterian leader, Cartwright, accepted the term as an honorary title. Cf. Perry, 293; McGinn, 27, 372.
[18] Marsden, 50, who quotes Neale, *History of the Puritans*, appendix, vol. i
[19] Perry, 293, who quotes: Strype, *Grindal*, appendix ixvi. Cf. Scott Pearson, 18, 108, 122, 123, who describes how Beza, Bullinger and Gualter from 1566 'were inundated with letters from Puritans and their opponents'.

In the same vein wrote Knox. In a letter to the bishops, he remonstrated on behalf of the 'dearest brethren in England who are deprived and forbidden to preach'. The letter contains some sharp expressions about the 'Romish rags', the 'vain trifles', and the 'dregs of the Romish beast'. Still, Knox deplored the vehemence with which the dispute was carried out on both sides, and entreated bishops and pastors 'to shew more forebearance'. He also wrote a letter to the suffering Puritans, in which he told them not to secede, not to be separatists, but to keep unity and peace 'for a time'.[20] The Church of Scotland was assuming its Presbyterian form at the time. Knox trusted that truth would soon prevail in England too, and that, with some patience from the side of the Puritans, the established Church would soon rid itself of all the relics of Romanism.

c. Open Defiance

However, the Puritan preachers were not as patient like that. Many persisted in their refusal to sign the declaration of conformity, appended to the Advertisements, and their ejectment remained a fact. At Cambridge, the cause of the deprived ministers was dealt with in an open and defiant manner. In October 1565, many students refused to wear surplices, and the Fellows appeared to have encouraged them. The students' action is often attributed to the sermons of the later Presbyterian leader, Thomas Cartwright. However, Scott Pearson is sure. That it was not until two years later that Cartwright -then Fellow at Trinity- preached so vehemently against the surplice.[21]

The Vestments' Controversy, or rather the *Uniformity Controversy*, and the subsequent deprivation of ministers, has contributed tremendously to the division of the Anglican Church. Many Puritan ministers no longer belonged to the beneficed clergy. They lost their official Anglican livings, and now they were dependent on the help of friendly patrons and sympathetic congregations. This fact has been of great importance for the development of Presbyterian structures of church-government. Itinerant deprived preachers went about the country preaching illegally. Puritan congregations or groups that gathered in private houses opened their pulpits to them. A climate was growing in which believers not automatically accepted the representatives of the Anglican hierarchy as their ministers and rulers. Congregations began to feel the desire of having more influence on the nomination of their own preachers. Congregations and ministers felt the need of lay-involvement in the government of the Church,

---

[20] Lloyd Jones, 277; cf. Marsden, 50
[21] Scott Pearson, *Thomas Cartwright*, 19, 20, 23. From the end of 1565, Cartwright was in Ireland, as chaplain of the Archbishop of Armagh. His absence in Ireland, while the *Vestments' Controversy* (Scott Pearson prefers: *Uniformity Controversy*) was raging, prevented him from taking a leading part in it. Cf. McGinn, 15

organised in independently ruling bodies. Parker's system of churchwardens was the only concession made by the Episcopate.[22] However, it was not worked out in a way, which could satisfy the Puritan desires for church-discipline and independence.

4. The first Congregations ruled by Elders

a. Shift from Dress to Rule

Among the deprived ministers and their friends there was an anxious deliberation concerning their policy for the future. According to Perry, they were divided on the question of complete separation or relative separation.[23] However, Collinson argues that the Puritan ministers at the time not yet identified themselves with some or other well defined principle of church-government.[24] They did not intend the establishment of a separated church-system, but they wanted to reform the existing system.

During the *Vestments' Controversy*, the attack on the Anglican Church shifted from matters of ceremony and clerical dress to the question of church-government. In 1566, among the London clergy a pamphlet appeared, entitled, 'A brief Discourse against the outwarde apparel and ministering garment of the popishe Church'. It was a direct attack on royal supremacy over the Church. If the magistrate insists upon conformity with regard to these 'idolatrous and offensive vestments ... then he exceeds his authority'. The Scriptures contain the complete plan for the building of the Church. The magistrate is subordinate in authority to the Church. Here the Presbyterian view of State-Church relationship is already indicated, that is, the external aspect of Presbyterian church-order, the independence of the Church and an Old Testament type of authority over the State.

The internal aspect of church-order, i.e. the government of the church and the exercise of discipline by chosen elders, was dealt with in a further exchange of pamphlets. In 'A briefe examination for the tyme of a certain declaration', an Anglican author defended the cause of the Episcopalian Church. This tract was answered by a booklet, which openly restricted the power of the bishops and likewise restricted the royal prerogative.[25] The special thing of this pamphlet is that in it for the first time reference is made to *seniors* or *elders* as

---
[22] Cf. chapter 4.3a. McGinn, 470: The system of churchwardens was not accepted by the Puritans. The *First Admonition* of 1572 condemned it and commented: 'You have to place in every congregation a lawful *seigniory*'.
[23] Perry, 292, 293
[24] Collinson, part II, chapter 3
[25] 'An answere for the tyme, to the Examination put in print without the author's name to mayntayne the apparel prescribed against the declaration of the ministers of London', 1566.

the proposed order for the Church. McGinn thinks that this reference probably was not a conscious expression of Presbyterianism, because 'the Calvinistic distinction between the orders of elders and ministers was still unformed'.[26] McGinn is right when he says that this distinction was not made until a few years later, by Thomas Cartwright. However, he is not right when he suggests that conscious Presbyterianism needs the idea that ministers and elders are essentially different offices. We remember Bucer who derived his various offices from the one central presbyter office, and he was one of the main architects of a Presbyterian order of the Church.

The pamphlets by the end of the Vestments dispute certainly did not contain a completely alternative church-order, but the external and internal aspects of the emerging Presbyterian vision were already apparent in them. The effort to limit the power of the magistrate 'was closely linked with' the refusal to conform to Episcopal authority.[27] In this struggle, the activities of Puritan preachers coincided with the activities of the Puritan members of Parliament. In 1566, the Puritans in the House of Commons introduced two bills, intended to reform the *Book of Common Prayer*. Eventually they were laid aside until the following Parliament in 1571.[28]

b. Circumstantial Separatists

Meanwhile the *Puritan Movement* within the Anglican Church began to assume certain organised forms. In London, a number of preachers resolved 'that they would not have the Word of God preached nor the sacraments administered with idolatrous gear'. They decided 'to break off from the public churches and assemble as they had the opportunity in private house or elsewhere to worship God in a manner that might not offend against the light of their consciences'.[29] John Field and Thomas Wilcox, dedicated Calvinists, belonged to the first leaders of this first Puritan congregation with an alternative church-order. In 1567 they began to preach, first in private houses, and then in London's Plumber Hall. They administered the sacraments, ordained ministers and elders, and exercised discipline. Their examples were Calvin, and especially Knox, whom Field called 'a worthy and notable instrument of God'.

---

[26] McGinn, 18-22
[27] Cf. McGinn, 21
[28] Cf. McGinn, 24
[29] Perry, 292, who quotes Neale, *History of the Puritans*, i, 181

Field and Wilcox were no real independentists or separatists.[30] They intended a Reformation of the Church of England from within. Scott Pearson calls them 'circumstantial separatists'. They were not real Congregationalists by conviction, although they were their forerunners.[31] In the Church they found a serious lack of preaching and discipline, and an unscriptural system of government by bishops. This they tried to mend by the formation of a voluntary nucleus congregation in which the Word of God could be preached and discipline could be exercised. A comparison with Bucer's *Christliche Gemeinschaften* [Christian Communities] in Strasbourg can be made[32], but we should not forget two things. First, Field's group did not yet reflect a balanced theory of Presbyterian church-order. The group only realised that the Church of England obstructed the true ministry of the Word of God and the government of the Church according to the Scriptures. Secondly, neither the participants of Field's 'experiment' nor the later Puritans and Presbyterians were believers in the 'ecclesiola in ecclesiae', i.e. little churches within the Church. Lloyd Jones comments: 'The Puritans were not concerned to form these nuclei within the Church. Many of them in practice seemed to be doing that, but ... that was not their intention, nor their objective. If it did happen, it was a kind of accident, because the majority of the Church did not respond to what they were anxious to do for them. They never consciously went out to set up these little churches within the Church. Indeed, their primary object was to influence the whole Church of England and to carry on the reform which they felt had stopped'.[33] Their position was different from the continental Reformers, who they recognised as their teachers.

One of the reasons why the *Puritan Movement* did not harbour a comprehensive church theory right from the beginning, is, that the foreign examples did not entirely fit to the English situation. Bucer and Calvin accepted the bishop, though in parity with other presbyters. However, the Puritans did not meet Reformed bishops who believed in equality with the other ministers. The Puritans realised that they were in a but halfly reformed Church', which was governed by an assumed elite of church-princes and a monarch, who had no real eye for the needs of the congregations. Bullinger's theory seemed to accommodate the Erastianism of the Elizabethan bishops. Knox's advice to

---

[30] Real and conscious separatism began in 1568, when a small group, led by one Dr. Richard Fitz, seceded from Field's congregation. They preceded the separatist Brownists of the 1580s; according to Collinson, they cannot yet be labelled as 'Independentists' or 'Anabaptists'. In general, the nonconformists did not agree with Fritz's separation. Cf. Collinson, part II, chapter 3; Perry, 293, 294
[31] Scott Pearson, 19
[32] See chapter 3.5.d
[33] Lloyd Jones, 138, 139

tolerate Episcopalian rule 'for a time' was not experienced as helpful. Moreover, the characteristics of the English Parliament made their position different from most foreign Reformers. The Puritans appreciated the representation of Puritan people in Parliament as theologically and practically important for the Reformation of the Church. Foreign Reformers like Calvin did not know institutions like those of the incipient English democracy. The continental Reformers experienced that the representative body of the city-council essentially belonged to the magistracy and not to the people. In England, this had been shaped differently, since long before. It has to be stressed indeed that the situation of the continental Reformers was not quite congruent to the situation of their English counterparts. This was true ecclesiastically as well as politically. Therefore, their theories needed to be adapted to the English scene. The man who could do this for Calvinism was Thomas Cartwright.

Chapter 8

The Admonition Controversy

1. The appearance of Thomas Cartwright

a. Cartwright as a Scholar

Now that the controversy has shifted from the questions of liturgy and apparel, to the questions of royal supremacy and episcopacy, the Puritans began to think of the theological formulation of their church-conception. They needed someone who could adapt the Genevan form of church-government and discipline to the English situation; someone who would not merely imitate the Scottish, Dutch and French derivations of Calvin. They needed a theologian who would formulate the independence of the Church as to the State more emphatically than Calvin did, at the same time evading the revolutionary consequences from Calvinism taken in Scotland, The Netherlands and France, and the revolutionary tendencies of Separatism and Anabaptism.

This man they found in Thomas Cartwright, an eminent scholar at the University of Cambridge, a true Puritan of independent mind. His biographer, Scott Pearson, calls him 'the chief exponent of Presbyterianism in England'. Cartwright's public appearance in the history of Puritanism began when he was already over 35 years of age. Probably born in 1535, in the neighbourhood of Cambridge, he was a student in the reign of Edward, and in the first period of Mary. Edward Puritan divines, like Lever, Ridley, Hooper, and foreigners like Bucer, influenced him deeply.

Cartwright had no personal share in exilic Puritanism in the days of Mary, and did not withdraw from university until after her accession. Some years after the accession of Elizabeth, he became a Fellow of Trinity-College, Cambridge. In 1564, he took part in a disputation before the queen. He did not take an active part in the *Vestments' Controversy*, because for some years he left England and was a chaplain of the archbishop of Armagh in Ireland.

Returning to England, he was appointed professor of divinity in Cambridge[1]. He was certainly a man of independent convictions. When the Swiss Reformers in 1566, adopted the second Helvetian Confession, which in the line of Calvin and Bucer recognised the possibly existence of bishops, Cartwright plainly commented that he did adhere to a certain view, simply because it was Calvin's.

---

[1] Scott Pearson, 1-25; McGinn, 49

Ministers and Elders

This is far from saying though, that Cartwright was a real Calvinist. In his later dispute with Whitgift he would call Calvin 'the notablest instrument that the Lord hath stirred up for the purging of his churches and of the restoring of the plain and sincere interpretation of the Scriptures, which hath been since the apostles' time'. He could have shown no greater respect for any earthly authority. However, in Cartwright's conception Calvin does not supersede the authority of God: 'And yet we do not so read his (Calvin's) works, that we believe any thing to be true, because he saith it, but so far as we can esteem that which he saith doth agree with the canonical Scriptures'.[2]

In 1570, Cartwright began to lecture on the early chapters of the book of *Acts*, dealing with the Church. 'The guiding principle running through his lectures was that the Church should be modelled on that of apostolic times. And the inevitable consequence of this principle, according to Cartwright, should be the total abolition of diocesan episcopacy and the establishment of Presbyterianism'.

Of course the protagonists of Anglicanism reacted fiercely against him. Lloyd Jones holds the view that there is some connection between the indignation aroused by Cartwright's early lectures and 'that many Anglicans today object to the drawing of any doctrine from the book of Acts'.[3] In 1570 Cartwright raised the whole question of the nature of the Church. The primitive Church of the New Testament is example and model for the Church of today.

b. Cartwright's First Debate with Whitgift

Cartwright's superiors at university got him to draw up and sign a statement of his doctrine in six articles. The gist of them is as follows: The names and offices of archbishops and bishops should be abolished. In their stead the offices of bishops and deacons, as described in the New Testament should be established. The bishop should have a purely spiritual function and the deacon should care for the poor. The government of the Church should not be entrusted to chancellors of bishops or officials of archdeacons etc., but to the minister and the presbytery of the Church. Each minister should be attached to a definite congregation. No one should, like a candidate, seek the office of a minister and none should be created ministers by the authority of bishops, but should be elected by a church. All should promote this reformation according to their several vocations, i.e. the magistrate by his authority, the minister by preaching and all by their prayers.[4]

---

[2] *Works of Whitgift*, vol. I, Parker Society, pp 214, 215, quoted by Cremeans, 72
[3] Lloyd Jones, 252
[4] Scott Pearson, 28,29, quoting the original Latin document in the Cambridge Registry

It was clear to conforming and nonconforming Anglicans that Cartwright 'was striking at the authority of the Crown, and of the episcopacy in spiritual matters and he was suggesting that this authority be spread out among the ministry more closely associated with the membership of the Church'.[5]

Congregations should have a voice in the election of their ministers. Ministers must be fit to teach, and be examined before their ordination. Every minister should preach to his own flock. In addition, the government of the Church should be entrusted to the minister and the presbytery. In other words: 'Every church ought to be governed by its own ministers. No man ought to solicit or to be a candidate for the ministry. Ministers should be openly and fairly chosen by the people'.[6]

It is noteworthy that Cartwright, in his six articles, had not yet stressed the importance of lay-elders. The ministry of the Word is still the only real office. This reminds us of the early Calvin, who during his first stay in Geneva and in Strasbourg, only knew the minister and had no room for elders.[7] These ministers could be called 'bishops', but not in an Episcopalian sense. They have a purely 'spiritual function'. More emphatically than Calvin, Cartwright completely rejected the existence of bishops in an Anglican sense. In Cartwright's view, there is absolute parity of ministers. Like Calvin's successor Beza, whom he was soon to meet in Geneva, he was very conscious of the dangers of Episcopalianism and Erastianism.

The Episcopacy was not slow in condemning Cartwright. The attack on him was led by Whitgift, the future archbishop and now his superior at university. He was barred from getting a doctor's degree and he was suspended from the professorship of divinity. In 1571, he left university. In 1572, after a sojourn in Geneva, the fellowship of Trinity-College was also taken from him. Whitgift used the fact that he had not fulfilled his fellowship-oath, which bound him to take priest's order within a stated time.[8] Indignant at the accusation of being a revolutionary, Cartwright complained in a letter: 'I hear that I am accused of seditious and schismatic practices. Oh, baseness'. (Marsden)

c. The First Exile: Geneva

After his suspension, Cartwright went to Geneva, where he stayed for several months. This short stay in the capital of the Presbyterian Reformation has been of great importance for the further development of his thought. In Geneva, we find Cartwright in the role of an academic teacher. Besides, he studied the

---

[5] Cf. Cremeans, 84
[6] Marsden, 77, quoting Strype, "Whitgift", appendix
[7] See chapter 3.6.c
[8] Scott Pearson, 63-65

details of the Genevan model of church-government and was allowed to be present at a meeting of the Consistory. Beza was impressed by his ability. In a letter, the Genevan Reformer gave expression to his admiration: 'the sun did not shine upon a more learned man than Cartwright'.[9] His contacts with Geneva and with Beza taught him the importance of the eldership in the Church. Beza's initial friendly relationship with some of the English bishops had changed, after the ejectment of Puritan ministers. This had led him to designate the episcopacy as a demonic institution. At the same time the seeds were sown of a conflict that sprang up between Beza and Erastus. In 1568 in Heidelberg, the Puritan George Withers had collided with Erastus on the question of church-discipline. According to Erastus excommunication was not of divine order, and offences by Christians should not be punished by the Church, but by the State. He excluded lay-elders from the exercise of discipline, because they were not to take the position that belonged to the civil magistrate. Gualter, the Zürich Reformer, sided with Erastus and warned the English bishops against Presbyterian Puritans like Wither. However, Beza maintained the necessity of discipline and excommunication, to be exercised by the elders of the Church.[10]

Beza's recent experiences influenced his view of the English situation. Beza's friendship, together with the daily ecclesiastical practice in Geneva, encouraged Cartwright to continue into a Presbyterian direction. Soon the elder would appear in his writings. His lectures on Acts and the six articles were a beginning. Before that time the feelings expressed in them were already alive. Now, for the first time they had been intellectually phrased and moulded into a more comprehensive theological attack on the Episcopalian system. The stay in Geneva consolidated his view, and led him to the further development of his idea of church-government. With Cartwright, started the history of formal Presbyterianism in England. In February 1572, his Puritan friends asked for his return, and Cartwright answered this call by leaving Geneva. Through Rouen, he travelled back and by the intervention of Puritan friends at the royal court, he was allowed to sail back to his homeland.

d. The Wandsworth Enterprise

In the meantime the situation in England had grown more favourable for the reception of Puritan thought. We already mentioned the formation of alternative congregations by John Field and Thomas Wilcox.[11] In June 1568, Field's

---

[9] Scott Pearson, 48
[10] Cf. Scott Pearson, 133,134; McGinn does not mention Beza's influence on Cartwright's vision of the variation of offices. He is sure, however, that 'the Calvinistic distinction between the orders of elders and of ministers was introduced in England by TC' (p.21).
[11] See chapter 7.4.b

London congregation was severely hit by persecutions. At the instigation of Elizabeth herself, more than a hundred members were arrested. However, this could not stop the movement. It rapidly spread over the whole district of London and found inroads to the rest of the country, e.g. in the county of Northamptonshire[12] where fertile soil was waiting.

According to Marsden, in 1572, Field, together with men like Wilcox and Travers, formed a church in the London area of Wandsworth on the bank of the river Thames.[13] Marsden and Scott Pearson don't agree on the question, whether this was the first Presbyterian church of England. Did the founders form a consistory or presbytery within the Anglican parish of Wandsworth? That would have been in accordance with the principle of non-separation and change from within, expressed by Presbyterian declarations, like the Admonitions to Parliament, in the same year. According to the second Admonition, presbyteries should be established in every parish and they should comprise ministers and elders. The elders should be inducted by the minister of the congregation that elected them. Scott Pearson thinks that the Wandsworth-congregation did not bear these characteristics of proto-Presbyterianism. It could have been a separatist, secret body 'containing Congregationalist as well as Presbyterian elements' and was probably not an embryonic presbytery or consistory in the modern sense.

In Scott Pearson's opinion, Wandsworth was a separatist enterprise. Its protagonists were not Proto-Presbyterians like Field, but probably one Crane, who would end up as a Greenwoodian. Therefore, Marsden's view that in 1572 at Wandsworth actually a Presbyterian meeting house was erected by Field, Wilcox, Travers c.s., is disputed by Scott Pearson. He calls this statement 'an interesting product of imagination, but not history'[14] He adds that the 'Wandsworth-Presbytery' probably did not occupy a place of importance, because Cartwright in his trial in the 1950's did not admit to have knowledge of it. We doubt, however, whether this argument of Scott Pearson is well founded. Why should Cartwright have admitted before his interrogators the knowledge of presbyteries, knowing that his opponents were out to suppress all forms of Presbyterianism?

The question of independent presbyteries of ministers and elders had a direct bearing on the Presbyterian demand that the authority of the civil magistrate in ecclesiastical matters should be restricted. However, in practice -as Cremeans shows-[15] the Presbyterians were very careful in admitting that they really organised consistories or presbyteries.

---

[12] Cf. Cremeans, 101 ff
[13] Marsden, 61 ff
[14] Scott Pearson, 76-81
[15] Cremeans, 109-112

> 'The Calvinists refused to be trapped into admitting that they denied all ecclesiastical power to the magistrate, and tried to evade admitting it, because they hoped eventually to establish a commonwealth in England in which the officers of the Church and of the State, each operating in their own spheres, would cooperate in guiding the people to obey the will of God'.

Scott Pearson's account of the rejection of the congregation of Wandsworth as the first Presbyterian church in England suggests that not only the theoretical aspect of Presbyterianism starts with Cartwright, but also the practical aspect of the phenomenon.

However, the practice of church-government independent of episcopacy and civil magistrate already existed before Cartwright's public appearance. It existed in independent groups that differed in degree of separatism and acceptance of state authority in ecclesiastical affairs. They all wanted to associate authority more closely with the membership of the Church. Cartwright's Presbyterianism did not represent all these groups. In the diverse multitude of Puritans, which ranged from moderate conformists to extreme separatists, he trod the middle-road.. He tried to evade the attitude of those Puritans that only accepted the salvation-doctrine of Calvinism, and left church-government to the monarch and the bishops. On the other hand, he rejected Puritan thought that denied all ecclesiastical power to the civil magistrate. In line with Calvin's conception, he restricted the authority of the State, and at the same time he gave the civil magistrate definite obligations concerning the rule of the Church. Cartwright was a nonconformist in between conformists and extreme separatists. He tried to go the Presbyterian *via media*, evading the dangerous cliffs of deadly conformity to the structures of the world and of poisonous revolution against the powers that God has ordained. His stance could be summarised by: no conformism and no separatism, no episcopacy and no people's democracy, no state-absolutism and no rejection of state duties.

e. The Second Exile: Heidelberg

There was also an evolution in Cartwright's thought. In the beginning of his public career he was closer to the left than at the end. His experiences abroad and the events in England made him more careful. After some violent years –on which we shall comment in the next section- Cartwright left England for the second time. While in Heidelberg from 1574 to 1576, he underwent the moderating influence of Reformed divines, like Tremellius, Ursinus, Zanchius, Olevianus, who under the pious Elector Frederick enjoyed full freedom for their

Presbyterian practices.[16] Cremeans mentions the possible impact on Cartwright: 'The Heidelberg Calvinists did not stress the idea of the right of resistance, and they probably inclined Cartwright himself to a less radically revolutionary attitude. The Heidelberg Calvinists felt no need to develop the doctrine of resistance, because their elector had set up the Genevan system for them, and the doctrine was unnecessary'.[17]

In his contemporary dispute with Whitgift, Cartwright did not promise obedience to the magistrate in things contrary to the will of God, but he said that he would submit to punishment by the magistrate, rather than actively resist him. He disapproved of the more radical Puritans, and did not like their manifestations of revolt and dissent. Schism and secession were loathsome to him.

Of course not all Puritans at home agreed with his changing attitude. He was criticised by some Puritan ministers. Gradually a rift was growing between him and certain sections of Puritanism, during the long period of his exile.[18] From 1577 to 1585 Cartwright was in The Netherlands, until 1582 in Antwerp and later in Middleburgh. As a minister to English sailors and merchants, he served as a clergyman to the Church of England.

f. Cartwright and Browne

In this period, contacts with English separatist groups, led by Robert Browne and Robert Harrison, cured him of remaining revolutionary sentiments. According to Browne the civil magistracy had no ecclesiastical authority at all. The spiritual rule of the Church and the outward power of the magistrate are to be completely separated. Taught by the chaotic schismatism in Brownist circles and by their furious proposals for destructive resistance, Cartwright took exception of Browne's views. Diametrically opposed to Browne he advocated the presbyterianisation of the Church of England 'with the help of civil magistrates and with constitutional means'.

Harrison was less radical than Browne. Cartwright had friendly discussions with him. However, unlike Harrison, he did not consider himself as a seceder. He did not accept Harrison's objections for not recognising the Anglican Church as a Church. He admitted that want of discipline, a dumb and unlawful ministry, an unscriptural system of government are deplorable facts. Nevertheless, he considered the Church of England to be Church of Christ.

Cartwright's contacts with Browne and Harrison expose the attitude of Presbyterian Puritans to the State-Church on one hand, and to radical dissent on

---

[16] Scott Pearson, 130-135
[17] Cremeans, 117
[18] Cf. Scott Pearson, 149, 153

the other.[19] In the meantime the Presbyterians did not renounce their ardent hope that -by way of gradual improvement- the English Church might become Presbyterian.

In 1585, the Privy Council granted Cartwright leave to return to England. Through the influence of Leicester he acquired an important preaching position at the hospital of Warwick, from where he could take a prominent part in the direction of the Presbyterian Movement. Although, according to Scott Pearson, his Presbyterian convictions were as strong as ever, he continued to be an opponent of separatism. The discussion with his sister-in-law, Anne Stubbe, is part of his further controversy with the Brownists. It was like 'a repetition in miniature of the discussion between Cartwright and Harrison in Middleburgh'.[20] In chapter 12 we shall comment on it.

Although it was increasingly evident that the Presbyterian Puritans were no Separatists, no extreme fanatics or revolutionaries, the Elizabethan government sought for a chance to crush them, together with the whole Puritan Movement. By 1590, internal dissensions and pressures of episcopate and monarchy, had seriously weakened the position of the Puritans. The conflict came to a head in the ultimate arrest and imprisonment of Cartwright and a number of other Puritan preachers. Until his release, in 1592, Elizabeth's High Commissioners and Star Chamber members interrogated him, in attempts to prove his responsibility for the establishment of independent or separatist consistories and presbyteries. Repeatedly Archbishop Whitgift turned out to be his chief opponent. However, his complicity to a system of Presbyterian meetings could not be proved. Perhaps it is true that Cartwright and most of his friends, though they 'believed in and hankered after Presbyterianism', never really practiced it themselves until this time.[21]

In the last decade of Cartwright's life we see him back at Warwick for some years, then in the Channel Island of Guernsey, and finally back at Warwick again, where he died in 1603. In Guernsey, outside the realm of direct Elizabethan control, a Presbyterian form of church-government could be realised with the help of Cartwright.[22] However, that story is beyond the scope of this study.

Scott Pearson concludes that Cartwright, in the period of his public appearance, 'changed the accent of emphasis from the destructive attitude of a revolting critic to that of a loyal constructive and friendly Reformer'. Cartwright 'modified his tactics many years before he died', but he 'never forsook his desire to presbyterianise the Church of England'. He 'dropped his controversial

---

[19] Scott Pearson, 211-231; cf. A. Peel, *Cartwrightiana*, London: Stewart Trust, 48-118
[20] Scott Pearson, 309
[21] Scott Pearson, 336-348
[22] Scott Pearson, 372

pen, but kept loyal to his Presbyterian ideals', and never showed favour to separatist Puritans and Anabaptists'.[23]

Cartwright's movement was not a popular mass movement like Puritanism in general. Although it had many influential supporters, it did not achieve its purpose of establishing a national Presbyterian Church, instead of the prevailing Anglican system.

2. The *Admonitions* to Parliament and the *Explicatio*

a. The House of Commons

Cartwright's lectures and articles of 1570 represented 'the first public expression of a new trend in Calvinist nonconformity'[24], although in the preceding pamphlets' war of the *Vestments' Controvery*, attempts were already made to formulate an adaptation of Calvinism to the English situation.[25] It was felt by the conformists that Cartwright's action was a direct attack on episcopacy and royal supremacy. The more so, because soon the Puritans in the House of Commons, inspired by the writings of Cartwright c.s., took the initiative. In 1572 they introduced two bills for 'rights and ceremonies', designed to cut away the Anglican ceremonies, and to reform the Church after the pattern of Geneva. With them, the bills of 1566 were revived. The conformists saw that this involved a dangerous assault on their establishment, and they counterattacked through a parliamentary act for the reformation of 'certain misorders touching ministers of the Church'. To the indignation of the Puritan faction, the queen commanded not to deal with the Puritan bills, and Parliament was prorogued.[26]

Now the bishops started a new campaign for the enforcement of the *Prayer Book* and the *Articles*. Certain Puritans, among them John Field, offered the signing under conditions. However, this attempt for a compromise was rejected.[27]

b. The First Admonition

In this highly explosive situation, in 1572, a very polemic document was published, *An Admonition to Parliament for the reformation of Church-*

---

[23] Scott Pearson, 387-389, 411
[24] See chapter 8.1.a; cf. Cremeans, 84
[25] See chapter 7.2.a
[26] Perry, 296, 297. In these bills, an attempt was made to revive and give authority to the 'Reformatio legum ecclesiasticarum', which had narrowly missed becoming the law of the Church of England in the reigns of Henry VIII and Edward VI.
[27] Collinson, part III, chapter 2

discipline. This writing, which served as the starting point of a long battle of words between Cartwright and Whitgift, marked 'definite revolt against the Elizabethan church-system as a whole, and resembles a declaration of war'.[28] It was divided into two parts.

The first part contained a description of the external notes or marks of a true Church, which are the preaching of the Word purely, the ministering of the sacraments sincerely, and the proper administration of ecclesiastical discipline. Particular emphasis was put on the last of these two points. A comparison was made of the Anglican Church and the Primitive Church of the New Testament and early church history. The tract did not contain a call for revolution. However, it demanded to 'remove whole antichrist both head, body and branch, and perfectlie plant that puritie of the Word, that simplicitie of the sacraments, and severitie of discipline, which Christ hath commanded and commended in His Church'.

The second part of the *Admonition* is entitled, 'A View of Popish Abuses, yet remaining in the Englishe Church, for which godly ministers have refused to subscribe'. It has three sections. The first section contains arguments against the Book of Common Prayer, which was called a book 'picked out of that popish dunghill'. The second section struck against the prescribed method of administering the sacraments and the prescribed clerical vestments. The third section contained comments on the *39 Articles*.

With the *Admonition* Puritanism entered its Presbyterian phase. It rejected the spiritual headship of the queen and of the Episcopalian system. The acts of the early Church in the New Testament were considered as not less binding in matters of church-government and discipline, than in matters of salvation doctrine. The tract could be called 'the first open manifest of the Puritan party', and it marked 'the determination to do away with the existing system of polity and worship in the English churches'.

The *Admonition* was published anonymously. However, when Field and Wilcox were accused of and imprisoned for writing it, they confessed that they were the joint authors. It has been said by Perry and others[29] that Cartwright was the author of the first Admonition of 1572, and that he participated in its composition. His biographer, Scott Pearson, rejects this thought, being sure 'that there is no evidence for such an assertion'. Cartwright knew that the book was the work of various persons. He defended its contents, but he also disapproved of certain wrongly used quotations from Scripture in the *Admonition*.[30]

---

[28] Cf. Cremeans, 84,85; Scott Pearson, 60: 'Its chief aim was the abolition of Episcopacy, and the erection of Presbyterianism'.
[29] Perry, 297
[30] Scott Pearson, 59

Although the *Admonition* can be looked upon as 'the point at which Puritanism began to be a hostile force'[31], it anxiously defended itself against the charge of radical Anabaptism. It 'openly struck at the Episcopal polity, including not only archbishops and bishops, but even the queen herself'. Yet it did not advocate revolution. Cremeans points to 'the fact that the rise of nationalism in the 16th century had produced an almost universal acceptance of the doctrine that subjects owe allegiance to their ruler, however good or bad he [or she] might be'.

Calvin himself had recognised the fact that revolutionaries against properly constituted sovereigns were in danger of being designated as outcasts. In his *Institutes* he repudiated those, like the Anabaptists, who refused to admit the royal supremacy. Calvinists were very sensitive on this point.[32] This was shown by the attitude of Field, who was in prison since he handed the *Admonition* to Parliament. From there he spread a defence against Whitgift's accusation that the *Admonition* was an Anabaptist document calling for violence. He pleaded loyalty to the confession and church-discipline that were constituted by the first French Huguenot Synod in Paris in 1559, which fenced off Anabaptism. From his prison cell, Field tried to organise opposition and mobilise the forces of practical Presbyterianism. Collinson is not sure whether the term 'elder', which was apparent in the *Admonition*, also occurred in Field's calls from prison.[33]

c. The Second Admonition

Before the year 1572 had passed, and by the time Whitgift was ready with an answer to the *Admonition*, a second *Admonition* appeared. It supplemented the first one, and elaborated on the Presbyterian reform, and the machinery whereby it was to be effected. Here the question of the authorship turns up again. Marsden, McGinn, and Perry join 'the general opinion' that Cartwright was the author of the *Second Admonition*.[34] However, Scott Pearson 'has no hesitation in breaking away' from this traditional view. Cartwright himself denied the authorship. Besides, its style of 'unsparing violence' is not that of Cartwright.[35] Scott Pearson is supported by Collinson in the assumption that the *Second Admonition* could have been written by Christopher Goodman, who during the Marian exile was a helper of John Knox in Geneva.[36] Goodman had seen

---

[31] McGinn, 25-27
[32] Cf. Cremeans, 113
[33] Collinson, part III, chapter 4
[34] Marsden, 83; McGinn, 42, 49, 52; Perry, 301
[35] Scott Pearson, 74. Cartwright distanced himself from certain points in the *Second Admonition*, e.g. as to the question of doctors of theology.
[36] Collinson, part III, chapter 4; Scott Pearson, 74; cf. chapters 3.2.b and 6.2.d

Presbyterianism in practice in Geneva, and later in Scotland, where he stayed at the invitation of Knox until 1565. After the accession of Elizabeth his revolutionary fervour, expressed in, How Superior Powers ought to be Obeyed, had diminished considerably. He even accepted the position of an archdeacon, and in 1571, before the High Commission, he signed a retraction of views 'which may be, and be offensively taken'. He wished that writings against 'the monstrous rule of women' had not been published, and affirmed that 'women may lawfully govern whole realms and nations'.[37] Cremeans says that his life in England after this 'was troubled, as he was in constant difficulty because of his nonconformity'. His influence on other English nonconformists must certainly have been significant.[38]

Goodman recanted his revolutionary political writings, but he did not abandon his Presbyterian views. Danner, in his description of Goodman's significance, concludes that 'he may have had a hand in writing the *Second Admonition*'. Anyway, he acted as a publisher of Presbyterian writings during the subsequent Cartwright-Whitgift dispute.[39]

The author(s) of the *Second Admonition* tried to work out the practical consequences of the *First Admonition*. The first declared what was in need of reform. The second told how the Reformation was to be carried out. It explained the function of parochial consistories, conferences (i.e. regional presbyteries, or classes), provincial, national and universal councils or synods. Presbyterian church-rule was described as the only system of church-government allowed by the Scriptures. In this, according to Cremeans, there is a different emphasis than with Calvin, who chose the Presbyterian system, but did not attack the Episcopalian system in principle'. The author(s) of the *Second Admonition* did not read Calvin like this[40], but assumed that the only possible consequence of Calvinism was the abolishment of Episcopalianism and the introduction of Presbyterianism. Throughout the *Second Admonition* Scott Pearson notes bitter antipathy toward the bishops: 'They are censured for their persecution of the so called *Precisians*; they are responsible for the manifold corruptions in the Church; they are its real enemies'. The author(s) condemn the Roman Catholic elements in the English Church. The *Book of Common Prayer* in particular is denounced 'as a product of the vile popish service book'. Such abuses 'as pluralities and the bestowal of degrees upon men who are unfit to be teachers in the Church are sharply criticised'.[41]

---

[37] Cf. D.G. Danner, 'Christopher Goodman and the English protestant tradition of civil disobedience', in: *Sixteenth Century Journal*, VIII, 3 (1977), 66.
[38] Cremeans, 39, 55, 63
[39] Danner, 66
[40] Cremeans, 94
[41] Scott Pearson, 73

The *Admonitions* were followed by severe royal measures. First the queen criticised the Episcopate for not being able to prevent the publication of seditious literature and the spread of Puritan thought. In a proclamation she openly charged the bishops with negligence, and in a letter to them she allowed them to be deliberately and publicly insulted, because they could not keep all churches ... in one uniform and godly order'. The proclamation appointed a special commission, and nominated certain lay commissioners for each diocese, who together with the bishops and their officials, were to make a strict search for nonconformists, and bring them before the judges. The suspected clergy were required to subscribe to a declaration approving of the *Prayer Book*, the *Articles*, and the royal supremacy, and, in addition, to making a sort of recantation.[42] In the meantime, the copies of the *Admonitions* were eagerly sought for, but in spite of the utmost efforts to repress them, they were printed and spread with alarming rapidity.

By the end of 1572, the *Admonitions* gave rise to a discussion of great importance between leading representatives of the Anglican and Puritan parties. It became known as the *Admonition Controversy*. Cartwright had returned from Geneva, and at the time, he worked as an itinerant preacher. Whitgift, gradually rising on the ladder of Anglican hierarchy, was employed by Archbishop Parker to procure an answer to the *First Admonition*. We already noticed that soon he produced a reaction. He named it, *Answer to a certain Libell entituled Admonition to Parliament*. In 1573 Cartwright issued his, *Replye to an Answere made of M. Doctor Whitgift againste the Admonition to Parliament*. His opponents were so much angered by the tract that Cartwright had to leave the country again. His exile would last until April 1585. In the 1574, the year of Cartwright's flight, Whitgift returned with his, *Defense of the Aunswere to the Admonition against the Replie of T.C.* While in Heidelberg in 1575, Cartwright wrote his, *Second Replie of Thomas Cartwright, against M. Doctor Whitgift's Second Answer touching Church-discipline*. In addition, in 1579, probably in Basel or The Netherlands, Cartwright published his, The Rest of the Second Replie ...'.[43]

McGinn, in his extensive study of the *Admonition Controversy*, indicates that the public appearance of Cartwright and the publication of the Admonitions were a turning point in the struggle between Puritans and Anglicans. 'Until 1570 the quarrel had been confined to the relative indifference of rites and ceremonies. From the *Vestments' Controversy* of 1566 had emerged two principles, which were to form integral parts of Puritan doctrine, first that the Scriptures contain the complete plan for the edification or building of God's

---

[42] Perry, 298-300
[43] Scott Pearson, 128-130, 145-148

Church, and secondly, that the authority of the magistrate [in church matters] is subordinate to that of the Church. The *Admonitions* had popularised and spread these views. The Episcopalian defence, on the other hand, maintained, 'first, that God in His Word has set forth all doctrine essential for salvation, but has left to His Church the ordinance thereof, and secondly, that the magistrate is the supreme governor of the established Church'.[44] The Admonition Controversy helped to make Puritan dissatisfaction with the Church of England grow rapidly. However, this did not always and everywhere lead to the formation of Presbyterian theories or to the introduction of Presbyterian practices. There were parts of the country where some kind of consistories and presbyteries came to existence, consisting of preaching and ruling elders. Collinson describes the reforming activities of Wilburn in Northamptonshire, where 'Rome and Geneva' were each other's direct opponents.[45]

d. Travers' *Explicatio*

Presbyterian practice was greatly encouraged by the publication of a Calvinist book of church-discipline by Walter Travers, which was no doubt the first English Presbyterian church-order after Knox's *Geneva Book* of 1556. Knox's book was essentially a directory for public worship, stemming from Calvin's *Catechism*.[46] However, the book of church-discipline written by Travers described the full Presbyterian conception of church-government. It was first published in Latin, in 1573.[47] In Heidelberg, Cartwright translated it into English, and published it again in 1574, under the title, *A Full and Plaine Declaration of Ecclesiasticall Discipline owt off the Word off God, and off the Declininge of the Churches off England from the same*. It became popularly known as the *Explicatio*, being the last word of the Latin title. The *Explicatio* exercised a determinative influence on the policy of the Puritan Reformers. Its author, Travers, belonged to the second generation of Calvinist nonconformists, just like Field, Wilcox and Cartwright. Cremeans suggests that he was, even more than Cartwright, the intellectual head of the Presbyterian-Puritan Movement, 'drafting nearly all the important papers'.[48] However, Scott Pearson seems to contradict this. He brings up the question of the authorship of the *Explicatio*. He says that the preface of the *Explicatio* is usually ascribed to Cartwright[49], who also moulded it to a piece of English literature. We conclude

---

[44] McGinn, 49
[45] Collinson, part III, chapter 4
[46] Cf. Cremeans, 50, 51
[47] Walter Travers, *Ecclesiasticae Disciplinae et Anglicanae Ecclesiae al illa Aberrationis plena e Verbo Dei et dilucida Explicatio*, 1573.
[48] Cremeans, 85
[49] Scott Pearson, 135, 136

that Travers wrote the *Explicatio*, and Cartwright extended it and influences its form.

Rechtien explains that the *Explicatio* is a characteristic specimen of changing literary forms, apparent among Puritan writers at the time. These Puritans were distancing themselves from medieval oratorical forms, and they shifted to 'a plain style of diction and syntax', and to the incorporation of 'dichotomous structures'. Rechtien notices this style with early Puritan theologians like Cartwright, William Whitaker, and William Ames. The antithetical literary structures of these men served a new dichotomous way of argumentation, which 'left no opening for debate'. They pictured thought in a methodical structure, which descends from the most general definition to its most minute particulars through a series of bifurcations. To the *Explicatio* charts are appended, which give an example of this use of bifurcations. Discipline, being 'an order for the good government of the Church of Jesus Christ', is divided into two parts, the first is of the ecclesiastical functions', the offices, and the second is 'the duty of the rest of the faithful'. The first requirement of any ecclesiastical office is vocation, then follow the requirements of election and ordination. Ecclesiastical offices are divided into general and particular. The particular offices are not elaborated on. The general or ordinary offices are divided into simple and compound ones. The simple one is reflected by 'deacons', the compound one by the 'bishops', that is to say bishops in a Presbyterians sense, so 'elders'. Apart from the division into offices that exercise the discipline of the Church, the charts of the *Explicatio* give a survey of the organisational form in which the office-bearers partake. This is the second topic of the dichotomy, 'the consistory of the Church'. It is bifurcated into 'elders' and 'the whole authority of the consistory'.[50] The charts containing these bifurcations are dichotomous fold-out summaries of the text.

Although Cremeans thinks that the *Explication* was not intended as a direct attack on the Church of England as the *Admonitions* were, he admits that it opposed the established Church in a very fundamental way.[51] It believed in the paramount importance of the ministry of the Word of God. Without that ministry, there can be no proper Church. Ministers must be men who have been 'specially set aside and chosen by God'. In order to avoid 'oligarchy and tyrannous rule', they should be elected. Apart from the ministry of the Word, there is the consistory, the body that is responsible for the disciplinary side of church-government. It is made up of pastors, elders and doctors of the Church. Its two main functions are the administering of the election, and 'taking heed to

---

[50] J.G. Rechtien, 'Structures in the Theology of Walter Travers', *Sixteenth Century Journal*, vol. VIII, 1 (April 1977), 51 ff.
[51] Cremeans, 86, 87

offences and removing them out of the Church'. The elders to whom the ruling of the Church is left, should 'not neglect the judgement of the rest of the Church'. They should put up their decisions to the vote of the people for acceptance or rejection. Cremeans emphasises that this does not mean that Travers and Cartwright wanted to establish a system of 'popularity' or a democracy. The *Explicatio* 'has caught the spirit of aristocratic Geneva', and confutes the ideas of a people's democracy. The elders are the rulers of the Church, together with the ministers. This not only excludes a government by the people, but also a government by the State. Travers emphasised the separation of the functions of civil and ecclesiastical officers. 'The magistrate has authority over the things of this life, his only spiritual function being to protect the Church. As for the officers of the Church, their authority is in the spiritual; they have none in civil matters'. Essentially the magistrate 'is subject to the Church in spiritual matters'.

> The *Explicatio* exhorts princes and monarchs of the world to 'give upp their sceptres and crownes unto Him whome God had made and appointed the Heyre off His Kingdome and Lord off heaven and earthe'.

Cartwright spoke similar words in his dispute with Whitgift.[52] These words are far from meaning that Cartwright and Travers were revolutionary Calvinists. According to Cremeans their form of Calvinism was 'not as extreme as that developed under pressure of completely intolerant magistrates in Scotland, France and The Netherlands'. He points to the possibly sobering effect of 'the Elizabethan compromise'. Elizabeth was still a Protestant, and the established Church still accepted most of Calvinist theology'. Concerning the situation in The Netherlands, Cremeans is certainly right, when he compares Calvinist opposition against the Anglican establishment and Dutch Calvinist resistance against Spanish suppression. In this sense, English Calvinism was not provoked to be as revolutionary as its Dutch counterpart. However, when Dutch Calvinism consolidated its Presbyterian Church under the protection of a free national State, liberated from Spanish-Habsburg suppression, it lost much of its revolutionary character and got characteristics of a State Church, intolerant to other churches. English Presbyterianism did not experience the protection by the State, on the contrary. It was a minority group within the Puritan Movement, which was looked upon as a consciously subversive danger for the established Church and its monarch. In this sense English Presbyterian Puritanism was may be more revolutionary than Dutch Calvinism in its later stages.[53] More than the

---

[52] Cf. chapter 7, note 7
[53] Cremeans (89), admits that he Calvinist nonconformists were seen as radicals in their desire for change. 'In spite of the fact that the nonconformists had worked out their own plan of action to

Dutch Church in its free State under Calvinist magistrates, the English Calvinist Puritans felt the need for the establishment of an independent Reformed Church, free of interference by tyrannical forces who despised the Presbyterian system of church-government.

Yet English Presbyterians were no advocates of violent revolution or of armed resistance. They were moderated by political circumstances and conceptions, but in the first place, their moderation stemmed from Calvinism itself. Calvin abhorred revolution and only hesitantly permitted his followers in France to defend themselves. Calvinism did not intend to reach its objectives by revolution, but by the ministry of the Word of God and by the establishment of true churches. Cartwright and Travers envisaged 'a divine plan for the government of the Church'. This plan was to provide for the gradual and evolutionary substitution of Episcopalianism for Presbyterianism. Patiently they waited for a change in the attitude of the political leaders. 'Tarrying for the magistrate', became a household word of the 16th century Presbyterian Movement, which disclaimed responsibility for separatism and revolution.

In Heidelberg where he translated the *Explicatio* in 1574, Cartwright was taught in anti-revolutionary Calvinism.[54] There under the protection of the Elector Frederick, a Presbyterian system had been put into practice, which in several aspects served as a model for the English proto-Presbyterians. In Frederick's Palatine Cartwright learnt to attach much importance to the consistory, i.e. the body of self-government of a local congregation. The elder and the consistory were to become cornerstones of the Presbyterian system of church-government. Travers and Cartwright were its builders in the English context, the first by formulating a comprehensive theory, the second by applying this theory to the practical situation in the English churches. In Travers' work, the emphasis is on the theory and in Cartwright's work it is on the practice of Presbyterianism. However, Cartwright was also a theoretician, and Travers also worked on the practical side. Cartwright, apart from his pastoral work in The Netherlands and later at Warwick hospital and in Guernsey, wrote his famous treatises. Much importance was attached to his *Confutation* of the Roman Catholic version of the New Testament, the 'Rheims translation'. By Anglicans and Puritans, the *Confutation* was considered as an impressive answer to the arguments of the Counter Reformation. Travers, apart from his work on the formulation of Presbyterian church-discipline, contributed to its practical realisation. In Antwerp, he worked as a minister among English sailors and

---

apply to the situation in England, and had not adopted the Scottish or French plan, the conformists soon realised that, ideologically they had carried their Calvinism through to its ultimate theocratic form'. The conformists 'naturally regarded the situation as highly dangerous for themselves'.

[54] Cf. chapter 8.1.e

merchants. While he was a preacher in the Temple Church in London[55], he did much for the defence of practical Presbyterianism against the Anglican views of the day, represented by Hooker c.s.[56]

e. Travers' *Directory of Church-government*

Travers' *Explicatio* of 1573/74 was the prelude to his famous book on church-discipline, which began to play a role of importance in the 1580s. Scott Pearson warns that this 'Puritan book of discipline par excellence' should not be confused with the *Explicatio*.[57] It became known as Travers' *Directory of Church-government*, and was not printed until 1644.[58] It was a Puritan kind of Prayer Book, a modification of Knox's *Geneva Prayer Book*, essentially a liturgy for the regulation of public worship.[59] The *Explicatio*, sometimes also called *Book of Discipline*, was not in the first place directed at the regulation of public church services. It formulated the government and the organisation of the Church as such. Just like the *Explicatio*, Travers' book on church-discipline showed the Puritans' dissatisfaction with the Anglican *Book of Common Prayer* and with diocesan Episcopacy. The Presbyterian church-order as already represented in the *Explicatio* was the foundation of this new Puritan Prayer Book by Travers. It provided directions 'for the appointment of pastors, doctors, elders and deacons. It recognised the weekly assembly of exercise as part of the system of a truly Reformed Church, and it implied that the true Church ought to be governed by local eldership, and by lesser and greater conferences'.[60] By the enormous influence of Travers' *Directory of Church-government* (i.e. Book of Discipline) the Puritan Movement 'was assuming the definite features of a Presbyterian organisation'. The Puritan leaders were pressing for its general recognition in the movement.

---

[55] Perry, 322, 323. Travers was chaplain and reader at the Temple Church in London. When Lord Cecil wanted to appoint him Master of the Temple, Whitgift opposed this plan. Finally, Richard Hooker got the nomination.
[56] Scott Pearson, 253
[57] Scott Pearson, 141, 142, 257ff
[58] The Latin title of Travers' Directory is: *Disciplina Ecclesiae sacra Dei verbo descripta* (the first part), and *Disciplina Synodica ex ecclesiarum quac eam ex verbo Dei instaurarunt usu Synodis atque libris de eadam re scriptis collecta, et ad certa queadam capita redacta* (the second part).
[59] Collinson, part VII, chapter 3. Unlike the Separatists, most of the Puritans wished fixed forms of worship and church-order. Travers' *Directory of Church-government* was more than a directory of common order, and less than a liturgy. It contained great similarities with the Scottish church-order. Liturgy was given a less important place than ministry, there would be no sacraments without a sermon. The emphasis was on simplicity, sincerity and purity. The Book differed greatly from the Anglican church-order in giving freedom for forms of public prayer and singing. It also contained a collection of devotional material and prayers, destined for the use in family circles and private gatherings.
[60] Scott Pearson, 156

Puritan leaders especially tried to presbyterianise the existing practice of gathering in conferences. In 1586 Travers' book, 'a manual calculated to provide the necessary regulations for the desired Presbyterian organisation', was sent to all conferences, with the request to put it into practice. Local and regional conferences were now referred to as Presbyterian *consistories* and *presbyteries* or *classes*. Other assemblies were designated as *synods*. Were these bodies of local and regional church-government indispensable parts of 16th century Presbyterian thought? Scott Pearson notes that this has often been denied. However, he is convinced that the Puritan leaders of the time aimed at the introduction of not only regional presbyteries or classes, but also of local consistories, according to the Genevan model. Already before the term consistories and classes came into use, Presbyterian proto-structures existed. These were conferences, often called *exercises* or *prophesyings*. The nonconforming Calvinists developed these organisations inside the Anglican structure from 1570 onward. They formed an essential part of the *Grand Design*, i.e. the Presbyterians' plan to reach their ultimate purpose: a Presbyterian State Church in a theocratic context.

Chapter 9

Failure of the Grand Design

1. The Use of Legal Means

a. The Grand Design

The Puritan leaders had developed a plan of introducing Presbyterianism by legal means, making use of lawful institutions. They rejected the idea of realising their theocratic ideal by revolutions and armed resistance. They believed in means of gradually convincing the magistrate and the episcopacy of the need for a Presbyterian church-order. Legal action, petitions, use of existing structures were their weapons. This was their *Grand Design*.

The Episcopalian defence was weak. Whitgift, in his dispute with Cartwright, did his utmost. However, many felt that the Anglican theologians could not offer a comprehensive and cohesive theory of church-government, which was able to strike at the proposals in the Admonitions to Parliament and in the Puritan books of discipline and liturgy. Archbishop Parker was unable to cope with the situation, he died in 1575. He was succeeded by Grindal. The new archbishop, though he was opposed to Puritanism in its radical Cartwrightian Presbyterian form[1], was more Puritan-minded than his predecessor was. Influenced by Bucer and Calvin, he did not see the bishop as an autocrat, but as a fellow-presbyter. When Grindal tried to reach an agreement between bishops and Puritan preachers, and took a number of reform measures, a most promising period, 'a golden time full of godly fruit', seemed to begin. However, the queen was quick to veto the Puritan tendency of her ecclesiastical servant. Finally, Grindal dramatically collided with Elizabeth on the issue of the *prophesyings*.

b. The Prophesyings

The practice of *prophesyings* had crept in from circles of the continental Reformation.[2] They were gatherings of ministers, or of ministers and other people of the congregations, intended for the strengthening of brotherhood and unity, and for mutual edification. In England, they were also called *conferences*, or *exercises*, or *assemblies*. They gathered in the first place to consider the Scriptures. One participant was appointed to expound a passage, and then, the

---

[1] In 1573, after the publication of the *Admonitions*, Grindal -then Archbishop of York- contributed to the organisation of an inquisition against the Puritan leaders (cf. Scott Pearson, 117).
[2] Cf. Collinson, part IV, chapters 5, 6; Scott Pearson, 237ff; Lloyd Jones, 252

others gave their criticism of the expositions, and they discussed it together. The *prophesyings* became very popular.

The increase of *prophesyings* after 1570 can be explained, according by the acceptance in many Puritan circles of Travers' *Explicatio* and proposals for introducing Presbyterian church-order.[3] Soon these gatherings developed to centres of church administration. They began to examine candidates for the ministry, and to play an important role in the nominations of ministers. There was a great lack of able preachers. The *conferences* tried to solve this problem. Often they acted with consent of the bishop. That there was and obvious Puritan climate in the Church of England is proved by the fact that ten out of the fifteen bishops were in favour of these gatherings.[4] At the same time the bishops sometimes hesitated to agree with the *prophesyings*, because they realised that these gatherings could be subversive to their own position.

Scott Pearson says that after the inquisition of 1573-1574, following the publication of the *Admonitions*, 'the exercises were among the best practical agencies for the spread of Puritan principles. Under cover of a legitimate conference, the zealous were enabled to advance their cause quietly and inconspicuously. ... These exercises with their moderators and their mild form of disciplinary jurisdiction, were really embryonic presbyteries [or: consistories, classes] of the modern type'.[5]

The *prophesyings* were approved of by Grindal and by many of his bishops, and this helped much to make them effective for the spread of church-discipline. Although Grindal supported them, he feared the subversive activity for which they might be used. Therefore, he issued a set of regulations, which excluded deprived and ejected preachers from taking part in the *prophesyings*. The lack of preachers and the ignorance of clergy was one of the reasons why Grindal supported the exercises. He also hoped that this practice would bring the Puritans to conformity. If his policy had been successful, the English Church perhaps could have made a silent transition to a system very close to a Presbyterian type of church-order. However, history took a different course.

The queen and some of the bishops realised that the *prophesyings* were dangerous for Episcopalianism. They were to upset the whole of the Elizabethan Settlement. In the end they would grow out to a system that left no room for a hierarchy of bishops and for royal supremacy over the matters of the Church. Even when regulated, the *prophesyings* were formed after the Calvinistic pattern of consistories and classes, and they were propaganda for the Presbyterian church-government. Therefore, in 1574, the queen commanded Archbishop

---

[3] Cremeans, 96ff
[4] Collinson, part IV, chapter 4
[5] Scott Pearson, 157

Parker to ask all the bishops of the church province of Canterbury to stop the *prophesyings*. However, the practice of these gatherings continued and extended. Then, in 1576, the queen forbade the *prophesyings* directly, and Grindal, the new archbishop, was ordered to remove them. The desire for more preachers and better preaching did not impress the queen. In her opinion, three or four preachers in one shire were sufficient.

When Grindal refused to cooperate, she brushed him aside, and neutralised him. She appointed a number of new bishops who were opposed to Puritan discipline. One of them was Whitgift. He became the bishop of Worcester. In the years of the *Admonition Controversy*, Whitgift's dispute with Cartwright had made him the chief defender of Episcopalianism against the dangerous disciplinarian system of the Presbyterian Puritans. A list of objections, drawn up by Whitgift, shows how the conformists feared the ultimate result of the spread of *prophesyings*.[6] They were the beginning of a competitive system, which 'would lead to particularism, each parish going its own way'.

Whitgift was afraid 'of the possibility of insult to the nobility, if they were chosen to be elders, and had to serve under an elected minister'. However, the argument of 'insult to the nobility' could not be used in support of Episcopalianism. Collinson points out that the majority of nobility and gentry were anti-clerically disposed. They not only resisted the Calvinist view of discipline and preaching, but also the government by bishops. In general, the nobility favoured the prophesyings, because this decentralised institution created possibilities for the cooperation between local magistrates and local congregations.[7]

Whitgift also feared that Presbyterianism might bring 'a new popedom and tyranny into the Church, because of the authority it gave to pastors and elders, even over civil magistrates'. Further objections were that the Presbyterian discipline 'smelled of Anabaptism'. 'It took all authority in ecclesiastical matters away from the prince. It aimed at popularising the State and government of the commonwealth. It opened the way to discord, by giving authority to many people'.

Elizabeth's measures had changed the situation. Now the Anglican hierarchy had stronger leaders, who did their utmost to arrest the Puritan Movement. Puritan strongholds came under interdict. Puritan preachers were suspended and ejected. How severe were these measures? McGinn holds, that 'the common Puritan allegation' that after the Admonitions their ministers were ejected in large numbers, for 'untrue'. He is convinced that the Episcopalians

---

[6] Cremeans, 99, 100
[7] Collinson, part IV, chapter 3

were more tolerant than Cartwright and his followers.[8] However, Collinson mentions the suspension of many preachers, e.g. all the ministers in Norwich.[9] Perry who is certainly not a friend of the Puritans, confirms this.[10] After the suspension of Archbishop Grindal in 1576, there was a new wave of ejectments.

Still some bishops did not cooperate in the suspension of the *prophesyings*. Neither did the royal Council, to which belonged influential Puritan-minded men, like the Earl of Leicester, Lord Cecil, Walsingham, Knollys, Huntington. The majority of the country's nobility opposed the queen's ecclesiastical measures. The same was true for Parliament. As a result of this, Elizabeth's campaign against the proto-Presbyterian structures ended in a failure. The *prophesyings* continued to be used, and the suspension of preachers broke the unity of the Anglican Church, thus stimulating Separatism. The *prophesyings* remained to be a channel for the influx of Presbyterianism. 'Notwithstanding some stops put to these exercises, they were generally so approved, in regard to the benefit of them, in bringing the knowledge of the Scriptures among both ministers and people, the better to confirm all against the errors and superstitions of popery, that it was not long before they revived again'.[11]

c. Browne and Harrison

The suspension of ministers led to a movement of secession. Its leaders became Browne and Harrison. They actually separated from the Anglican Church, and at the same time divided the Puritan Movement. Robert Browne was an itinerant preacher from Norfolk. He denounced those who were satisfied with the prevailing Church system. He also condemned those who were contented to remain in a Church with ceremonial laws and an Episcopalian government of which they did not approve. To this criticised category belonged Thomas Cartwright, and the *Admonitioners* like Field. Against them, Browne published 'a treatise of Reformation, without tarrying for any, and the wickedness of those preachers that will not reform themselves and their charge, because they will tarry with the magistrates, and compel them'.[12] Browne was an extremely

---

[8] McGinn, 123, 124
[9] Collinson, part IV, chapter 4
[10] Perry, 298, 299, gives more information on the suspensions. The queen's proclamation of October 1573 appointed a special commission of Oyer and Terminer, and nominated certain lay commissioners for each diocese, who together with the bishops were to make a strict search for nonconformists. Even bishops who were Puritan-minded, like Parkhurst, found themselves 'constrained to act vigorously against them' ... 'So vigorously did the work proceed in the diocese of Norwich that not less than 300 clergy are said to have been suspended'.
[11] Strype, 'Annals', 481, quoted by Cremeans, 98
[12] Perry, 314ff

radical Puritan. Although in practice the Anglican Church offered possibilities for structures like the prophesyings and for a certain involvement of lay people in the local church-government, Browne refused to condone to the Episcopalian system any longer. The lack of discipline and preaching, the government by a hierarchy of bishops the ecclesiastical supremacy of the monarch, those were the things Browne did not want to bear any longer. As a result of his unhidden opinion, he was constantly arrested and in prison. In 1581 he retired to The Netherlands, first to Antwerp and later to Middleburgh, with a band of his followers. His disciples fell into all sorts of quarrels and divisions among themselves. Cartwright, during his years in Middleburgh, disputed with Browne and his successor Harrison, and tried to let the seceders join his group of Presbyterians within the Anglican structure.[13] Eventually, Browne was condemned by his own congregation. He returned to Britain and finally he conformed to the Anglican Church.

d. Greenwood, Barrowe and Penry

In the meantime, in England a different strand of seceding Puritans emerged. Their leaders John Greenwood, Henry Barrowe and John Perry, because of their fearless criticism of the Anglican system, were practically forced out of the Anglican Church. They did not flee to the European continent, and therefore had to bear the full wrath of queen and bishops, without being supported by their fellow Puritans in the Presbyterian camp. They were put in prison, where they produced a rich multitude of Puritan writings on church-discipline and government, before they were executed in 1593. This literature shows that the accusation that they were no radicals or Anabaptists, is untrue. Greenwood, Barrowe and Perry were very close to the ideas of Cartwright c.s. However, there were differences. The seceding Puritans refused to compromise in matters of the Church by bowing before the monarch and the bishops even for reasons of expediency. Moreover, in their view the power of the minister was more embedded in the wider structure of the congregation, and more dynamically related to the other elders and to the office of the priesthood of all believers.[14] Their violent death terminated a further development of their thoughts, which otherwise could have joined and positively influenced the Presbyterian main stream. Deprived of their leaders many Greenwoodians and Barrowists fled to the European continent after 1593. There they gradually deviated from the thought of Greenwood and Barrowe, individualising the congregation and its ministers. As such they belonged to the instigators of the Movement of Congregationalism.

---

[13] Scott Pearson, 215
[14] Paas, *De Gemeenschap der Heiligen*, 205-380, has researched their ecclesiological views.

Failure of the Grand Design

Even in Cartwright's own family circle, there were those who sympathised with the Barrowists and Greenwoodians. This is shown in the correspondence with his sister-in-law Anne Stubbe. In the next chapter we shall review these letters, which throw light on the Presbyterian attitude towards Separatist Puritans.

There were also other Separatist sects, like the *Familists*, or the *Family of Love*. They were an off shoot of Dutch Anabaptists. In addition, there were the Anabaptists proper. Brownists, Greenwoodians and Barrowists, though also Separatists, were different from these groups. They did not share with them the Anabaptist view of perfection and of demonising of the civil magistracy and the State. Many Anabaptist seceders had suffered death under the preceding Tudor monarchs, and also under Elizabeth some were executed. They were especially bitter against the Puritans in the State Church, whom they considered unscriptural and unspiritual compromisers. However, the sects of Anabaptism do not appear to have had many followers in England.

e. The Dedham Papers

The appearance of Separatist groups and the continuation of the prophesyings made clear that the queen's policy had failed. Elizabeth and her bishops must have realised that their actions could not stop the Puritan Movement. The prophesyings not only increased in number, but together they also gradually assumed the form of an underground secret network. It became more and more difficult to check the activities of the Puritan preachers. In 1582, at Cockfield, 300 ministers met for a discussion about the *Book of Common Prayer*. In the same year other conferences took place in Cambridge and Wethersfield. Presbyterian activities in the Stour Valley led to the formation of the so called *Dedham Conference*, a permanent body, which existed until about 1590. The interesting thing is that this conference took extensive minutes, which have been preserved. Collinson studied the *Dedham Papers*.[15]

The *Dedham Papers* give insight in the *Grand Design*, the Puritan plan of action to change the Church of England. Edmund Chapman, lecturer at Dedham, belonged to the foremost initiators and leaders of the conference.[16]

---

[15] Collinson, part IV, chapter 6; cf. Scott Pearson, 239ff
[16] A contemporary guide, entitled, *The Parish Church of St Mary at Dedham*, pp. 21, 27, says: 'In the Anglican Church of Dedham a tablet commemorates Edmund Chapman. He was probably the first of the regular lecturers, appointed in 1577 or 1578. The origin of the institution of lecturers lies in the time of Henry VIII, when it became apparent that before the Reformation the parish clergy in England were not trained to preach sermons. In subsequent years, many towns and parishes hired lecturers to fill the gap. Actually, they were preachers, hired by a parish to assist the parish priest, i.e. the rector or vicar. This office must have been quite common. The lecturer's pastoral duties included delivering sermons, synonymous with lectures'.

Ministers and Elders

The minutes show that the conference was a transitional structure. Its transitional character appears from the attitude of the conference members to the formal authorities of State and Church. They were loyal to their great design, which was to be realised by legal means, making use of legitimate institutions. However, as it became increasingly clear that monarch and bishops would never allow Calvinist discipline and church-government, they felt more and more tempted to change the Church if necessary in defiance of the law. In the end, most of the Dedham divines would keep loyal to the commonwealth law of the *Elizabethan Settlement*, and conform to the State Church.

The essential reason why the Dedham-conference should be called transitional is the absence of elders in it. It was not yet a full Presbyterian classis, because it had no lay-elders. However, many things that made it approach very closely to a Presbyterian classis. The Dedham-conference tried to govern the Church in a Presbyterian way, in a large region without recognising the boundaries of Episcopal dioceses. Episcopacy was not yet excluded, but the Dedham jurisdiction and administration were largely independent of the Anglican church-government by the bishops. There was a strong tendency of *independentism* and *congregationalism*, with an emphasis on discipline, fellowship, and the examination and nomination of new preacher. In practice, the conference only accepted the existence of bishops, if these church officers would loosen themselves from the hierarchical Anglican structure and accommodate themselves to a system in which there was parity of ministers.

However, the conference did not lay the government of the Church into the hands of elders, chosen by the congregation. The introduction of chosen elders would have substituted and completely excluded the authority of bishops, and this would have turned the conference into an illegal revolutionary organisation. That was what the Dedham-divines wanted to avoid. That is why they never came to a complete acceptance of Presbyterian church-order, as proposed in the Admonitions, in Cartwright's writings, and in Travers' books on church-discipline and church-government. The Dedham brothers were afraid to incriminate themselves by officially accepting the *Book of Discipline*. They did not sign. Instead, they used a reduced form of the *Book of Common Prayer*. However, there was much more acceptance by other conferences, like those in London, Oxford and Cambridge. Collinson mentions the *Acta* of 1587 of the Cambridge conference, which denounced the bishops as anti-Christian, and the *Decrees of Warwickshire* that advocated the Reformed practice of Presbytery within Episcopacy'.[17]

Nevertheless, Collinson thinks that in this period there were only indications and no proofs of a calculated Presbyterian conception of the Church.

---

[17] Collinson, part IV, chapter 6

Considering the facts, we wonder whether he is right. It is true that the Calvinist Puritans did not intend to build a separate independent Presbyterian Church. However, from the time of the *Admonitions* onward, their vision of the Church of England must have been definitely Presbyterian, including the ideal of church-government by ministers and elders. Preserved correspondence shows that the Dedham-divines were in contact with other conferences and with the group of Field and Wilcox in London. Although there is much obscurity with regard to frequency and quality of these contacts, one can say that the conferences cooperated in a way that reminds of the working of a network of Presbyterian classes. Anyway, Presbyterian-minded ministers made use of this subversive network for their attempts for a silent realisation of a Presbyterian takeover.

f. Expulsion or Subscription

In these circumstances Archbishop Grindal died, after a long period of humiliation by the queen. Whitgift succeeded him, the prelate who had already shown that he was a faithful servant of Elizabeth. He was soon called 'the queen's little black husband'[18], because of his loyal obedience to the monarch's desires with regard to the Church. With a set of three demands, Whitgift forced the Puritan clergy to choose between expulsion and conformity with the State Church. All ecclesiastical officers had to subscribe to royal supremacy, to the *Book of Common Prayer*, and to the *39 Articles of Religion*. If they refused to sign, they would lose their benefices and livings, and be ejected. After the initial expulsions in the 1560s and 1570s, these severe demands were a major blow against Puritanism. Those Puritan preachers, who still had an official beneficed position in the State Church, found themselves in a very difficult situation. It seemed to be a question of to leave it or to take it. Especially the *Book of Common Prayer* they could not accept unconditionally. The subscription text runs as follows:

> '... that the *Book of Common Prayer* and of the ordering of bishops, priests and deacons, containeth nothing in it contrary to the Word of God, and that the same may be lawfully used, and that he himself will use the form of the said book prescribed in public prayer and administration of the sacraments, and none other'.[19]

Whitgift's measures contributed to the increase of division in the ranks of the Puritans. Those whom Lloyd Jones calls 'the true Puritans' were led into the

---

[18] McGinn, 31
[19] Perry, 318, who quotes Strype's *Whitgift*, b.iii,2; cf. Scott Pearson, 241ff

directions of Presbyterianism or Separatism.[20] However, a large number of Puritans came to a conditional subscription in the end. According to Collinson, the majority of the Puritan preachers -among them Chapman and other Dedham divines- finally came to a settlement through conditional subscription.[21] They preferred reconciliation with the bishops to expulsion. To them belonged those who eventually would give up Presbyterianism and submit to Episcopalianism. Lloyd Jones calls them 'Anglican Puritans', in distinction from the 'true Puritans' of the Presbyterian and Separatist categories. Collinson indicates that these two directions in Puritanism, after one generation would belong to opposed sides of the cleavage between Establishment and Dissent.

In the 1580s the 'Anglican Puritans' abandoned their original positions with regard to church-government. They continued a Puritanism of moral and pastoral teaching only. They were still Puritans, but not nonconformists. To the majority the ideal of Presbyterianism became irrelevant. Only after 1640 Presbyterianism would revive among them for a while. However, their style of Presbyterianism was much more pragmatic than that of the 'true Puritans'. The majority of them remained in the State Church until after the middle of the 17th century. Collinson calls them 'non-separating Congregationalists'. These people were on their way to independency.[22] The real Puritans, however, did not give up the struggle for a different discipline and a different government of the Church. They believed that it could still be done.

g. Whitgift's Inquisition

Whitgift, to his chagrin, did not reach the unconditional surrender of the majority of the Puritan ministers. Pressures from the side of Court members, like Cecil and Walsingham, forced him to certain concessions. However, now he tried to prove the inconformity of those who conditionally signed the declaration of conformity. For the use of the Ecclesiastical Commission, which had to execute a programme of church-visitations, he drew up a body of twenty-four articles. Conditional subscribers who were accused or suspected of nonconformity were called upon to purge themselves of the charges of these articles under oath. If they refused to swear the oath, they were immediately deprived from the office of a minister in the Anglican Church. When they swore, they were cross-examined. In case of dissimilarities between their answers and the articles, they were accused of perjury and accordingly punished.[23]

---

[20] Lloyd Jones, 253
[21] Collinson, part V, chapter 3
[22] Collinson, part VIII, chapter 5
[23] Perry, 319, 320

Great was the indignation of the Puritan ministers. A pamphlet appeared, entitled, 'The unlawful practices of the Prelates', probably written by Field. At Court, there was also disapproval. Elizabeth's chief-counsellor, Cecil, wrote a letter to Whitgift: 'In think the Inquisition of Spain use not so many questions to comprehend and trap their preys. According to my simple judgement this kind of proceeding is too much savouring of Roman Inquisition, and is rather a device to seek offenders than to reform any'.[24]

The Presbyterian Puritans tried to resist Whitgift trough Parliament. In 1584 and 1585, bills were introduced in the House of Commons, which proposed a change to Presbyterianism according to Travers' *Directory*, i.e. to a Presbyterian church-government with ministers, elders, consistories and classes.[25] Then a petition was drawn up in which the points of the bills we urged upon the Upper House (House of Lords), with a view of being presented to the queen. The petition amounted to

> 'a request ... that priests should be put on a level with bishops in the matter of ordination, that no ordination should take place without a call from the congregation, that subscription [of Whitgift's uniformity declaration] should be done away with, ... all Whitgift's disciplinary suspensions cancelled, *prophesyings* restored, and all dispensations abolished'.

Perry indicates that this petition by the Commons 'shows the strong Puritanical spirit which animated the majority of the House'.[26] The House of Lords, however, rejected the petition. Then the Puritans brought a number of new bills into the Commons. However, the queen, at the suggestion of Whitgift, resolutely commanded that this 'irregular legislation' should be stopped. Soon afterwards she dismissed Parliament.

Then the Puritan leaders realised that the official ecclesiastical and political channels were useless for them. The *Grand Design* of the introduction of Presbyterian church-discipline and government could not be put to practice with the help of lawful means and legitimate institutions. Therefore, they turned to other means. When it was absolutely clear that the supreme civil magistrate and the ecclesiastical authority left no room for legal plans, they began to set up 'a godly discipline outside the law'. The Puritan Movement in its nonconformist appearance, and especially the conscious Presbyterians among them, were forced to continue their activities underground.

---

[24] Perry, 321, who quotes 'State Papers of Elizabeth', clxxii, 1
[25] Scott Pearson, 251ff; cf. Perry, 323
[26] Perry, 324

2. 'A godly Discipline outside the Law'

a. Presbyterian Experiments

Presbyterian Puritans had discovered that the queen and her bishops would never tolerate the introduction of Presbyterian forms of discipline and church-government, even when this could be reached by legal means. However, they were not discouraged by their defeat. When their attempts failed to get Presbyterian church-order enacted by law, those who favoured it, decided 'to uphold it by a solemn mutual pledge'[27], outside the law of the country. In this way, illegal Presbyterian structures began to be organised, with consistories, ministers and elders.

According to Cremeans 'the success of Calvinist disciplinarians in introducing their system of church-government in the Church of England was remarkable in some places'. Of course their success was most apparent in those places where lower magistrates and ecclesiastical officers, in defiance of the queen and the archbishop, supported Presbyterianism. Cremeans mentions 'the outstanding' example of the Church of Northampton, 'where with the consent of the bishop of Peterborough, the mayor of the town, and the justices of the peace of the county and the town, a complete Calvinistic system of discipline was established ...', giving a picture of a community, which was organised almost exactly as Geneva was. The amazing fact of the Northampton Church is, that entirely outside the law of Elizabethan England, 'a close cooperation could exist of the civil authority and the ecclesiastical, in a true Calvinistic fashion'.[28] Handwritten copies of Travers' *Directory* circulated and served as the binding document of these Presbyterian structures. Perry notes that 24 ministers of the conferences -now classes- of Northampton and Warwick subscribed to the *Directory* as binding upon them. 'They were followed by others to the number of 500'.

Some of the conferences, e.g. the one at Dedham, were afraid to accept the *Directory* as their book of discipline, but in general, it was widely received. However, the intention to organise consistories and presbyteries within the Episcopalian Church, was not easy to realise in practice. It was practically impossible to avoid collisions with the representatives of the Anglican structure. Collinson says that it did not come to free election of ministers. Puritan ministers often accepted that the bishop played a certain role in their ordination. With regard to the election of elders, there were many serious problems. Many congregations did not succeed in the nomination and introduction of elders. Therefore, the exercise of discipline was organised in various pragmatic ways,

---

[27] Perry, 331
[28] Cremeans, 101ff

which were not always in accordance to the Genevan conception. As to public worship, the principles of the 'Genevan Forme' as represented in Travers' *Directory* were accepted. However, according to Collinson, in practice the *Directory* as such was not often used in public services. A selective usage of the Anglican *Book of Common Prayer* seems to have been the common thing. The *Prayer Book* was reduced until a Calvinist form was left. In other words, they omitted many liturgical elements, thus adapting the *Prayer Book* to Presbyterian practice. Collinson gets the impression that in general there was 'not a clean break with Anglicanism', but an attitude of 'pragmatic compromise'.[29]

In this way the nonconforming Puritans tried to evade collisions with the ecclesiastical and political authorities. They trusted that Presbyterian practice would continue to creep forward under the Anglican skin of the Church. Their policy was the gradual establishment of 'Presbytery within Episcopacy', until the Episcopalian structure of the Church would be completely undermined. That was the strategy of the leaders of the nonconformist Calvinists. However, after 1585 it became increasingly clear that this strategy could not succeed. Presbyterianism within the State Church was impossible without the cooperation of bishops and civil magistrates. In the last resort, it was impossible without cooperation by the queen. However, Elizabeth was very far from condoning Presbyterian experiments. Neither was Whitgift, the primate. Collinson characterises the Presbyterian Puritans of this period as adherents of a 'non-separating congregationalism', and he holds that their position was practically untenable.

b. The Martin Mar-Prelate Papers

The defeat of the Armada in 1588 delivered England from the threat of foreign[30] Roman Catholic aggression. However, the consequences for the Presbyterians were not all that positive. The designers of the *Elizabethan Settlement* got their hands free for an attempt to crush all nonconformist opposition. Soon they found an occasion. The more violent and exasperated section of the Puritan party, also embittered by the temporising policy of their brethren, determined to precipitate matters. They produced a series of seditious and often libellous attacks directed against the bishops. These tracts became known under the general name, *Martin Mar-Prelate Papers*. Scott Pearson notes that the Mar-Prelate Papers contained two elements. The one element was animated by the Presbyterian ideals of Cartwright c.s. The other element 'was mingled with gall and represented the quintessential ire, bathed in wit and irony of the Puritans against the bishops'. It has been stated that 'the Presbyterians or the Puritans

---

[29] Collinson, part VII, chapters 3, 4
[30] Scott Pearson, 263ff

proper' had no part in the tracts. Scott Pearson says that this view is misleading. Undoubtedly, moderate men, like Cartwright, did not favour the Mar-Prelate Papers, 'but that was because of the manner and form in which they were composed', which 'hurt the cause of Puritanism and hastened the fast ebbing tide'.[31]

Obviously, these tracts were of Puritan origin. However, the Presbyterian leaders realised that they were harmful to their cause. Although the use of abusive words and libellous attacks was quite common in the disputes and quarrels of those days, many people were struck by 'Martin's' bold language. Perry notes some of the most violent passages.

> Anglican church laws are 'popish and to be abandoned, a froth and filth to be spewed out of the commonwealth'. It was said that the Church of England was 'no true Church in as much as it lacked discipline'. Cathedral churches 'must be put down, where the service of God is grievously abused'. The archbishop was called 'Beelzebub of Canterbury, pope of Lambeth, the Canterbury Caiaphas, Esau, a monstrous anti-christ, a most bloody opposer of God's saints, a very anti-christian beast, most bloody tyrant'. The bishops were described as 'unlawful, unnatural, false and bastardly governors of the Church, the ordinances of the devil ... proud, popish, profane, presumptuous, paltry, pestilent, pernicious prelates and usurpers, enemies of God and the State'. The clergy who supported the bishops were characterised as 'popish priests, proctors of anti-christ, greedy dogs to fill their paunches, desperate and forlorn atheists ...', etc. The *Book of Common Prayer* was called 'a book full of corruption, many of the contents against the Word of God, the sacraments profaned therein; the Lord's Supper not eaten but made a pageant and stage play; the form of public baptism full of childish and superstitious toys'.[32]

These shocking statements indicate the degree of frustration to which many in the Puritan Movement had come. The series contained seven tracts. Especially the first one, *Epistle to the Terrible Priests*, was directed against Whitgift, and his conforming bishops like Cooper and Aylmer. The Puritan ministers realised that the archbishop and the queen would take revenge. According to Collinson, practically all of them rejected the way in which Martin Mar-Prelate attacked the Episcopalian establishment.[33]

Yet, it is almost certain that some Puritan ministers contributed to these writings. The name Martin Mar-Prelate did not necessarily represent any one single writer. There are different opinions on the question of the authorship.

---

[31] Scott Pearson, 277ff
[32] Perry, 331-335
[33] Collinson, part VIII, chapter 1

Collinson suggest that their names have not been found. Perry, however, supposes that the chief writers were two Puritan ministers, Penry and Udal.

Sometimes Cartwright is mentioned as one of the accomplices. Scott Pearson, however, is sure that 'Martin himself is still shrouded in mystery'. Yet the writer or writers must have belonged to the left wing of the Cartwrightian school. One of Martin's special demands was that permission be granted for the publication of Cartwright's *Confutation* of the Roman Catholic 'Rheims translation' of the New Testament. Cartwright's name was mentioned frequently and reverently in the tracts. That is why the ecclesiastical High Commission was quick to accuse him of complicity. However, there is no proof at all that Cartwright had a hand in the production of the papers. Although 'it is evident that the main purpose of the writings was the same as that cherished by Cartwright', he and others 'disliked the satirical and abusive means adopted and ... he objected to the unheard of pitch of scurrility that marked the tracts'.[34]

After investigation by the archbishop, Udal and Penry were arrested and charged with the authorship of the papers. Penry was liberated, because nothing could be proved against him. However, in 1593, he was arrested again, brought to trial, and executed. Udal died in prison.

c. The Proto-Presbyterian network Discovered

The publication of the *Martin Mar-Prelate Papers* provoked the Elizabethan government to intensify and widen its campaign against Puritanism. The queen ordered a thorough investigation, and this led to the discovery that the Puritan Movement was much more organised than was assumed by the authorities thus far. Elizabeth's High Commissioners found that there was a systematic attempt to introduce the 'Puritan Book of Discipline'. They began to realise that the phenomenon of prophesyings, exercises, conferences, catechisings and lectures was more than occasional. There was a 'gadding abroad' or a 'gadding to sermons' of small groups within the Anglican parishes, which like the *Christliche Gemeinschaften* [Christian Communities] in Bucer's Strasbourg, tried to uphold Presbyterian government and discipline, under then guidance of ministers and elders.

It had been very difficult for the State and the established Church to discover the organised pattern of these gatherings, leave alone to keep in check their potential separatism. The search for Martin Mar-Prelate unearthed much information on the clandestine *Puritan Movement*. Now, the whole Elizabethan judicial, political, and ecclesiastical system was mobilised in an attempt to uproot these subversive groups and to apprehend their leaders. Searches in

---

[34] Scott Pearson, 281-287

Northamptonshire and Warwickshire, the centres of Presbyterian activity, produced books, documents, acta and decrees, which were incriminating the Puritan leaders. Severe measures were taken, which removed the upper-structure of the Presbyterian Puritan Movement.

However, the Elizabethan government never succeeded to suppress Presbyterianism completely. Scott Pearson describes the victory of Presbyterian church-rule in the Channel Islands Guernsey and Jersey, and Cartwright's involvement in its development in the last few years of the 16th century.[35] In England, not any government would have been able to destroy the lower structure of conferences and exercises. Although the Dedham-conference was dissolved, Presbyterianism maintained itself in the Sour Valley. In Warwickshire, Northamptonshire, Hertfordshire, Cornwall and Devon, Presbyterian structures remained intact. The political aspirations of the Puritans had failed for the time being, and their public appearance was broken. However, underground the Puritan revolution continued. It changed England in such a way, that it could revive as a movement in the next century.[36]

The Presbyterian leaders were in a difficult position. They were in constant danger of being arrested and imprisoned. Therefore, in their public activities, they tried to be conformist and nonconformist at the same time, conformist when they were accused of Separatism and sedition, nonconformist when they were forced to submit to Episcopalianism. Sometimes, when they wanted to make clear that they were no Separatists, they came very near to recognising the Anglican Church, and conforming to it. Consequently, they publicly distanced themselves from Puritans like Barrowe, Greenwood and Penry, who suffered in prison, and eventually were executed. However, they never abandoned their Presbyterian principles of church-government and discipline. Because of their cautious attitude, the Elizabethan magistrates had no definite grip on the Presbyterian Movement as such.

d. Cartwright's Trial

This was most apparent in the trial against the movement's intellectual leader, Thomas Cartwright. In autumn 1590, Cartwright was suspended and summoned before the ecclesiastical High Commissioners. Thirty-one accusations were brought in against him. He had renounced Episcopalian ordination ant Antwerp and Middleburgh, and established Presbyterian churches there. At Warwick, he had not respected the Church of England, and condemned bishops and the *Prayer Book*. He had had knowledge of the *Martin Mar-Prelate Papers* and he was an accomplice in the conference movement. He had also written the

---

[35] Scott Pearson, 157-166
[36] Collinson, part VIII, chapter 4

Directory of Church-government (or, the Book of Discipline).[37] When he was confronted with these charges, Cartwright refused to take the expurgatory oath, and was then put in prison, together with sixteen other ministers. There he was to remain until May 1592. Meanwhile the debate continued.

While a prisoner, Cartwright had an important discussion with Bancroft, one of Whitgift's assistants. The discussion showed the progress in the self-consciousness of Anglican thinking. Whitgift, in his dispute with Cartwright in the 1570s had not advocated Episcopalianism as the only possible derivation from the Scriptures and early church history. He had only claimed that the Anglican system was the best and most legitimate expression of the Scriptures for the Elizabethan era. This 'feeble line of defence' of the government of the Anglican Church was not abandoned until the public appearance of Bancroft. In a sermon Bancroft had asserted 'that there was no scriptural basis whatever for the Presbyterian platform, and he claimed this for Episcopacy'. According to him 'there is no man living ... able to show where there was any Church planted ever since the Apostles' time, but there the bishops had authority over the rest of the ministry'. In his defence of 'the divine right of Episcopacy' Bancroft was supported by a Dutch divine, Adrian Saravia, who stated: 'It is certain that the Apostles did not appoint anything which they had not received from the Lord, but they appointed bishops, such as were Timothy and Titus, wherever there was need'. Bancroft, in his Survey of the Holy Discipline (1593), attributes the institution of bishops to Christ himself and stated that the Church of England was based on warrants of Antiquity'.[38] Cartwright, on the other hand, defended the legitimacy of eldership. It is based on Scripture, and in the times of the Emperor Constantine and Augustine of Hippo the practice of ruling elders flourished. However, before his examiners of the High Commission and the Queen's Star Chamber Cartwright denied that he himself had erected any eldership or presbytery.

In the end, his interrogators found it impossible to prove that Cartwright and his friends were guilty of putting into effect the system of meetings as prescribed in the Book of Discipline. Neither could they prove that the Cartwrightians had any connection with Martin Mar-Prelate, or that they belonged to a seditious conspiracy of schismatics or rebels.[39]

e. Separatists in Exile

The failure of the trials did not end the government's campaign against the Puritans. In 1593, the House of Commons -now also afraid of sedition and

---

[37] Scott Pearson, 312-319
[38] Perry, 343, 344, 348
[39] Scott Pearson, 327-349

rebellion by the Separatists- contributed to the enacting of a law by which nonconformists were threatened with severe punishment. Those who within three months should not submit to conformity and continued to refuse 'to repair to some church, chapel, or usual place of common prayer', would be banished from the country, and if they had returned without leave, they would suffer death. Many of whom who had already been arrested, and 'of whom the prisons were full', decided to 'abjure the country'. A number of Brownists and Barrowists were allowed to emigrate to America. Perry notes that the greater number of abjurers went to The Netherlands. They formed congregations in Amsterdam, Arnheim, Middleburgh, Leyden, and other places.[40]

In the meantime, Cartwright's moderate attitude caused misunderstanding on the left and on the right. The emergence of Separatist groups and the excesses of Martin Mar-Prelate refrained Cartwright from using his pen in defending Presbyterianism and radical Puritanism. As a result, the Brownists and Barrowists soon accused him of inconsistency and unfaithfulness.

f. Anglican attacks: Bancroft, Hooker

However, the fiercest attack came from the side of the Anglicans. Matthew Sutcliffe, Dean of Exeter, wrote a series of hostile tracts against Cartwright. Scott Pearson calls them the *Martin Mar-Presbyter Papers*, as they were not less slanderous than those written by their Puritan counterparts in 1588.[41] When Cartwright, before leaving for the Channel Islands in 1596, wrote a pamphlet in which he confessed certain weaknesses of old age, Bancroft rejoiced to see that 'the chiefe man that began this course in England, is drawing homeward'. Cartwright's answer to Harrison was mistakenly seen by Bancroft 'as a sign that he had departed from his original tenet that discipline is a necessary part of the Gospel'. However, Bancroft did not understand the motives of Presbyterianism. The Presbyterian denouncements of radicalism and separatism were explained by him as weaknesses that indicated the disintegration of a purely subversive movement.

This cheap bias and lack of understanding was not shared by the most famous Anglican theologian of the time, Richard Hooker. He was a much more dangerous adversary of Puritanism in general and of the Calvinist idea of church-government in particular. His series of books, *The Laws of Ecclesiastical Polity* (1594-1597), represented a classic defence of the Church of England. In a calm scholarly way he gave his analysis of Cartwrightian Puritanism. Perry notes that Hooker in this controversy occupied a middle place between Whitgift

---

[40] Perry, 336, 337
[41] Scott Pearson, 363-370

and Bancroft. Whitgift stressed the preference for Episcopalianism in the circumstances of the day. However, he had to concede that the Presbyterian pattern could be derived from Scripture. Like Cartwright, he accepted the Scriptures as the only foundation of his theory, but he was not able to prove his case out of the Scriptures. Bancroft stated that Episcopalianism was indispensably necessary to the Church at any time of history, and that Christ himself had commanded it in His Word.[42]

Hooker's conception, however, was different, because it was based on a different view of Scripture and of early church history. Contrary to Whitgift and Bancroft, he conceded that those church fathers, who introduced Episcopalianism, were not necessarily in line with the letter of Scripture. However, this did not deny the validity of Episcopalianism, because in Hooker's view the church fathers had a consensus with regard to this form of church-government. In general, the church fathers agreed that the Church should be ruled by a hierarchy of bishops. They were entitled to share this view, because human reason had taught them that Episcopalianism is not against Scripture, but is grounded in it. Scripture prescribes no form, but helps to establish it by the consensus of reason in those who guide the Church, according to the line of apostolic succession. Scripture is the revelation of salvation. Church-government and discipline are formulated by reason. Together with the revelation in Scripture, this consensus of reason has authority over the Church of Christ. The tradition of the Church is apostolic and, like the Word of God, it is in accordance with the work of the Holy Spirit. Hooker coordinated reason and revelation as the one activity of the Holy Spirit. In his vision, the authority of the Word of God was paralleled by the authority of reason. Luoma, in his treatise, 'Who owns the Fathers?', concludes that Whitgift could not beat Cartwright, because he shared with him a similar understanding of the authority of Scripture. Therefore, he lost when he tried to refer to Episcopalian practices in the early Church in support of his theory.[43] Hooker, however, did not need a command in Scripture for his Episcopalian system. The government by bishops is not derived from Christ's commandment, but it is instituted by the power of reason, which is given to the Church. The power of reason gives the Church the authority to choose a system of government that suits the circumstances of time and place.

However, according to Perry[44], Hooker 'did not admit the indispensable necessity' of the government by a hierarchy of bishops. In Hooker's opinion, things like church-government are mutable in a way. The

---

[42] Perry, 345
[43] J.K. Luoma, 'Who owns the Fathers?', in: *Sixteenth Century Journal*, vol. VIII, 3 (1977), 45-59
[44] Perry, 346

Church has the power, 'if it so willed to abolish the order of bishops, although that order is most agreeable to the teaching of the Holy Scriptures and to the ancient practice of the Church'. However, this does not mean for Hooker that there is a possibility for Presbyterianism. In his opinion, the Puritan view of the Scriptures was too narrow. He rejected the Presbyterian Puritan conviction that an unalterable polity of church-government was laid down in the Scriptures. He also denounced the Presbyterians' objection to a dumb ministry. According to him, the value they attached to preaching was exaggerated. There were other means that the Church could use for the salvation of souls, like the observance of the *Book of Common Prayer*.[45] Although Hooker never mentioned Cartwright by his full name, he frequently cited the writings of the Presbyterian leader, and criticised his 'disdainful sharpness of wit'.[46] He was also the definite opponent of Travers. Hooker and Travers used to preach regularly in the Temple Church in London, where they attacked each other's views.[47] Lloyd Jones emphasises

> 'that with Hooker, and by Hooker, Anglicanism received clear definition'. Hooker created the 'ultimate pattern for Anglicanism. ... The temporary positions were becoming hardened. Anglicanism as defined by Richard Hooker was something very different indeed from the ideas of Parker and Grindal, and those men who came back from the Marian Exile on the continent. A real change had taken place, ... an inevitable change. The temporary accommodations and compromises of 1558-1563 [and of the 1570s] had to lead to Hooker's position'.

The change in Anglicanism not only pertains to the questions of church-order, but also to those of salvation-doctrine. Controversies on the subject of predestination and election led to a conference at Lambeth Palace, where a number of articles were drawn up. These *Lambeth Articles* show that the Anglican Church still accepted the Calvinist thought on predestination. However, by the end of the century, under the influence of theologians like Peter Baro, a party was growing that protested against some of the 'terrible doctrines' contained in the *Lambeth Articles*. Whitgift himself withdrew his active aid from the Calvinist party. In the universities of Oxford and Cambridge, purely Calvinist teaching gradually receded to the background.[48]

---

[45] Cf. Scott Pearson, 271
[46] Scott Pearson, 272
[47] Cf. chapter 8.2. d and e
[48] Cf. Perry, 351-356

g. The Grand Design kept alive

The *Grand Design* of the Presbyterian Puritans of replacing Episcopacy by Presbytery had failed, at least for the time being. Scott Pearson summarises the reasons: Whitgift's coercive measures, the writings and the detective work by Bancroft, Sutcliffe's accusations, the argumentation of Hooker, the defeat of the Armada, the death of important patrons like Leicester, the rigours of the High Commission and the Star Chamber, the Mar-Prelate Papers which robbed Presbyterianism of the sympathy of moderate men, the vogue of extreme radicalism and separatism.[49] Other reasons could be added. Collinson thinks that the Puritans were victims of their own strategy. They underestimated their own strength, did not dare to use it.[50]

Apart from the breach between conforming Calvinists and nonconforming Calvinist-Puritans, a deep cleavage began to divide the nonconformists themselves. Many Puritans seceded from the State Church, and many of them had to leave the country.

However, the non-separating Presbyterians did not give up the hope of completion of the Reformation through the ultimate establishment of a Presbyterian State Church, which would bring every aspect of the English commonwealth under the beneficial discipline of the Word of God. They conceded to temporary concessions and compromises, and 'began to concentrate on pastoral teaching and pastoral theology without neglecting general protestant theology'.[51] This is the position of Cartwright in his later years. The big issue, the original idea, seemed impossible for the time being. However, he and his friends 'hoped that ultimately times might change, and true reform of the Church might be possible'. Collinson's view that they failed because they underestimated their strength, is true, at least in part. They probably lacked a clear sight of their incipient political power and possibilities. Some use of revolutionary means, including armed resistance, would probably have led to the victory of a kind of Presbyterian church-order.

The Cartwrightians did not think in these terms. The 'godly order', which they envisaged, was not to be realised by revolution or secession. Scripture taught them to respect the magistrate and to reject sedition and separation. The 'godly order' was to embrace the whole society, including the civil and ecclesiastical authorities, in a theocratic pattern. Their vision of society was different from the prevailing tyrannical structure of Monarchy and Episcopacy, and was also different from the chaotic situation that, in their view,

---

[49] Scott Pearson, 413ff
[50] Collinson, part VIII, chapter 5
[51] Lloyd Jones, 252; cf. McGinn, 138: Hooker's theology approached the Roman Catholic theory of cooperation between nature and grace.

would be the consequence of the ideas of the Separatists. Both denied the form of discipline, which they recognised in the Bible and in the early Church. Both represented a view of church-government and discipline, which was not in accordance with the Word of God. The Anglican hierarchy was based on worldly power, and had lost sight of the invisibility aspect of the true Church of Christ. The Separatists broke the unity of State and Church, and tended to unscriptural spiritualism, losing sight of the visibility aspect of the Church of England. A completely different order was to be introduced, not based on worldly power or on false spiritualism. In establishing this order, there was no hope in resorting to means used by Anglicanism and Separatism. No violence of revolution and suppression. No violence of schism and separation. Their strategy was the preaching of the Word of God, followed by the peaceful introduction of a Presbyterian church-order. That was the *Grand Design* of the early Presbyterians by the end of the 16th century.

However, the queen and the leaders of the Anglican establishment did not recognise this design as non-violent and peaceful. For them the practice of the network of *prophesyings* remained a danger. In addition, the majority of Calvinist-minded clergy in the Church of England, accused the Puritans of sedition and deviation from Calvin. In a way, Puritan activities were seditious indeed. The Puritan attempts of upholding the *prophesyings*, especially the inherent conscious Presbyterian efforts, were really undermining the English governmental system. Is this sedition or the inevitable working of the Word of God preached in a worldly society? After all, the same Word, which establishes the Church, also brings near the vision of the Kingdom of God.

h. Followers of the Genevan Example

It remains to be seen how Calvin himself would have looked at this. Cole and Moody describe the *prophesyings* 'within the Puritan tradition as an ongoing dynamic of the Reformers' sola scriptura', but also 'within the counter dynamic of Calvinism, whose independence of ordered discipline left of the Church, Calvin would have found strange and disturbing'.[52] However, this view is based on speculation. It is impossible to say how Calvin would have reacted in times and circumstances which were not his own and for which he bore no responsibility. Anyway, Calvin did not reject completely the rising against a prevailing regime, provided that in it there was some representation by the magistrates. It seems the Puritans of the 16th century acted in accordance to this, which may not deny differences of emphasis. The Puritans, including the early Presbyterians, tried to be true followers of the Genevan Reformer, not only

---

[52] C.R. Cole and M.E. Moody, *The Dissenting Tradition*, Ohio University Press, 197, 15ff. They refer to the significance of Collinson's view of the prophesyings.

concerning the doctrines of salvation, but also concerning the order and government of the Church. Consequently, their position towards the State and the civil magistrate was differently accentuated than the original version of Calvinism. The same is true for their proposed system of church-government. However, in their comprehensive view of mutual independence of State and Church, who at the same time were called to cooperation, and in their rejection of separatism and revolution, they clearly showed that they understood the original meaning of the Genevan Reformer.

Chapter 10

Attacks from Two Sides

1. Godly Discipline

The title of this chapter does not suggest that Cartwright's conception of church-order represented a third way, a conscious *via media*, between the positions of the Anglican episcopacy and the independent separatists. Cartwright did not build a structure of compromise, consisting of useful elements of both extremes. Of course, his Presbyterian church-doctrine was developed in the process of reaction and counter-reaction between both sides. But he did not derive from them, and he was not essentially guided by them. His idea of church-government was independent of the principles of *clerical hierarchy* and of *populism*. He was not orientated on the ideologies of *absolutism* and *democracy*.

Cartwright envisaged a system of government that was rooted in the Word of God. Government rests in God. He planted His Church on the earth and in His Word He commanded how the Church should be governed. Ministers and elders are its officers. They are servants of the Word of God, and they exercise church-discipline. Church and State, although belonging to different spheres with different responsibilities, should submit themselves under the Word of God and the discipline of the Church.

This *godly discipline* was not to serve the power of ecclesiastical and political rulers, as in the Elizabethan Anglican settlement. Nor was it to serve the personal influence or independence of individual human beings, as in the Separatists' churches. It was a theocratic conception directed towards the honour of God and the salvation of people. Presbyterian church-order was not seen as stemming from God's revelation, destined for the world. Its objective was to give back to God what He Himself had laid in it by His sovereign will, i.e. the honour of His name, presented to Him by His chosen people. His people continually thank Him for their sanctification and for the assurance of their justification. The Presbyterian system of church-government and discipline, considered to be a gift from God Himself, would consequently be suited best for the expression of thanksgiving to God. Because of its *godly order*, it safeguards the ministry of the Word and the discipline of people. Therefore, it is the best instrument for guiding sinners to God.

2. No Imitator

By his opponents, Cartwright was sometimes accused of being an imitator. We have seen how Bucer, Calvin, Beza and others promulgated ideas that were incorporated in Elizabethan Presbyterianism. Cartwright adapted the theories of his teachers to the English situation. Scott Pearson says: 'T.C. represented the nexus between English Puritanism and the continental Reformation'.[1] Especially Calvin was his example. He was even of the opinion that the writings of other famous men of the age, e.g. Bucer, need not be read, if the student confines the attention to Calvin, who 'hath in a manner that which is fittest in them'[2]

Calvin was put first, but this does not mean that Sutcliffe was right, when he called Cartwright a servile 'borrower of Calvin'[3] We would like to call him an independent follower of Calvin. 'Whereas Calvin's system was designed for a city-state only, Cartwright had a vision of an English Presbyterian State-Church'[4] Cartwright adopted the four orders, ministers, doctors, elders, deacons including widows, which were outlined by Calvin, but he worked out their positions in a wider system of church-government. One could wonder whether Cartwright, in his emphatic preference for Calvin, would have lost sight of the basic unity of the Church's office as taught by Calvin's teacher, Martin Bucer.

3. Inconsistent or Planned?

Apart from the suggestion of inappropriate dependence on others, Cartwright has also been accused of inconsistency. There is a remarkable contrast between the first period of his public activities and the later years. The sharpness of his original publications against the Anglican Settlement seems to contradict the meekness of subsequent writings. After the *Admonition Dispute* with Whitgift, which ended in 1577 with the publication of his, *The rest of the Second Replie*[5], a complete change of attitude and style was brought about. Moreover, the number of works bearing his name after 1577 was few. In 1590 before the *High Commission*, he declared: 'From the writing of my last book which was thirteen years ago, I never wrote nor procured anything to be printed which might be in any sort offensive to her majesty or the state'.[6] During the last quarter of century of his life, Cartwright 'published next to nothing that was controversial'.[7] However, this does not mean that his pen was idle. From later writings, one can conclude that he had changed his strategy. He had discovered that a direct confrontation with the queen and her bishops was counterproductive for the cause of Presbyterianism. England was not to be presbyterianised by violent action, but by silent and peaceful progress. 'Religion to him was more than controversy'. Ministers and elders had the cure of souls and their august office

---

[1] Scott Pearson, 409
[2] Scott Pearson, 226
[3] Scott Pearson, 369 ff
[4] McGinn, 135
[5] See chapter 8.2.c.d
[6] Peel, 2
[7] Peel, 7

would be damaged by direct disobedience to the commands of the queen and those in lawful authority. Cartwright had stopped his direct attacks on Anglicanism and the open defence of Presbyterianism. Although one can doubt whether his change of strategy was a lucky one in all its aspects -it sometimes fed the impression of cowardice-[8] it is evident that the charge of inconsistency is not justified. Cartwright never abandoned his Presbyterian principles of church-government. He put them forward in a very cautious way, trying to avoid controversy with Whitgift and the queen. Often he used the writing of letters, which were not printed or officially published, and he did not write his name on them, only the initials T.C. Because his leadership was recognised abroad as well as at home, these letters and other writings were silently spread among a large public of readers. His apparent position of influence continued to make him a dangerous opponent in the eyes of Whitgift, who 'was watching him as a cat does a mouse, always ready to pounce'.[9]

At least one work Cartwright liked to publish officially and widely, the *Confutation* of the 'Rheims translation'. This was a Roman Catholic version of the New Testament, incorporated in the Douay Bible, and a product of the Counter Reformation.[10] However, in 1586, when the work was partly finished, Whitgift forbade him to proceed and much to the disappointment of his Puritan friends, Cartwright conceded.[11] The *Confutation*, 'a storehouse of protestant learning'[12], was eventually published after Cartwright's death.[13] Although the author had left out most of the arguments in favour of Presbyterianism, it contained indications to the Genevan discipline. The office of the Church was divided into two classes, bishops and deacons. The bishops included doctors and pastors. The deacons were non-preaching elders and deacons proper. In the organisation and position of various offices, there is a striking difference as to

---

[8] Peel, 5

[9] Peel, 3

[10] Scott Pearson, 198-210; Peel 4,5. Cartwright's return from The Netherlands connected to this. Queen Elizabeth had requested Beza to answer the 'Rheims translation', but the Genevan Reformer had replied that 'she had one on her kingdom, far abler than himself to undertake such a task and upon further enquiry declared that it was master Thomas Cartwright'. Walsingham then wrote to Cartwright saying that the queen wanted his return to answer this Jesuit translation and commentary of the New Testament.

[11] Peel, 6, thinks that 'Whitgift's instinct that a rebuttal of the Roman position would reflect also on the Anglican, was thoroughly sound'.

[12] Scott Pearson, 398; Cf. M. Orru, 'Anomy and reason in the English Renaissance', in: *Journal of Historical Ideas*, vol. XLVII, 1, 1986, pp. 177-196. Cartwright's Calvinistic vision of sin and guilt is compared to Hooker's ideas, which essentially dissented from Calvinism into the direction of Roman Catholicism.

[13] Cartwright's *Confutation* was eventually published in Leyden, 1618. Scott Pearson, 204. In the circles of Dutch Calvinists Cartwright had met with a congenial atmosphere. In 1580, he was asked by the University of Leyden to accept a professorship. Scott Pearson, 190-194.

previous writings by Cartwright and as to Travers' *Explicatio*. Perhaps fear of the Anglican censor led Cartwright to placing the elder as far as possible away from the most central office of authority in the Church, the ministry. Bishops, i.e. pastors and doctors, 'are the highest offices of the ecclesiastical presbytery'. The non-preaching elders assist the bishop. Although they constitute with the bishops a senate or eldership, they 'do not meddle with the ministry of the Word'. They belong to the class of *deacons*, i.e. 'those officers who are not occupied in teaching', together with the deacons in a narrower sense. By this change of emphasis, not refuting a more exalted position of bishops, Cartwright tried to accommodate his Anglican inquisitors.

4. Elevation of the Minister

At the same time, here, Cartwright struck a notion that was stressed by Calvin himself. More than Bucer, Calvin had emphasised the difference in origin and position of ministers and elders[14] However, with Calvin and Cartwright this did not mean the denial of the equality and parity of ministers and elders in the Church's governing bodies, the consistories and presbyteries. The centrality of the ministry of the Word emphasised the parity-idea, especially when the ruling elders were excluded from it. This view cannot deny, however, that in practical situations a certain hierarchy had crept in, at the level of preaching and teaching the office of ruling elders had become second, after the minister. This was a compromise, which shifted the position of Cartwright's Presbyterianism into the direction of Episcopalianism

Nevertheless, Archbishop Whitgift realised that the book contained Presbyterian elements. He suppressed it. Whitgift feared that a rebuttal of Roman Catholicism by the able pen of Cartwright would reflect on the Anglican position too. Cartwright's *Confutation* is considered as a monumental refutation of Rome. As such, it was closer to Anglicanism than in his previous writings.

Cartwright had not abandoned Presbyterianism, but he had shifted to the defence of it in a more indirect way. Peel re-edited part of his later work. To it belonged commentaries, catechisms, pastoral letters and private instructions. In these writings, Cartwright would say nothing in direct disobedience to the authorities, although he would always seek ways to exercise his teaching and pastoral ministry. Presbyterian principles were always apparent; as may be indicated by the following quotation from a Cartwrightian catechism:

> 'G: Who are the governors? (of the church)
> A: They are such as deal in the Word and the Sacraments or deal not.
> G: What are they that deal?

---

[14] See chapter 3.6.a

A: They are the ministers who are also of two sorts, the pastor and the teacher
G: What is the teacher's duty?
A: To teach the people the whole will of God by opening the true meaning of the Scriptures
G: What is the pastor's charge?
A: To teach likewise, joining exhortation with his doctrine.
G: Who are the governors that deal not in the Word?
A: The elders and the deacons.
G: What is the elder's part?
A: To see good orders kept, and manners reformed and godliness increased throughout the whole Church.
G: What do the deacons?
A: Some of them look to the poor and some to the sick and impotent.
G: What are the rest of the body of the church?
A: They are people, which are governed.
G: What is their duty?
A: To yield obedience in all lawful callings to the governors, so far forth as comeliness and honesty will permit'.[15]

The essential elements of Cartwright's conception of Presbyterian church-government are expressed here. In theory, there is a parity of office-bearers. However, in practice the minister has acquired a position of dominance. Peel notes that in the Presbyterian-Puritan system of the theoretical equality of offices, 'the supremacy of Scriptures placed the ministers in a position of great advantage'. As the Scriptures were accepted by them as a rule for the Church and for daily life, 'those qualified to interpret them were in a position of unusual power'.[16]

The Anglican leaders not only felt threatened by the introduction of *lay-elders*, but also by the central position of the Puritan ministers. They felt that the Presbyterian conception of *bishops* or *ministers* would undermine the hierarchy of Anglican bishops.

The attacks on the Presbyterian minister came from the other side as well. The Separatists accused the Presbyterians that their ministers were not correctly chosen by the whole of the congregation and that they constituted a new elite of clerical tyrants.

---

[15] Peel, 156,157, notes that the use of catechism in religious instruction was common in the 16th century in all the churches. He mentions a large number of Elizabethan catechism-writers, among whom Edmund Chapman, one of the foremost leaders of the Dedham conference (cf. chapter 9.1.e). Chapman's 'Little Catechism' was approved by the Dedham 'classes', 'for the use of the people of Dedham especially'. The quotation from Cartwright's catechism can be found on page 171 of Peel's collection of Cartwrightiana.

[16] Peel, 18.

5. Change of Strategy

Cartwright and his friends were attacked from both sides, the Anglicans and the Separatists. They tended to direct their defence against the weaker of the two opponents. Until the end of the 1570s the Anglican party was not in a strong position. It was scarcely able to ward off the fierce assaults of the Puritans. At that time the Separatists -still few in number- did not get much negative attention in Presbyterian Puritan writings. This situation changed when Whitgift became archbishop and when the Puritans incriminated themselves with the libellous *Martin Mar-Prelate Papers*. Gradually the Anglican party recovered ground. The years 1590 and 1591 'were a watershed'. Then Whitgift, with the aid of Bancroft and the High Commission, broke the Presbyterian Puritan movement, after a sustained attack on the ministers who were its leaders.

In the meantime, Cartwright c.s. had begun to change their strategy. Direct attacks on the Anglican settlement were not launched anymore. It became necessary to take away the occasions of offence and persecution, in order to provide for a silent and peaceful progress of 'clandestine' Presbyterian activities in the State-Church. All ground for suspicion of extremism, schismatism and revolution should be removed. This urged the worried Presbyterian leaders to direct their attacks against the left side of the ecclesiastical scene. The battle-field had changed. However, the battle was still the same. The changing emphasis and direction of Presbyterian apologetic literature is reflected by a shift in Cartwright's work.

In the next chapters we will deal with Cartwright's apologetic writings, first against the Anglicans in the 1570s (chapter 11), and then against the Separatists in the years after (chapter 12).

Chapter 11

Defence against the Right

1. Rotten Pillar or Apostolic Model

In chapter 8.2 we saw that the publication of the *Admonitions to Parliament* was followed by an extensive literary duel between Cartwright and Whitgift during the years 1572-1577. The abridged contents of their polemic tracts is available in McGinn's, *The Admonition Controversy*. Whereas Scott Pearson holds that the dispute ended in a victory for Cartwright[1], McGinn is not impressed by the quality of Cartwright's part in it. He charges Cartwright with omitting or misrepresenting his opponent's arguments, and with a lacking scholarly approach, inconsistency, abusive rhetoric and a false rationalisation of the Scriptures. Cartwright's technique would have resembled that of other 'famous masters of propaganda, who are more interested in winning converts, than in seeking the truth'.[2]

These accusations illustrate the sensitivity of the Anglican-Puritan debate. The *Admonitions to Parliament* of 1572, particularly condemned the *Book of Common Prayer*, i.e. mass, the name of priest, the prescript prayers, the use of surplices, the Roman-like ritual, the homilies, the way of ordering ministers.[3] The *Admonitions* were essentially an attack on the entire government of the Church of England. The Church should be reformed according to the apostolic model and this model was Presbyterian. Whitgift called this the rotten pillar of Cartwright's programme.

In the subsequent dispute, the bones of contention were widely discussed. Some elements are of special interest for a better understanding of the struggle of Presbyterianism in the Elizabethan age. We concentrate on the dispute of the Presbyterian *minister* and the dispute on the Presbyterian *system*; both were defended to replace Anglicanism.

2. Sacrificing Priest or Preaching Minister

The *First Admonition* rejects the name of *priest*. It says: 'The office of priesthood is ended, Christ being the last priest that ever was. To call us therefore priests as touching our office is either to call back the old priesthood of the law, which is to deny Christ, ... or else to keep a memory of the popish priesthood of abomination still amongst us'. Whitgift attacked this statement by

---
[1] Scott Pearson, 87,88
[2] McGinn, 64-110; Cf. Scott Pearson, 83-103
[3] Cf. Scott Pearson, 93

saying that the word 'priest' was simply a translation of the New Testament *presbyteros*. Cartwright, however, said that this would be hard for Whitgift to prove, and he stated: 'The case standeth in this that forsomuch the common and usual speech of England is to note by the word priest not a minister of the Gospel, but a sacrificer'.[4] In the eyes of the Puritans, the function of a priest comes from *sacerdos*. To them, the *sacerdotal* character of the Anglican priesthood was a monstrosity which enslaved the congregation to the clergy and barred the development to a government of the Church by the preaching of the living Word of God. The *Admonition* compared the Anglican priests to the priests of the Old Testament:

> 'In those days no idolatrous sacrificers or heathenish priests were appointed to be the preachers of the Gospel; but we allow and like well of popish mass-mongers, men for all seasons, King Henry's priests, King Edward's priests, Queen Mary's priests, who of a truth, if God's Word was precisely followed, should for the same be utterly removed'.

The Anglican reaction was that the Puritans tried to imitate the Old Testament. However, Cartwright did not consider the true Old Testament priests as 'idolatrous sacrificers'. When they were no true priests, they were to be compared to the Anglican clergy.

At great length, Cartwright and Whitgift discussed the subject of *preaching*. First, there was the issue of the *homilies*. Whitgift defended a liturgy in which preaching only took a minor part and was to a large extent replaced by reading the homilies of the *Book of Common Prayer*. Cartwright rejected the *homilies*, not in the first place because of their contents, but because they took the place of lively preaching.[5]

The power of the Anglican hierarchy was very much apparent in the ordering of ministers i.e. of priests by the bishops. We already referred to the injunction, 'Receive the Holy Ghost ...', in the *Ordinal* of 1552. This is how the *Admonition* commented on the ordination phrase:

> 'They take upon them blasphemously, having neither promise nor commandment, to say to their new creatures: Receive the Holy Ghost. As though the Holy Ghost were in their power to give without warrant at their own pleasure'.

---

[4] Cf. chapter 5.3.c; cf. McGinn, 165-167
[5] McGinn, 149-151, 277

Whitgift thought that these words -as they were used by Christ Himself when He appointed His apostles- were not meant to provide the bishops with power to give the Holy Ghost in a mechanical way:

> 'The bishop, by speaking these words doth not take upon him to give the Holy Ghost, no more than he doth to remit sins when he pronounceth the remission of sins'.

Cartwright was not satisfied by Whitgift's assurance:

> 'As the apostles did use to pray that the grace of God might be given unto men, the bishop should not use this manner of speech, which containeth the form of a commandment'.[6]

The *First Admonition* contains a general attack on the Episcopal hierarchy as such:

> 'For certain men there are of great countenance, which will not lightly like of them, because they principally concern their persons and unjust dealings, whose credit is great and whose friends are many. We mean the lordly lords, archbishops, bishops, suffragans, deans, doctors, archdeacons, chancellors and the rest of that proud generations whose kingdom must down, hold they never so hard, because their tyrannous lordship cannot stand with Christ's Kingdom. ... For they whose authority is forbidden by Christ, will have their stroke without their fellow-servants, yea, though ungraciously, cruelly and pope-like, they take upon them to beat them and that for their own childish articles, being for the most part against the manifest truth of God'.

Cartwright underlined the Admonitioners' desire for a 'true ministerie', and with them he considered the archbishop, the bishops 'and the rest of that proud generation' as the chief enemies of the project to assimilate the English Church to Presbyterian standards.

Whitgift denied that the Anglican system gave legal ground to 'tyrannous lordship'. He replied that Christ's words 'do not condemn superiority, lordship or any such like authority, but the ambitious desire of the same and the tyrannical usage thereof'. Time and again, he tried to prove that the Anglican system was in harmony with the ideas of Calvin. According to him Calvin did not conclude to the equality of ministers. There had always been and must be degrees and superiority. Calvin was quoted as having said in his *Institutes*, that the twelve apostles had one among them to govern the rest and

---

[6] McGinn, 251,252

that *Acts* 1 does not mention the electing of ministers by any common consent of the whole church.[7]

Cartwright retorted that Calvin did not mean that Peter was a moderator and that ministers ought to abstain from all civil offices.[8] The question of civil offices performed by clergymen was very important. How could there be parity of chosen ministers if they operated at the various levels of the civil magistracy? Contrary to Whitgift, Cartwright claimed that the civil magistrate had to be severed from the ecclesiastical officer. There should not be one minister over the other. 'The civil magistrate is severed from the ecclesiastical officer by bearing dominion; therefore bearing dominion doth not agree to the position of ministers, for they are all here. Cartwright in one stroke combined his vision of the Church and his view of the State. Bearing dominion is the duty of the State. The ministry of the Word of God and the exercise of discipline pertain to the regiment of the Church.

Whitgift rejected Cartwright's divisions and distinctions. In his opinion, the civil magistrate should not be distinguished from the ecclesiastical officer in this way. He tried to develop a theory that would fit the supremacy of Queen Elizabeth and the Erastian conception of State-Church relationship: The dominion of Christ concerns the State as well as the Church. The ecclesiastical office 'signifies a peculiar office of superiority and government under the prince, at the appointment of the prince'. Whitgift granted 'that there is a great difference between the dominion of kings and princes and the jurisdiction and authority of bishops', but this was not the same difference as in Cartwright's view. 'Kings have power over life and goods; so have no bishops. Kings have authority over all persons within their dominions without any limitation; if bishops have such dominion, especially in civil causes, it is not in the respect they be bishops, but it is from the prince and limited unto them'. This was how Whitgift defended the exercise of two kinds of dominion by the bishops, civil and ecclesiastical.

Cartwright however, denied 'that the ecclesiastical person can exercise any dominion at all'. In the Church, there could not be a hierarchical system with an inequality of ministers, who at the same time are members of the hierarchy of the civil magistracy. The *Admonition* puts it like this: 'If you will restore the Church to his ancient officers, this you must do. Instead of an archbishop or lord bishop, you must make equality of ministers'.

Whitgift did not deny that touching the ministry of the Word of God all ministers are

---

[7] McGinn, 322-325, 440
[8] McGinn, 332, 354

equal, but he distinguished this ministry from the office touching the order and government of the Church, and he declared that in the latter there were degrees and superiority.

Cartwright compared his opponent's view to the Roman Catholic conception. He said that New Testament details show that there were no archbishops and bishops at the time.

Whitgift's reaction was: 'Although the apostles had not this name of archbishop among them, yet they had the same authority and office; for they had the government and directions of divers churches, both in matters of doctrine and discipline'.

On this Cartwright asked: 'If this distinction came up in the apostles' time and by them, how cometh it to pass that they never mention it?'

Then the two protagonists of Anglicanism and Presbyterianism began to approach the question under the aspect of the *visibility* of the Church.

Whitgift granted to Cartwright that Christ is the Head of the Church 'and spiritually governeth the same in the conscience' of the office-bearers. However, in his opinion this spiritual government only pertains to the inward, invisible form of the Church. He challenged Cartwright to 'gather from Calvin that the government of the Church is only spiritual'.[9] There is also an outward and visible form of the Church and this form 'requireth an outward and visible government, which Christ does not execute as well as by the civil magistrate as He does by the ecclesiastical minister'. This led Whitgift to the conclusion that 'Christ governeth by Himself spiritually only, and by His ministers both spiritually and externally'. Here the spirituality of the Church is almost exclusively identified with its invisibility. The external visible aspects of church-government are not really the domain of the Spirit. External church-government is merely a question of human reason and tradition.

Cartwright however, was convinced 'that God by the ministry spiritually governs His Church'. Therefore, civil magistrates could not govern the Church.

In Whitgift's opinion, this desire for a spiritual church-government was dangerous, because it undermined the external, visible government of the Church. According to him, Cartwright's ideas reflected the revolutionary tendencies of Anabaptism: 'If you mean that there need [to be] no civil magistrates, no civil and political laws, no external discipline, no outward ceremonies and orders, you are greatly deceived and join with the Anabaptists'. He added: 'To conclude that the civil magistrate is secluded from the government of the Church, or that there needeth no external regiment, is dangerous and savoureth Anabaptism'.

---

[9] McGinn, 344, 345

Cartwright, however, did not want to neutralise the civil magistrate, nor did he want to remove external, visible church-government. He only emphasised the spiritual character of the Church's visibility:

> 'The government of the Church is spiritual. ... Christ ruleth by His Spirit in the hearts of His elect, but there is also spiritual government which is in the whole church visible and to be seen, exercised by those who God hath appointed in His stead, called spiritual because, whereas the civil magistrate useth the sword, this useth the Word and where the civil governor addresseth himself to the body and hath that for special matter to work on, the spiritual governors be occupied in reforming the mind and subduing that whith those punishments and corrections, which God hath appointed for that purpose'.

Cartwright's vision implied the limitation of the civil magistrate's authority over the Church and it excluded the holding of civil offices by church-officers. Actually, in ecclesiastical matters, the magistrate was to be subordinate to the presbytery of ministers and elders. This political implication was felt as threatening to the framework of the Elizabethan State and it explains much of the severity the Presbyterian-Puritans were dealt with by the authorities. It was feared that the Presbyterians would set up a clerical State with tyrannical features, like in those countries where Roman Catholicism swayed the sceptre.

However, Cartwright's church-officers were not meant to absorb the civil-magistrate and to govern the country. His opposition against the holding of civil offices by church-officers should have given the Anglican prelates the assurance of this. The exercise of civil order and the execution of punishment pertain to the civil-magistrate only. That church-officers 'have civil offices joined to the ecclesiastical is against the Word of God. ... The Scripture teacheth that ministers ought not to meddle with civil offices'.

Whitgift's answer to this confutation of the accusation of Presbyterian political clericalism shows the confusion of the Anglican position. Although reproaching Cartwright of political clericalism, he himself because of his loyalty to the Erastian structure of the Elizabethan settlement, had to defend the holding of civil offices by the clergy. Even the execution of civil punishment pertained to the responsibility of clerical courts. He complained that Cartwright had said that it is against God's Word to have prisons in the disciplinary system of the Church:

> 'But your margent is very bare of proof. ... Did not Peter punish Ananias and Saphira ... surely far more grievous than if he had put them in prison ... Peter punished with temporal punishment, being a minister of the Word ... therefore there is nothing repugnant to the office of a minister of the Word to punish with temporal punishment'.

Cartwright reacted to this: 'What Peter did, was ecclesiastical power and this was done by virtue of ... one of those functions that the Lord pleaseth in His Church for a time'.

In this vein, the *First Admonition* to Parliament was discussed by Whitgift and Cartwright. Its direct attack on the Anglican system was intensified by the explanations of Cartwright and the tension was increased by Whitgift's counter-attacks.[10]

3. Government by Elders Disputed

Now we turn to the debate on the *Second Admonition*, which describes the church-structure to be put instead of the Anglican system: The institution of 'a right ministry of God and a right government of His Church, according to the Scriptures set up'.[11] A right ministry and a right government, 'which the Lord Himself in His Word commandeth'. The first question, of course, was how Scripture should be interpreted and used. Should only those things be allowed in the Church that God explicitly has commanded in His Word or is there an area free for human interpretation regarding things that God did not forbid or even did not mention in His Word?

Whitgift was quick to react to this question as follows: 'That no ceremony, order, discipline or kind of government may be in the Church, except the same be expressed in the Word of God, is a great absurdity and breedeth many inconveniences in the Word of God, is a great absurdity and breedeth many inconveniences'.

Cartwright did not enter the trap set by his opponent and did not say that he only accepted those things that were explicitly expressed or commanded in the Bible. In such cases as are not particularly mentioned in the Scriptures, four rules should be applied. The first was that all ceremonies 'should not offend any', the second, 'that all be done in order and comeliness', the third, 'that all be done in edifying', and the fourth 'that they be done to the glory of God'. Cartwright stressed that all things in the Church ought to be appointed according to the Word of God. He did not deny 'that certain things are left to the order of the Church, because they ... could not at once be set down and established forever'. He acknowledged that certain indifferent things are not regulated in the Bible. However, he was convinced that the questions of preaching, church-government and discipline were no indifferent things. Here the Church was bound to the commandments of God in His Word. The orders of the Church should be framed in accordance to the Bible and the primitive

---

[10] McGinn, 278-368
[11] McGinn, 369-539

Church. Cartwright declared and Whitgift denounced the idea that the church-government of the apostles' time pertained to all times.

Whitgift argued that the Apostolic Church was not a model for all times. He granted that the primitive Church knew the existence of elders. They were necessary because there were no Christian magistrates at the time. But as England was ruled by Christian magistrates now, the English Church had no need of elders.

Cartwright, because of his Calvinistic two-kingdoms-theory, was convinced that then and now the Church required elders. He divided the functions of the Church into two parts, the elders who 'govern or take charge of the whole Church', and the deacons, who 'take charge of one part of the Church, which is the poor'. The elders are called *presbyters*. They teach and preach the Word of God and govern too, or else they govern only and do not teach or preach. Of the first kind are *pastors* and *doctors*. Of the second are those who are called *elders* or *seniors*, or *ancients*. Cartwright worked out the words of the *Admonition*: 'To these three jointly, that is the *minister*, the *seniors* and the *deacons*, is the whole regiment of the Church to be committed'. The presbyters or elders, i.e. the ministers and the seniors or ancients, 'govern, admonish, correct and order all things pertaining to the congregations'.

Cartwright now explained the difference between these offices. From 1 *Cor.* 12: 28 he derived the authority for his government by seniors or elders. From *Eph.* 4: 11 he derived his ministers. The seniors were not to preach in public worship but together with the ministers, they governed the whole Church. A senior was essentially a bishop and a pastor. He exercised discipline and held the principle sway touching the elections and the throwing out of elders. The preaching elders were ministers of the Word and also pastors. A special calling and training qualified them for the public ministry of the Word. However, the other elders too were ecclesiastical officers.

Whitgift disdainfully asked: 'How can you make your seniors ecclesiastical , seeing your *seigniory* (consistory) must consist of noblemen, gentlemen, merchantmen, handcrafts men, tailors, shoemakers, carpenters etc., even such as the most of the parish will choose?'

Cartwright answered that although the solely ruling elders did not preach in public, they were ecclesiastical persons and that they governed the whole Church. Actually, they were superior to the civil magistrate in ecclesiastical matters. The magistrate must conform to the elders in the affairs of the Church. Reacting to Whitgift's suggestive question where this left the authority of the civil magistrate, Cartwright returned that his opponent apparently hoped 'to draw us into displeasure with the prince'. He assured him that he recognised the queen's authority as 'the greatest in the earth', adding a restriction at the same time: 'Yet it is not infinite, but it is limited by the Word of God'.

Cartwright's limitation of royal power did not mean that he denied to the civil magistrate all responsibility for ecclesiastical matters. He did not separate the realms of State and Church, but only stressed the distinct responsibility of each. In this context, the State has certain duties with regard to the Church. 'The prince and the civil magistrate hath to see that the laws of God touching His worship and touching all matters and orders of the Church be executed and duly observed, and to see that every ecclesiastical person do that office whereunto he is appointed and to punish those which fail in their office accordingly'. In Cartwright's vision, the civil government had to serve the Church wherever she herself could not operate, in order to safeguard her existence, ministry and discipline. The civil government was not to be given any authority concerning the making of orders and ceremonies of the Church, because these things 'pertain to the ministers of the Church and to the ecclesiastical governors'. Again and again, Cartwright stressed the distinction of Church and State: 'As they (i.e. the elders) meddle not with the making of civil laws for the commonwealth, so the civil magistrate hath not to ordain ceremonies pertaining to the Church'. As to the orders, Cartwright, like Calvin accepted the idea that the civil magistrate could contribute to the ordering of elders, but unlike his Genevan teacher, he claimed the making of orders as an exclusive right of the Church.

The idea that in ecclesiastical matters the State is less important than the Church tasted of *Romanism* to the Erastian tongue of Whitgift: 'I have heard of it, for I have read of it in the books of the papists'.

Cartwright did not intend to revive some sort of Roman Catholic ideology of the Church being placed above the State. Like Calvin in Geneva, he wanted a Church and a State both working for the realisation of the Kingdom of God, though in different and distinguished areas. Like Calvin, he heralded the self-government of the Church by consistories, classes and synods. Even more than Calvin, he stressed the right of the congregation to elect its own ministers and seniors. The prevailing situation was criticised by the *Admonition*, like this: 'Touching the ministry of the Word of God, it must be confessed that the substance of doctrine by many delivered is sound and good. Yet, herein it faileth, that neither the ministers thereof are according to God's Word proved, elected, called or ordained'.

It should be acknowledged that in the 1570s, the *Admonitioners*, Cartwright and other Puritan divines, did not so much criticise the quality of preaching in the English Church. Preaching has been improved by the impact of Puritan-minded ministers, who had remained in the Church. Calvinistic Puritanism had influenced most of the Anglicans theologians, including the bishops and archbishops.[12] Conformists did not differ with regard to the message of personal salvation. In questions of predestination, justification, regeneration, sanctification and in the estimation of the value of preaching, there was not yet a rift between them. The appearance of lecturers and the activities in *prophesyings* had been very beneficial to the quality of preaching.[13]

Cartwright and the Admonitioners, however, wanted to go much further than this. In ministry and church-government many abuses and false structures had remained. The *Admonition* concluded:

> 'Unless they be removed and the truth brought in, not only God's justice shall be put forth, but also God's Church in this realm shall never be built, ... therefore remove ... the bishop's authority, claiming to themselves thereby right to ordain ministers and to bring in that old and true election which was accustomed to be made by the congregation... Let a lawful and godly seigniory [consistory] look that they preach not quarterly or monthly, but continually'.

Free elections of office-bearers and authority by consistories, were added to the demands. In their dispute, Cartwright and Whitgift of course, opposed each other as to the question of *election* of office bearers Cartwright declared that Scriptures prove 'that no minister was placed in any congregation, but by the consent of the people'.

Whitgift answered that the Bible does not disclose definite regulations and that the way in which ministers and congregation were related, was a thing indifferent:

> 'I say that in the whole Scripture there is no commandment that it should so be, nor any example that maketh herein any necessary or general rule, but that it may be altered as time and occasion serveth'.

If time and occasion and not the Bible are the criteria of the making of church-order, one could ask why the Anglican hierarchy found it necessary to suppress a Presbyterian church-order, because there could be freedom in this matter.

---

[12] McGinn, 33. 'Whitgift never was an exponent of the Genevan form of ecclesiastical polity and only paid due respect to Calvin as an interpreter of Scriptures'. Although he moved away from Calvinism -cf. McGinn, 137, 138- Whitgift often quoted Calvin in support of his arguments against Cartwright. The opponents regularly accused each other of misrepresenting or misinterpreting Calvin. Cf. McGinn, 95, 126, 134, 135, 178, 322-325, 332, 354, 440. According to McGinn, in his last years as an archbishop, Whitgift 'at least tacitly approved of Hooker's denunciation of other Calvinistic doctrines', i.e. the doctrines of salvation.

[13] Lloyd Jones, 252. 'Lecturers were simply preachers and did not have the responsibility of the parish and the pastoral side of the work. Their work was to preach the true doctrine as they understood it. These lecturers became soon popular, especially in market towns'.

Cartwright c.s. often asked this question. The answers they got betrayed an arrogance of power. Whitgift denounced the right to free election of officers:

> 'In ecclesiastical affairs, it is much meeter that such as have knowledge zeal and care for the people should place over them a meet and fit pastor than that the choice of him should be committed to the multitude, which is not only for the most part ignorant, but careless in such matters, yea and oftentimes evil disposed and commonly led by affections, as friendship, hatred, fear, etc'.

Whitgift granted that in the Early Church congregations chose their own ministers, but this practice was not to be applied to Elizabethan England.

> 'In the apostles' time the Church was under the cross and therefore very few in comparison was there that embraced the Gospel, ... and they themselves could best judge who among them was fittest to teach and instruct. ... Now the Church is in prosperity and therefore the number that professeth is great, ... and in most parishes not one is fit for the ministry among them or known them, so that they could call they know not whom'.

This comparison of the Early Church and the Elizabethan Church was crippled on both sides. It was the typical reaction of an Elizabethan church-prince, who held to the conviction that royal supremacy and Episcopalianism are the best solutions for the order of the Church. In that view the queen was the supreme governor of a hierarchy of bishops that governs the Church. There was no room for the right of 'the multitude' to some form of representation by free elections.

Cartwright's reaction was two sided. On the one hand, it is evident again that he did not defend his Presbyterian ideal with the arguments of democracy. Whitgift's insinuation that he desired a government by 'the multitude', was denied by his Presbyterian principles. In his conception, church-officers did not need the full consent of the entire membership of the congregation. Here Cartwright clashed with the Separatists. His idea of election did not imply that power was laid in the hands of the people. The authority over the Church, including the regulation of election, he entrusted to the consistories, presbyteries and synods of ministers and elders, and if necessary in certain circumstances, even to the civil magistrate.

> 'If it should happen that any church should desire or choose or consent upon by the most part some that is unmeet either for doctrine or manners, then the ministers and elders of other churches round about should advertise first and afterward, as occasion should serve, sharply and severely charge that they forbear such election, or if it be made, that they confirm it not by suffering him to exercise any ministry. And if either the churches round about do fail in this

duty... they ought to drive that church from that election to another which is convenient'.

When the churches 'round about' failed altogether, the civil magistrate was to organise the election and nomination of true officers. It is clear that Cartwright was no populist and no advocate of separation of State and Church, like the Separatists were said to be.

On the other hand, in this period Cartwright fully rejected the supremacy of the Elizabethan State and the Episcopacy. He was a staunch defender of independent spiritual self government by the Church in its visible and invisible aspects, according to the Presbyterian principles, which he derived from Scripture. At this junction, he did not only show Calvin's but also Bucer's influence: 'All the faithful are members of the one mystical Body of Christ which ought to have a mutual care one of another'. This scriptural truth led him to the conviction that ministers and elders should be elected by the congregation, though not by every individual member, and that there should be a government by consistories, classes and synods. As the government of the Church is spiritual, it should be essentially independent of the State. Chosen elders were to govern the Church and not the civil magistrates with bishops as their executors.

Whitgift continually tried to defend the Erastian role of the State, although he granted that the Early Church did not know such a structure.

> 'In the apostle's time', he wrote, 'there was no Church established, being then no Christian magistrates; but now there is Christian magistrates and a Church established and subject to rulers'.

The dilemma was church-government by queen and bishops or church-government by ruling and preaching elders. This was the central theme of the great dispute. Whitgift not only rejected the idea that the office of elders was the only possible derivation from Scripture, but he was also convinced that the authority of the queen and the bishops made the elders superfluous.

Cartwright boldly spoke of the absolute necessity of elders. They should replace the bishops, and with that, the whole structure of the English Church was to be reformed. Indeed, the *Admonition* proposed the removal of 'the whole anti-christ, both head, body and branch and perfectly plant that purity of the Word, that simplicity of the sacraments and that severity of discipline, which Christ has commanded and commended to His Church'. These words indicate that the Presbyterian Puritans wanted to be builders and not destroyers of the Church. The Admonitioners said:

> 'We declare our good will to the setting forth of God's glory and the building up of His Church ... hoping that God who has begun in us this good work, will not only in time hereafter make us strong and able to go forward therein, but also move others upon whom He has bestowed greater measure of His gifts and graces, to labour more thoroughly in the same'.

No doubt the latter part of this phrase points to Cartwright and other Puritan divines, who were determined to continue the defence of the Presbyterian cause.

Whitgift, Cartwright' great opponent and inquisitor, feared 'a heavy plague of ... schisms and heresies' and ultimately 'ruin and destruction', if Presbyterian practice would be allowed in the Church. However, the Presbyterian movement never intended to break away from the English Church. It was largely responsible for the restoration of preaching and discipline, by which any church stands. When in the 17th century -after an almost victory- the Presbyterians seceded from the State-church, it was not because of their schismatism and heresies, but because they were ejected or voluntarily left because of the Anglican stubbornness, which did not leave any room for elders and presbyteries within the Episcopalian structure and also because many Anglican divines ultimately turned their backs on Calvinism as a whole, even regarding the doctrines or personal salvation.

At that time, for nearly a century, the Presbyterians had been defending themselves, not only against Anglicanism on the right, but also against their opponents on the left. They had done so, because they were of the opinion that schism and separatism could not be elements of a Presbyterian vision of the Church. Anyway, Cartwright's discussion with the Separatists of his day makes clear that Whitgift's charge of schismatism was not justified.

Chapter 12

Defence against the Left

1. Struggle within Puritanism

a. Cradled in Presbyterian Climate

The suppression of those Puritans who refused to conform to the Anglican system contributed to the strengthening of separatist tendencies. In addition to Anabaptism outside the State-church, which appears to have never been very strong in England, there were the radical sections of Puritanism within the Church. Gradually these Puritans moved from a position of 'circumstantial separatism' to real separatism. Examples are the 'privy churches' of Mary's reign and Richard Fitz's group in the beginning of the Elizabethan era.[1]

The real Puritan Separatist were the groups of Browne and Harrison. They literally seceded from the State-church in the end of the 1570s and with their leaders many had to flee to the continent[2], where they established their own congregations, e.g. in The Netherlands, which bore Congregationalist characteristics. Browne and Harrison should be distinguished from John Greenwood and Henry Barrowe. They were also separatist leaders, but they did not emphasise Congregationalist ideas; they also did not migrate to the continent and ended their lives as prisoners in 1593.

When looking at the momentum of the *Separatist Movement* in the 16th century, one should realise that these groups were cradled in a Presbyterian climate. Their leaders carried out many of Cartwright's principles to what they considered to be their logical conclusions. With regard to the Brownists, however, ultimately 'the gulf between Browne and the Presbyterians was complete'.[3] The Brownists severed links with their former Presbyterian antecedents. Their vision of the Church and its offices and of State-Church relationship became different from the Cartwrightian conception. Whereas Cartwright wanted to establish a national Church under the government of ministers and elders with the help of the civil magistrate and with constitutional manners, the Brownists did not want such a Church, they did not emphasise the importance of special ruling and teaching offices, and they absolutely rejected all authority of the civil magistrate in ecclesiastical matters. Ruling and teaching in the Church should not be given to the civil government, and certainly not to

---

[1] See chapter 7.4.b
[2] See chapter 8.1.f
[3] Scott Pearson, 223

an apostate system of bishops. These matters were not even in the first place a duty of ministers and elders. In the first place, they are to be done by every member of the congregation. The ministry of the Word, the government and disciplining of the congregation were to get shape in the activity of teaching and disciplining by all church-members among themselves. Teaching and ruling officers derived their authority from the general consent of the whole congregation, i.e. from every member. Every form of ecclesiastical community with those who had remained in the State Church was forbidden, because this Church had lost its Christian characteristics and had turned anti-christian. A rigid use of punishment, eventually by excommunication, against sinners should be practised.

These were the views of Browne and his successors. They were in opposition to Cartwright's ecclesiastical conception, as well as to his strategy. Harrison seems to have been less intransigent than Browne. He 'represented more faithfully the genealogical connection with Puritan Presbyterianism', and 'seemed to sympathise with Cartwright's view that while then Church of England was imperfect, it was not therefore wrong to attend its services and account it Christian'.[4]

b. Separatists differed from Anabaptists

Cartwright's position with regard to the Separatists was not entirely similar to the position of the 'magisterial'[5] Reformers on the continent. The Reformers had to deal with Anabaptists, who consciously seceded from the main line Reformation, demonising Church and State, and claiming perfection for themselves. As we have seen, nearly all first-generation-reformers, after a period of friendly relations with incipient or real Anabaptist Radicals, were forced to turn against them, because the political and doctrinal consequences of their revolutionary attitude threatened the progress of the Reformation. In England, *Anabaptism* was found outside the *Puritan Movement*; as such, it remained a rather insignificant group in the 16th century. Within the *Puritan Movement*, a radicalism of a different type emerged. Some Puritans radicalised, not so much because of disappointment with the salvation theology of the main line Puritans, but because of their 'tarrying with the magistrate' for reform of the Church's governmental structure. Different conceptions of church-rule and church-government gradually came to the surface. However, for a long time the ecclesiastical struggle was mainly fought between Puritans.

Cartwright had important discussions with separatist leaders during his stay in The Netherlands. In the beginning of the 1580s, the Dutch city of

---

[4] Peel, 49
[5] Cf.chapter 3.2.b and d. Cf. Williams, *The Radical Reformation*

Middleburgh received from Norwich the congregation of Browne and Harrison. Before his return to Britain in 1583, Browne wrote a number of treatises.[6] Cartwright's answer in letter-form was published by Browne probably in 1585, together with his reaction: 'An answer to Master Cartwright his letter for ioyning with the English Churches: whereunto the true copie of his sayde letters is annexed'.

2. Church of Christ or False Church

a. The Church is Founded on Christ

In those years, Cartwright also exchanged letters with Harrison. Although less radical than Browne, Harrison doubted the church-character of the English Church. This was an important question. If it could be proved that the State-Church lacked the notions of a true Church, then the Radical Separatists were justified in separating from it and then the Cartwrightians were rightly to be criticised, because of their 'tarrying for the magistrate' and their rejection of separation. Peel printed an answer by Cartwright 'unto a letter of Master Harrison.[7] In this answer, Cartwright agreed that the English Church wanted discipline, that its ministry was unlawful and dumb. Nevertheless, the Anglican Church was still the Church of Christ and its ministers were still ministers. Against Harrison he argued that the assemblies of the Church of England 'which have Christ for their Head and the same also for their foundation, are God's churches'. The Lord in his mercy 'hath set up divers burning lamps in those assemblies, whereby light is conveyed more or less into all the parts'. The presence of divine grace and light, even when rarely found, makes a church a Church of God. 'If there were but in every church one truly ... faithful, ... yet should all those churches be unto us the churches of God'. Although the assemblies of England 'had deserved through want of discipline and of teaching ministry to be cast out from the accompt of the churches of God', yet Cartwright holds that 'the communicating with them should not make them [i.e. the other churches and church-members] guilty of falling away from the Lord'. Weak discipline does not make a church a false church. The most essential part of the

---

[6] Browne wrote 'A treatise of reformation without tarrying for anie and of the wickedness of those preachers which will not reform till the magistrate commaunde them; a book which sheweth the life and manners of all Christians and a treatise upon the 23 of Matthewe'. Scott Parson, 211 ff, calls this book 'a direct blow at the Presbyterian party and its constitutional manners'. Towards the end of his stay in The Netherlands, Brown wrote 'A true and short declaration, both of the gathering and ioyning together of certain persons, and the lamentable breach and division which fell amongst them'. Cf. Peel, 48, 49

[7] Peel, 49-58, 'An answere to a letter of Master Harrison's by Master Cartwright, being at Middleborough'.

church is the church's foundation on Christ. There is no discipline, no church, if there is no faith in Jesus Christ. Of course 'it is a piece of that discipline ... that there should certain be chosen out of the rest to preach the Gospel'. Without the ministry of the Word, 'it is plain that there are not visible and apparent churches'.

These two things, the foundation on Christ and the ministry of the Word, make that a church 'retains the right of the Churches of God'. This is true, even when 'other points may want, yea, although there may be some defect in these two'. The sacraments ministered by dumb and unlawful ministers are nevertheless sacraments.

b. The Objectivity of the Church

Cartwright here defends the objectivity of the Church and its ministers. Although their ministry is lacking, 'they are ministers of God so far as the good things they offer to us'. Jesus Himself commanded 'that the Scribes be heard in that they taught truly'. Our Saviour, who 'lived in the corruptest times of the Church ... yet commanded the man whom He purged from leprosy to show himself unto the priest'. Jeremiah, being suspended for a time from coming into the temple, 'sent Baruch to read his sermons in the temple'. Cartwright not only defends the receiving of good things out of the hands of unlawful and dumb ministers; he also says that a minister, although he was not chosen and nominated in the right way, 'may be held for a minister who has the Church's calling'. If he is an impious or a dumb minister, communication with him is not forbidden. When you are not able to avoid him, you 'may communicate with a minister that is an adulterer, without being partaker of his adultery. Even so also, I may communicate with a dumb minister and yet nevertheless be free from his impiety'.

3. The Position of the Minister Disputed

a. Full Consent

In Cartwright's writings against the Separatists, full emphasis was laid on the position of the minister. The Separatists tend to deny the objectivity and authority of the office of the ministry. They seem to replace it by the subjectivity of *the inner light* in the heart of every individual believer. Therefore, they lose sight of the principal characteristics of the Church and the essence of salvation. The Church lives by the Word of God and its ministry. The believer lives by the same Word. Church and believers are not made by inner experiences and convictions, but by obedience to and faith in the Word of God. The origin of Church and faith is not within man, but outside him in the Gospel, and is applied by the Holy Ghost. The work of the Holy Ghost does not diminish the objectivity of the Word. When the Word is preached or read, the Holy Ghost builds the Church. Therefore, the Church of Christ is there where the Word and the sacraments are ministered. Even when the minister is lacking or not correctly chosen, this does not mean that the Church is absent.

The Separatists reproached Cartwright that his minister was not based on the full consent of the congregation. They feared that Presbyterian ministers might become a kind of tyrants. When he defended the authority of the minister against the Episcopalians, Cartwright heard the same argument. By them he was accused of giving 'to the ministers in their several charges, an absolute power of doing what them likes best, without controlment of either civil or ecclesiastical authority'.[8]

b. Eldership and Democracy

Thus, the Presbyterian ministry of the Word was attacked by both sides. The Separatists thought that the position of the Presbyterian minister did not do justice to the authority of the individual believers. The Episcopalians feared that the Presbyterian ministers and their presbyteries undermined the authority of queen and bishops. One side considered the Presbyterian minister as a hindrance to democracy, whereas the other side saw him as a symbol of it. In his debate with the Episcopalians, Cartwright tried to safeguard the ministry, by stressing the importance of eldership. Ruling elders were to replace the bishops and the civil magistrate in church-matters. In this way, he hoped to realise the independence of Church and ministry. However, in the controversy with the Separatists the argument of eldership was not very useful for the defence of the Presbyterian ministry, because Cartwright -deriving from Calvin- had practically construed a hierarchy of ministers over elders.

In the opinion of Cartwright, the Separatists misused the idea of eldership. Their office-bearers tended to reflect a complete *democratisation* of the congregation, at least in theory. In his view, this weakened the objectivity and authority of the ministry. Therefore, the necessity of elders is not stressed in Cartwright writings against the Separatists. On the contrary, he tries to teach his opponents on the left that the absence of ruling elders in a system that is still essentially Episcopalian, is not to be regarded as ground for the accusation that the Church is a false church. The essence of the Church of Christ exists in an imperfect Church.

---

[8] Scott Pearson, 198

4. Debate with Anne Stubbe

a. Imperfect, yet True Church

Separatists were to be found in the circle of Cartwright's relatives. In 1578, when in Antwerp, he married Alice Stubbe, sister of a notable radical Puritan, John Stubbe. The latter's wife Anne, was a follower of Browne and Barrowe. Her defence of the Separatists cause was answered by Cartwright. The last stage of their correspondence happened in 1590, when Cartwright was harassed by the interrogators of the *High Commission*.

Peel thinks that Cartwright's relationship with Stubbe may have injured him with the queen and may have been one of the reasons why he stayed abroad for so long.[9] In 1579, John Stubbe had written a book, *The discoveries of a Gaping Gulph*, against the queen's proposed marriage with the Roman Catholic duke of Anjou. As a result of this the writer and his book-seller were ordered to have their right hands struck off. No doubt, the queen's displeasure was increased by Cartwright's tract 'Whether it be lawful for a Protestant to marry a Papist?', which referred to the same subject as Stubbe's book.[10] By these events, Cartwright, in the opinion of the authorities, seemed closer to the Separatists than he really was.

Peel printed the original texts of the correspondence in 1590 by Anne Stubbe and Cartwright.[11] They show mutual respect, but at the same time, they illustrate the difference between the Separatists' view and Cartwright's Presbyterian conception.

In her letter, Anne Stubbe explains her separatist stance, by declaring that the Church of England 'is not the Church of God by agreement of His Word, in that they obey not but resist the voice of Christ'. Its ministers have no authority of Christ, nor the keys of His Kingdom. The main reason is that they are not elected by the free choice of the people of God', i.e. not everyone in 'godliness and sobriety' has his free choice. So, these ministers are forced upon them. General consent of the congregation is required for the making of a minister. If there was one member who 'did find justly fault with him, then he could be no minister of the people of God'. Separation from the State-Church, 'come out from among them' is a necessity, 'for a great number of both ministers and people have no knowledge of the true faith'. Anne Stubbe denies to these ministers the power to exercise discipline.

---

[9] Peel, 59
[10] Scott Pearson, 183 ff
[11] Peel, 60-75; Cf. Scott Pearson, 305 ff

> 'You have not the power of Christ to excommunicate any but by your lords the bishops and their courts, even the power of anti-christ'.

Of her own separatist congregations Anne says that they have the truth, not 'because they were taught by some pastor under Christ', but 'by our Saviour Christ and His apostles' and because the Lord taught him to teach one another. She grants that separatist teachers may not have knowledge of the original tongues of Scripture, but she confutes that this knowledge safeguards the Church.

> 'Consider your own ministers', some of whom are learned men, but 'truly my heart mourns to see the general hardness of hearts'. Knowledge of the original tongues does not guarantee true knowledge of the Word. 'Scriptures of God are not like men's words ... we see our own hearts in the Word of God, ... so we of the Church of God have the knowledge of the interpretation of the tongues'.

Cartwright, in his answer tries to make clear that Anne's reasons are not justified. You are wrong when you claim 'that you may not communicate with us in the worship of God, for that we are none of the Church'. The first reason, disobedience to the voice of Christ, cannot be used, because

> imperfect obedience does not shut people from the Church. The children of God not only suffer from infirmity, ignorance, error and deception, but they 'have also their proud and presumptuous sins'. Nevertheless, they remain children of God. The same is true for the Church. In it, all true believers are not on the same level and hypocrites are also among them. Although the Church ought indeed to be obedient unto the voice of Christ, 'yet it does not follow that whatsoever company does not obey to the voice of Christ, is therefore none of the Church'.

The second reason why the Separatists consider the State-Church as a false Church, is that it has *'no authority* of Christ, *nor the keys* of His Kingdom'. Cartwright is far from saying that the English Church sufficiently applies the Scriptural rules of discipline. However, he denies that lack of discipline makes her a false Church.

> Even Paul 'does not cross out the name of the Corinthians, from being a church, because it has ceased the censure of excommunication against the incestuous person'. The most important elements of discipline have been left in the Church of England. 'For first it binds by declaring the judgement against the unrepentant and secondly it loosens in the preaching of the glad tidings of the Gospel to those who believe'. In addition to that, another part of the keys and of the authority of Christ is still functioning, namely the private

admonishing of brethren mutually. These things make the Church of England a Church of God.

The third argument concerns the question of *election*. Cartwright with irony says to his separatist sister-in-law:

> If we are not the Church of Christ, because we have no free election of ministers, 'how much more are you not of Christ's Church, which have no ministers at all and therefore no elections at all, neither free nor bound?' Christ has given to the Church ministers. However, amongst you 'there is not so much as one that is fit for the function of the ministry'. You do not know the true exposition of the Scriptures, 'nor have any to teach you to translate them to you'.

By these phrases, Cartwright admonishes the Separatists to be careful with their accusation that an imperfect church is a false church. If the absence of ministers is a token of a false church, the separatist congregations are false themselves. When the Separatists demand the election of ministers, they should not forget this.

b. The Voice of Christ is heard

Cartwright grants that the choice by the people ought to be free and full. Does this mean that all ministers who were not chosen are false? This is a wrong conclusion. Lea was trust upon Jacob, but afterwards she was accepted. 'Lawful acceptance of a lawful and able minister makes his ministry lawful as if the election were full'.

The Separatists misinterpret the term of 'free and full election'. They think that 'if the minister be not chosen by the whole congregation, it is no free choice'. Scriptures prove that the Church chose its ministers in a manner 'taken from the civil elections', by the 'lifting up of hands'. Not the full consent of the whole congregation was required, only a majority of votes in the presbytery. If the 'consent of every single person of the church' would be necessary for the elections of a minister, this would be also necessary for his subsequent ministerial activities. For 'if any of the church shall fall to a mislike of the ministers, forthwith his ministry must be broken off'. This would mean that individual sinners and hypocrites could 'withstand the rest of the church' and neutralise the ministry of the Word of God.

Apart from this, Cartwright mentioned other reasons why 'our churches are the Churches of God'. In the English Church, the voice of Christ is heard. From this, people in true faith receive comfort and hope. Another reason is that the continental Churches of the Reformation have 'given us the hands of fellowship'. They 'acknowledge our Church as their sister'. Of course, it is possible that the fellowship of Christ's Church on earth errs in certain questions, but 'it is not possible for them all to err in the principle and fundamental points of salvation'. The Church of God on earth 'cannot discern the invisible Church and the company of the elect', but for the Church it is 'an easy thing to discern ... the testimony of the Church'.

In this way, Cartwright refutes Anne Stubbe's allegation that she may not join the English Church's 'un-spiritual worship of God'. He warns her that by abstaining from the ministry of Word and the Sacraments, she may 'run in danger of spiritual famine'. Her conception of the scriptural demand of separation is one-sided. Scripture does not command 'so much the separation by place', but 'a departure from our own corrupt natures as well as from the corruption of others'. He concludes his correspondence in a conciliatory tone and style:

> 'Yet I have not written this, either to condemn your judgement in all things you hold, nor to justify the sundry corruptions, that are in our churches of England'. However, his sister-in-law should not 'bring an evil report of her ... in charging upon her the evil which she does not, as in taking away the good things which she does or rather which the Lord does in her heart'.

Cartwright rejects the Brownists' claim that the Church of England is altogether anti-christian. The Separatists' alternative, pure congregationalism is unworkable. The authority of the ministry of the Word is frustrated in the State-Church by the hierarchy of bishops and archbishops, but it is also undermined by the separatist vision of the Church and its functions. Rejection of church-government by bishops does not mean the sacrifice of the authority of ministers. Opposition against Episcopalians does not necessarily lead to the acceptance of the doctrines of Separatism.

5. Fading Authority of the Elder

a. Do Elders Preach and Teach?

The Presbyterian conception of the eldership of the Church is two-sided. The elders represent the aspect of government and discipline. They share these duties with the ministers, who in addition to this are charged with preaching and teaching. An important question is whether the exercise of government and discipline by elders also pertains to the preaching and teaching activities of ministers. Do elders in this concern have authority over ministers? In what way, they themselves are responsible for preaching and teaching?

In the Reformed tradition, the answers to these questions are not unanimous. The relative unity of elders and ministers was stated by all, but there were different views as to the distinction of these offices. Let us look at some examples.

As we have seen, Bucer and à Lasco stressed the office of the Church as derived from the community of believers. With them, the elder is not essentially distinguished from the minister. Consequently, their elder has more authority than the elder in Calvin's system.

According to van Ginkel the practice in the Reformed Churches is disappointing when compared to the promising Presbyterian theories. His statement that Calvin himself took away from the elder the disciplinary responsibility for the doctrines of the Church, may sound too harsh, but he seems to be right in declaring that 'in Calvin's thought the elder does not bear the central office' and that 'the minister in Calvin's thought is definitely a more important officer than the elder'.[12] Calvin's elder has a disciplinary function. However, this function only pertains to the 'common' members of the congregation. The elder has no authority over the ministers in matters of preaching and teaching of the Word of God.[13]

b. Clericalist Tendency

In the Huguenot Church of France Calvin's emphasis was applied. The French Protestants did not stress the idea that the offices are a representation of the congregation. They preferred election by the consistory to election by the congregation[14]

In Reformed churches in e.g. The Netherlands, Germany, Switzerland, Africa, and North America, apart from Calvin's influence, the line of Bucer and à Lasco is definitely visible. Yet, the high estimation of lay-eldership was weakened soon.[15] The elder represented an anti-hierarchical as well as a democratic tendency, but in practice, he was pushed back by the ministers of the Word to a second rank position. At classes and synods the ministers dominated. The formulation of church-orders was adapted to this situation. In this way the position of the elder as to governmental and pastoral duties, was greatly limited. Van Ginkel says that they even could not perform the exercise of discipline without the authoritative support of the ministers.[16] The 'insignificant role of the

---

[12] Calvin's view of the dispension of the charismata is different from Bucer's conception. Cf. chapter 3.5 and 3.6.a
[13] Cf. van Ginkel, 137, 147
[14] Van Ginkel, 162
[15] Cf. Van Ginkel, 183
[16] Van Ginkel, 260 ff b

elders' in present day classes and synods, leads Van Ginkel to the conclusion that the danger of a new hierarchy of church-officers, was not warded off by the Presbyterianism of the Reformed Churches, but by their *Synodicalism*[17] a new hierarchy of higher and lower ministers was perhaps prevented. However, concerning the relationship of ministers and elders, a certain hierarchicalism has crept in. Elders do not share the advantages of ministers. They are excluded from the ministry of Word and Sacraments, and in general, they are not trained in theology. These are the very points that gave authority to the ministers. Moreover, the elder only serves temporarily and he receives no salary. As a result, the practice of the Presbyterian office of the Church is not in accordance with its theory. It cannot be excluded 'that ministers consciously contributed to the decay of eldership'[18], i.e. of the 'elder-side' of Presbyterian governmental system. The ways how ministers are addressed, as 'reverend' (exalted one), or 'dominee' (lord), are indicative for their elevated position.

This clericalist tendency is even stronger in those churches that derived much of their Presbyterianism from the English scene. An example is the *Church of Central Africa Presbyterian* (C.C.A.P.) in the countries of Malawi, Zambia and Zimbabwe. External and internal authority in the Church is almost completely in the hands of the ministers. Because the number of ministers is small, elders necessarily preach and supervise pastoral aspects of day-to-day local church life. They cannot have official church-session meetings without the presence of a minister, who has to be the moderator. All sacramental acts and disciplinary measures have to be executed and blessed by a minister. Often the local congregation and its elders cannot decide which minister to receive, because ministers are posted by the synod. The church is organised in a top-to-bottom-structure, leaving the elders of the local congregation without significant influence at presbytery and synod levels. Practically, the ordained clergy take all the decisions, in their presbyteries and synods. Full time clerical officials at synod level are particularly powerful.[19]

Van Wyk has explained that the *clericalism* in 'the Reformed Churches in Central Africa', is a result of the heritage of the Scottish Presbyterian churches, which through their missionary effort were at the cradle of Central African Presbyterianism. English early Presbyterianism, through John Knox, has become the father of Scottish Presbyterianism and consequently also of Presbyterianism in this part of Africa. The Scots were influenced by incipient

---

[17] Van Ginkel, 297
[18] Van Ginkel, 299
[19] Steven Paas, *The Faith Moves South: A History of the Church in Africa*, Zomba: Kachere, 2006, cf. 189-197, for a brief history of the C.C.A.P.

English clericalism, and after Knox they also added to it themselves.[20] Van Wyk comments:

> 'The Scottish Reformers followed the Genevan model, but they had to act in the context of an Episcopalian State Church. Attention for the local congregation was replaced by attention for the Church as an institution. ... Consequently, the clericalist approach of the office of minister and the conception of the other offices as assistants to the higher office, have made it impossible for the offices of elder and deacon to develop in their own right. ... Scottish Presbyterianism reflects the consequences of replacement of the government by Christ by a government by man and the consequential idea of office-bearers as servants of an institution'.[21]

6. Cartwright and Calvin

a. The Same Principles

Having in view the problematic tendency of clericalism in the tradition of Reformed and Presbyterian churches, it is helpful to study Cartwright's ideas on the offices of the Church. In a way, the English situation was unique. The Presbyterian conception was not only under pressure of the populism on the left, but also of the hierarchy of bishops on the right. The context was determined by Separatist revolt and by Anglican suppression. Not much room was left to Cartwright, who refused to join both extreme positions. The circumstances in which English Presbyterianism was born, were different from the context of the cradles of Presbyterianism in other parts of the world. This led to differences in Calvin reception and in reception of Presbyterianism.

Calvinistic Churches on the European Continent had to defend their positions into two directions, Anabaptism on the left and State-supremacy on the right. Cartwright did not encounter radicalism in its Anabaptist form. Yet, he adapted Calvinism to the English situation by working out to greater detail the Presbyterian system of church-government. He did not deviate from Calvin's principles, but adapted them to the situation. This is also true for his view of the relationship of ministers and elders. Like Calvin, he considered the ministers of the Word as the most central office-bearers of the Church. In this conviction, he was very consistent. His estimation of the elder shows a similar pattern of development as with Calvin and with Calvinism generally.

---

[20] Paas, *From Galilee to the Atlantic*, 214, refers to Andrew Melville, who in his *Second Book of Discipline*, 'put more emphasis on the power of the minister and other elders' than Knox had done in the *First Book of Discipline*.

[21] J.J. van Wyk, *The Historical Development of the Offices according to the Presbyterian tradition of Scotland*, Universiteit van Stellenbosch, 1995, in 'Samevatting'.

Defence against the Left

b. Shifts of Emphasis

During the initial period of defence against Episcopalianism, Cartwright advocated the involvement of the *lay-element* and the introduction of elders as the only solution for the Church of England. After the *Admonition Controversy* and his encounter with the Separatists on the continent, he did not abandon the ideal of church-government by chosen elders, but Cartwright got 'convinced of the inexpediency or futility of publishing any writing of a pro-Presbyterian nature'[22] and from then on 'more earnest than ever he tried to preserve the integrity of the Church of England'[23] and its ministry. By the end of the 1570s, he shifted his emphasis again; or rather, then he began to re-emphasise his original position.

Calvin's development is more or less similar. During his first stay in Geneva and his period in Strasbourg, he only knew the minister of the Word. Then, after his return to Geneva, confronted again with the supremacy of the Genevan State and the lack of discipline among the Genevans, he designed his famous structure of eldership. Finally, when the Church had won a certain independence of the civil magistrate, the office of the elders tended to lose its paramount significance in favour of the positions of the ministers.

Cartwright, in his 1570 lectures on *Acts*, stressed the importance of the ministry. In 1572, at the instigation of the *Admonitions to Parliament*, he began to defend the eldership. But after the *Admonition Controversy*, he was almost completely silent with regard to elders, completely concentrating on the introduction and defence of a 'true ministry'.

It should be admitted, however, that Cartwright's shifts of emphasis were inspired by circumstances that were much less congenial to Presbyterianism than those in Calvin's last period in Geneva. Not the victory of Calvinistic church rule, but the impossibility to have it in short terms, made Cartwright decide for a strategy by which the government by ministers was more heavily stressed, at the expense of the elders, whose authority was not stressed anymore.

7. Theocratic Vision weakened

a. Not a Lost Cause

That Cartwright did not live to see the results of his strategy, does not necessarily justify Scott Pearson's statement that his life-work was 'the pursuit

---

[22] Scott Pearson, 204
[23] Scott Pearson, 231

of an apparent lost cause'.[24] The Elizabethan Presbyterians -though a severely beaten minority by the end of the century- belong to the indispensable representatives of the Christian Church whose pious struggle against tyranny and anarchy should be never forgotten. Their cause is not lost, because it is the cause of the Church of Christ. We agree to Lloyd Jones' conviction that the Presbyterians were the core and the essence of the Puritan movement. Their first concern was the essence of God's plantation on earth, 'the nature of the Church that is, a desire for full and complete Reformation'[25], founded on the acceptance of the Word of God as the supreme authority in all matters. The essence of God's work on earth is the establishment of 'a pure Church, a gathering of the saints', by means of the preaching of the Word and the exercise of a godly government and discipline. Lloyd Jones warns that if we fail to put the Presbyterians' doctrine of the Church in a central position, we are departing from their attitude, outlook, spirit and understanding.[26]

b. Vision of the Church Changed

However, their faithfulness to the centrality of the doctrine of the Church did not prevent the Presbyterians from considerably changing their emphasis in the course of time. This especially pertained to their vision of the relationship of ministers and elders. In the 16th century the Presbyterian idea was non-separatist and theocratic. The State-Church was looked upon as the leading and guiding agency of the whole political and ecclesiastical community. The high estimation of the Presbyterian principle of the Church was defended into two directions, on the one hand forwarding the *elder* against the tyrannical powers of bishop and magistrate, and on the other hand, forwarding the minister against the anarchical disorder of separatism.

From the angle of the proclamation of the Word, the minister held a major sway in both areas of defence. Gradually, when the danger of anarchy increased and also the repression by the authorities, the balance of ministry and eldership changed. Certainly, the elder did not disappear from Presbyterian thought, but he became less important. This affected the vision of the Church. Because the elder was connected to the exercise of government and discipline in the community of the commonwealth, his decrease in importance went with a fading of the theocratic conception of the Church. From a position of external authority embracing the whole commonwealth of Church and State, the elder retired to a position of internal authority only.

---

[24] Scott Pearson, 338
[25] Lloyd Jones, 256
[26] Lloyd Jones, 258, 259

In the Anglican structure, the elder was not allowed to exist. There where he was formally accepted, his position was overshadowed by the minister. His position was limited to the exercise of discipline among the 'common believers' of a certain congregation only. If blessed by the minister, he had some say in questions of government and election. At classes and synods the ministers -especially because they were directly dependent on the bishops- outweighed the elders. After the ejectments and secessions in the 17th century, the authoritative position of ministers over elders and congregations would become the normal situation in Presbyterian Churches. The ideals of theocracy and non-separatism almost completely faded away, and together with them the original ideal of Presbyterian eldership.

8. Conclusion

The Presbyterian reformation of church-government was a serious attempt for a Scriptural answer to those doctrines that advocated tyranny and anarchy in Church and State. However, perhaps Presbyterianism was clearer in expressing its objections against the structures that it rejected than in putting forward the scriptural system that it wanted to substitute for them. The pattern of relationship between ministry, eldership and common priesthood is of central importance. It has been a subject of theoretical reflection and a challenge to the practice of the Church. As such, it has touched the very existence of the Church until the present day. There is a danger of underestimating the vital necessity of the ministry of the Word, in its unbreakable connection to the government and exercise of discipline by congregation-chosen officers. When the Presbyterian search for Biblical answers is neglected, the congregation of believers may fall victim to an anarchical individualism, or to be submitted again under 'lordly lords'.

The 16th century Calvinist Reformation wanted to honour the Presbyterian vision of the New Testament and the Early Church. However, definitions of the minister and the elder were not always conclusive. Presbyterian churches should continue to look for a transparent picture of the relationship between ministers and elders. We are especially challed to get in view the *office of all believers*, and how it is related to the offices of ministry and eldership. Therefore, Calvinist tradition challenges Calvinists and others to rethink their church-orders in obedience to the Word of God.

Table of Events

597	Augustine arrives in England
664	Synod of Whitby
1066	Norman Conquest
1215	**Magna Charta**
1330	Birth of Wycliff
1461-1483	Wars of the Roses
1483	Birth of Luther
1484	Birth of Zwingli
1491	Birth of Bucer
1509	Birth of Calvin; Accession of Henry VIII
1513	Birth of Knox
1518	Luther's writings reach England
1520	Luther's **Babylonian Captivity**
1521	Burning of Lutheran books at St. Paul's; Henry VIII, 'Defender of the Faith'
1525	**Zürcher Ehegericht** established
1526	Tyndale publishes a translation of the New Testament
1527	Wolsey's proceedings against heretics; Beginning of Henry's divorce proceedings
1529	Fall of Wolsey
1531	Zwingli dies
1532	Henry VIII submits clergy
1533	Cranmer becomes Archbishop of Canterbury; Henry's divorce pronounced; Birth of Elizabeth
1534	*Acts of Supremacy*; Papal Supremacy formally abjured by clergy
1535	Visitation of the monasteries; Publication of Coverdale's Bible
1535(?)	Birth of Cartwright
1536-1559	Publication of various editions of Calvin's *Institutes*
1536	Supression of monasteries; Henry divorces Anne Boleyn; Henry's *Ten Articles*; The Northern Rebellion
1538-1541	Religious conferences in the Habsburg Empire; Calvin's stay in Strasbourg
1538	Discussions by Henrican and Lutheran divines; Henry VIII's excommunication published; Bucer's *Von der waren Seelsorge*; Henry's *Six Articles*; Publication of the *Great Bible*
1545-1563	Council of Trent
1546	Luther dies
1547	Henry VIII dies; Visitation of the Church; accession of Edward VI
1549	Habsburg Interim; Bucer c.s. to England; first Edwardian *Book of the Common Prayer*
1550	First Edwardian *Ordinal*; Altars ordered to be removed; Hooper and the first *Vestments' Controversy*

1551	Bucer dies; Knox becomes Chaplain of Edward VI
1552	Second Edwardian *Book of Common Prayer*; second Edwardian *Ordinal*; Reformation of church-laws proposed
1553	*42 Articles*; Edward VI dies; Accession of Mary; Repeal of Reformation Statutes
1554	Married clergy deprived; arrival of Cardinal Pole
1555	Persecutions and exile; burnings of Ridley and Latimer
1556	Knox's *Geneva Book*; burning of Cranmer
1558	Mary dies; accession of Elizabeth; return of refugees
1559	Disputation of Marian and Elizabethan divines; Parker becomes Archbishop of Canterbury; Elizabethan *Acts of Uniformity and Supremacy*; revision of the Book of Common Prayer
1563	Convocation agrees upon *39 Articles*
1563-1567	Second *Vestments' Controversy*
1564	Calvin dies; Cartwright's oration before the queen
1565	Cartwright to Ireland
1566	Parker's *Advertisements*; 'A briefe discourse against the outwarde apparell'
1567	Field and Wilcox form congregation at Plumber's Hall; separation of Fitz's group; dispute by Erastus and Wither in Heidelberg
1570	Cartwright's lecturers on *Acts*, and *Six Articles*; Cartwright suspended from professorship
1571	Enforcement of subscription to *Elizabethan Settlement*; Cartwright to Geneva; Parker's ecclesiastical canons (*churchwardens*)
1572	*Admonitions to Parliament*; Knox dies; Cartwright back in England and deprived of fellowship; Formation of Wandsworth-congregation
1572-1577	*Admonition Controversy*; inquisition against nonconformists; warrant for Cartwright's arrest
1572-1576	Cartwright in Heidelberg
1573-1574	Travers' *Explicatio*; its translation by Cartwright
1575	Parker dies
1576	Grindal becomes Archbishop of Canterbury; queen forbids prophesyings; Grindal suspended
1577	Cartwright in Basel; Chapman lecturer at Dedham; Cartwright to The Netherlands
1578	Cartwright marries Alice Stubbe
1581	Browne to The Netherlands
1583	Grindal dies; Whitgift becomes Archbishop of Canterbury; enforcement of subscription; Browne back to Britain
1584	Hooker becomes Master of the Temple Church in London
1585	Cartwright back to England; appointed Master of Leicester's hospital at Warwick; Whitgift does not allow Cartwright to proceed with *Confutation* of *Rheims translation*; Travers' Book of Discipline sent to all conferences
1587	Greenwood and Barrowe become prisoners and start their writing career
1588	Defeat of the Armada; *Martin Mar-Prelate Papers*
1590-1592	Cartwright c.s. interrogated by High Commission and Star Chamber
1590	Last stage of Cartwright's correspondence with Anne Stubbe

1592	Sutcliffe's attack on Cartwright
1593	Severe statute against the Puritans; execution of Greenwood, Barrowe and Penry; flight of Separatist congregations to the Continent
1594-1597	Hooker's *The laws of ecclesiastical polity*
1595	Cartwright to the Channel Islands
1596	The *Lambeth Articles*
1601	Cartwright back to Warwick
1603	Elizabeth dies; accession of James I; Cartwright dies; Whitgift dies
1604	Hampton Court Conference; Bancroft becomes Archibishop of Canterbury

Bibliography

Augustijn, C., *De godsdienstgesprekken tussen rooms-katholieken en protestanten van 1538-1541*, Haarlem: De Erven Bohn, 1967
Blunt, J.H., *The Reformation of the Church of England*, London: Rivingstons, 1882
Bohatec, J., *Calvins Lehre von Staat und Kirche*, Breslau: Marcus, 1937
Carlson L.H, *Elizabethan Nonconformist Texts*, delen I t/m VI, London: Allen and Unwin, 1953-1970
Collinson, P., *The Elizabethan Puritan Movement*, London: Cape, 1967
Cremeans, C.D., *The reception of Calvinistic thought in England*, Urbana: University of Illinois Press, 1949
Dankbaar, W.F., *Calvijn, zijn weg en werk*, Nijkerk: Callenbach, 1982
Danner, D.G., 'Christopher Goodman and the English Protestant Tradition of Civil Disobedience', in: *Sixteenth Century Journal*: vol. VIII 1977
Davies R.E, *The problem of Authority in the Continental Reformers - A study in Luther, Zwingli, and Calvin*, London: Epsworth, 1946
Dickens A.G. and D.Carr (eds), *The Reformation in England in the Succession of Elizabeth I: Documents of Modern History*, London: Arnold, 1991[10]
Friedman, R., *The Theology of Anabaptism*, Scottdale: Herald Press, 1975
Ginkel, van, A., *De Ouderling*, Amsterdam: Ton Bolland, 1975
Hague, D., *Protestantism of the Prayer Book*, London: The Book Room, 1912
Hoak, D.E., *The King's Council in the Reign of Edward VI*, Cambridge University Press, 1976
Hollerbach, M., *Das Religionsgespräch als Mittel der Konfessionellen und politischen Auseinandersetzung im Deutschland des 16. Jahrhundert*, Frankfurt am Main: Lang, 1982
Hope, C., *Martin Bucer and the English Reformation*, Oxford: Blackwell, 1946
Krusche, W., *Das Wirken des Heiligen Geistes nach Calvin*, Göttingen: Vandenhoeck und Ruprecht, 1957
Lindsay, T.M, *The Church and the Ministry in the early centuries*, 1867
Lloyd Jones, D.M., *The Puritans, their Origins and Successors*, Edinburgh: The Banner of Truth Trust, 1987
Locher, G.W., *Huldrych Zwingly in neuer Sicht*, Zürich: Zwingli Verlag, 1969
Lohse, B., *Martin Luther, eine Einführung in sein Leben und sein Werk*, München: Beck, 1981
Luoma, J.K., 'Who owns the Fathers?: Hooker and Cartwright on the Authority of the Primitive Church', *Sixteenth Century Journal*: vol. VIII, 3, 1977
Marsden, J.B., *The History of the Early Puritans*, London: Hamilton, 1850
McGinn, D.J., *The Admonition Controversy:* New Brunswick, 1949 (original documents)
Murray, I.H., *The Reformation of the Church: A Collection of Reformed and Puritan Documents on Church Issues*, Edinburgh: The Banner of Truth Trust, 1987[2]
Niesel, W., *Die Theologie Calvins:* München: Kaiser Verlag, 1957
Paas, Steven, *De Gemeenschap der Heiligen: Kerk en Gezag bij Presbyteriaanse en*

Separatistische Engelse Puriteinen 1570-1593, Zoetermeer: Boekencentrum, 1996 [extended bibliography, including original sources]

Paas, Steven, *From Galilee to the Atlantic: A History of the Church in the West*, Zomba: Kachere 2006[2]

Paas, Steven, *The Faith Moves South: A History of the Church in Africa*, Zomba: Kachere, 2006

Peel, A., *Cartwrightiana*, London: Stewart Trust [original document]

Perry, G.G., *A History of the English Church*, London: Murray, 1891

Quanbeck, W.A., 'The Formula of Concord and Authority in the Church', *Sixteenth[h] Century Journal*: vol. VIII, 4, 1977

Ranke, von, L., *Maria Stuart en haar tijd*, Amsterdam: Borkam, 1944

Rechtien, J., '*Structures in the Theology of Walter Travers*', Sixteenth Century Journal: Vol. VIII, 1, 1977

Scott Pearson, A.F., *Thomas Cartwright and Elizabethan Puritanism:* Cambridge University Press, 1925

Spijker, van 't, W., *The Ecclesiastical Offices in the Thought of Martin Bucer*, Leyden: Brill, 1996 [transl. of: *De ambten bij Martin Bucer,* Kok Kampen, 2nd edition, 1987]

Stephens, W.P., *The Holy Spirit in the Theology of Martin Bucer*, London: Cambridge University Press, 1970

VanderSchaaf, M.E., 'Archbishop Parker's Effort towards a Bucerian Discipline in the Church of England', *Sixteenth Century Journal*: vol. VIII, 1 1977

Westcott, B.F., *A general view of the history on the English Bible,* London: MacMillan, 1868

Whitaker, E.C., *Martin Bucer and the Book of Common Prayer,* Great Wakering, 1974

Williams, G.H., *The Radical Reformation:* Philadelphia: TheWestminister Press, 1962.

Wyk, van, J.J., *The Historical Development of the Offices according to the Presbyterian Tradition of Scotland:* Universiteit van Stellenbosch, 1995

Index

à Lasco, Johannes, 49, 51, 67, 94, 182
absolutism, 64, 118, 154
adiaphora, 38, 48, 81, 102
Admonition Controversy, 16, 69, 75, 89, 107, 109, 113, 121, 122, 123, 124, 125, 126, 134, 155, 160, 161, 162, 163, 166, 167, 168, 169, 171, 185
Advertisements, 104, 106, 107, 108
Alexander III, 15
Alexander, Peter, 15, 67
Ames, William, 127
Amsterdam (congregation), 15, 36, 148
Anabaptism, 36, 37, 38, 39, 42, 46, 47, 48, 55, 113, 123, 134, 137, 164, 173, 174, 184
apostolic succession, 40, 87, 89, 90, 149
Arnheim (congregation), 148
Augustine (missionary to Anglo-Saxons), 14
Augustine of Hippo, 147
Avignon (Popes of A.), 11, 15
Bancroft, Richard, 24, 147, 148, 149, 151, 159
Barrowe, Henry, 9, 37, 136, 137, 146, 148, 173, 178
Becket (Thomas B.), 15
Beza, Theodorus, 43, 59, 74, 75, 81, 101, 107, 115, 116, 154, 156
Black Rubric, 83, 84, 103
Boleyn, Anne, 102
Boniface VIII, 12
Bonner, Edmund, 91, 92
Book of Common Prayer, 65, 84, 85, 86, 87, 90, 95, 96, 97, 103, 110, 122, 124, 130, 137, 138, 139, 143, 144, 150, 160, 161
Browne, Robert, 37, 111, 119, 120, 135, 136, 137, 148, 173, 174, 175, 178, 181
Bucer, Martin, 23, 32, 34, 35, 38, 41, 44, 45, 46, 47, 48, 49, 50, 51, 52, 53, 54, 57, 58, 59, 64, 65, 66, 67, 68, 69, 70, 79, 80, 81, 86, 87, 88, 94, 110, 111, 113, 132, 145, 154, 155, 157, 171, 182, 192
Bullinger, Heinrich, 31, 32, 35, 43, 44, 59, 61, 70, 79, 81, 86, 95, 106, 107, 111
C.C.A.P (Church of Central Africa Presbyterian), 183
Calvin, John, 9, 22, 23, 31, 32, 35, 38, 41, 43, 44, 46, 49, 50, 51, 52, 53, 54, 55, 56, 57, 58, 59, 60, 62, 63, 64, 65, 68, 69, 70, 71, 72, 73, 74, 75, 76, 77, 79, 81, 82, 86, 87, 97, 98, 100, 101, 106, 107, 110, 111, 112, 113, 114, 115, 118, 123, 124, 126, 129, 132, 152, 154, 155, 157, 162, 163, 164, 168, 169, 171, 177, 182, 184, 185
Cartwright, Thomas, 14, 16, 17, 24, 36, 69, 73, 75, 81, 87, 89, 94, 101, 102, 107, 108, 110, 112, 113, 114, 115, 116, 117, 118, 119, 120, 121, 122, 123, 124, 125, 126, 127, 128, 129, 132, 134, 135, 136, 137, 138, 144, 145, 146, 147, 148, 149, 150, 151, 154, 155, 156, 157, 158, 159, 160, 161, 162, 163, 164, 165, 166, 167, 168, 169, 170, 171, 172, 173, 174, 175, 176, 177, 178, 179, 180, 181, 184, 185
Cathari, 106
Cecil (Robert Dudley, Earl of Leicester), 104, 105, 130, 135, 140, 141
Celtic Church, 13, 14
Chapman, Edmund, 137, 140, 158
Christliche Gemeinschaften [Christian Communities], 48, 51, 58, 111, 145
churchwardens, 66, 67, 109
clericalism, 26, 165, 182, 183, 184
Colet, 19
commonwealth (Christian c. of Church and State), 38, 42, 43, 44, 48, 55, 60, 62, 63, 64, 68, 71, 72, 75, 100, 118, 134, 138, 144, 151, 168, 186
Conforming Puritans, 69, 77
Congregationalism, 136
consistories, 25, 58, 71, 73, 74, 76, 77, 117, 120, 124, 126, 131, 133, 141, 142, 157, 168, 169, 170, 171
Constantine (Constantinian), 38, 147
Contarini, Casparo (Cardinal), 34
Convocation (House of C.), 66, 104, 106
Counter Reformation, 103, 129, 156
Coverdale, Miles, 30, 95, 105, 107
Cox, Richard, 95, 97, 105
Cranmer, Thomas, 30, 60, 63, 67, 78, 79, 80, 82, 83, 84, 85, 87, 92, 93, 94, 95, 97
Dedham (conference, papers), 137, 138, 139, 140, 142, 146, 158
democratisation, 18, 23, 36, 39, 54, 64, 112, 118, 128, 154, 170, 177

Directory (by Travers), 130, 141, 142, 143, 147
dominee, 183
Douay Bible, 156
Dryander, Francis, 67
Edward I, 15
Edward III, 15
Edward VI, 39, 45, 61, 63, 65, 67, 70, 78, 86, 91, 121
election, 35, 42, 70, 115, 127, 142, 150, 169, 170, 171, 180, 182, 187
Elizabeth (Queen E.), 26, 32, 65, 66, 69, 70, 75, 91, 93, 95, 98, 99, 100, 102, 103, 104, 106, 107, 113, 117, 120, 124, 128, 132, 134, 135, 137, 139, 141, 143, 145, 156, 163
Episcopalianism, 23, 28, 48, 63, 64, 66, 68, 70, 72, 100, 115, 124, 129, 133, 134, 140, 146, 147, 149, 157, 170, 185
episcopos(pl. episopoi), 23, 49, 50
Erasmus (Desiderius), 19
Erastianism, 43, 44, 48, 55, 60, 61, 63, 64, 68, 70, 75, 78, 100, 107, 111, 115, 116, 163, 165, 168, 171
Explicatio(by Travers), 121, 126, 127, 128, 129, 130, 133, 157
Fagius, Paul, 67
Field, John, 110, 111, 116, 117, 121, 122, 123, 126, 135, 139, 141
Fitz, Richard, 111, 173
Frederick (Elector), 118, 129
Gardiner, Stephen, 91, 92, 93
Goodman, Christopher, 74, 75, 98, 123, 124
Gospellers, 63, 104
Grand Design, 131, 132, 137, 141, 151, 152
Gratianus, 11
Greenwood, John, 9, 136, 146, 173
Grindal, Edmund, 23, 64, 65, 66, 69, 95, 97, 105, 106, 107, 132, 133, 134, 135, 139, 150
Gualter, Rudolf, 79, 95, 107, 116
Habsburg Empire, 12, 56, 59, 78
Harrison, Robert, 119, 120, 135, 136, 148, 173, 174, 175
Henry II, 15
Henry VII, 18
Henry VIII, 18, 20, 29, 30, 31, 61, 78, 83, 91, 92, 102, 105, 121, 137
hierarchicalism, 183
High Commission, 106, 124, 145, 147, 151, 155, 159, 178

Hooker, Richard, 24, 28, 130, 148, 149, 150, 151, 156, 169
Hooper, John, 20, 30, 31, 63, 78, 79, 80, 81, 82, 93, 94, 95, 106, 113
House of Commons, 18, 104, 110, 121, 141, 147
House of Lords, 104, 141
Innocentius III, 12, 15
Inquisition, 31, 94, 140, 141
Institutes (Calvin, I. of the Christian Religion), 22, 55, 57, 58, 123, 162
Jewel, Melanchthon, 95, 105
Kilchören, 43
Kirchenpfleger, 48, 57, 58
Knox, John, 63, 67, 68, 69, 74, 75, 83, 84, 94, 95, 96, 97, 98, 99, 101, 108, 110, 111, 123, 124, 126, 130, 183, 184
Lambeth Articles, 70, 150
Latimer, Hugh, 20, 80, 94
Leicester (Cecil Robert Dudley), 105, 120, 135, 151
Leyden (congregation), 44, 148, 156, 192
Lollards, 17, 18, 39
Luther, Martin, 12, 18, 19, 21, 31, 32, 35, 37, 38, 40, 41, 43, 44, 45, 46, 59, 60
Magister Reformation, 38
Magna Charta, 15
Malawi, 2, 8, 183
Marian Exile, 63, 68, 95, 96, 105, 150
Mar-Prelate Papers, 143, 145, 146, 151, 159
Martyr, Peter M. Vermigli, 67, 81, 86, 94, 95
Mary (Queen), 31, 65, 68, 75, 78, 86, 91, 92, 93, 94, 97, 98, 103, 104, 105, 113, 137, 161, 173
Middleburgh (congregation), 119, 120, 136, 146, 148, 175
More (Thomas), 19, 30, 40, 44, 51, 54, 63, 70, 95, 98, 115, 128, 157
Netherlands, The, 8, 12, 51, 62, 67, 71, 73, 74, 94, 113, 119, 125, 128, 129, 136, 148, 156, 173, 174, 175, 182
Norman Conquest, 14
Northumberland (Lord Protector), 68, 78
Novatians, 106
Ochino, Bernard, 67
Oecolampadius, Johannes, 35, 44
Olevianus, Caspar, 118
oligarchy, 26, 36, 43, 53, 127
Ordonnances Ecclesiastiques (by Calvin), 57

194

Parker, Matthew, 48, 64, 65, 66, 67, 86, 94, 104, 107, 109, 114, 125, 132, 134, 150
Parkhurst, John, 95, 135
Penry, John, 136, 145, 146
Philip II (King of Spain), 93
Philip of Hessen, 33
Pilkington, James, 95
Plumber Hall (congregation), 110
Precisians, 100, 105, 106, 124
predestination, 70, 150, 169
presbyteries (classes, seigniories), 25, 27, 30, 43, 50, 69, 71, 73, 74, 77, 117, 120, 124, 126, 131, 133, 142, 157, 170, 172, 177, 183
presbyteros, 23, 42, 49, 50, 66, 89, 110, 132, 161
prophesyings, 63, 66, 69, 73, 106, 131, 132, 133, 134, 135, 136, 137, 141, 145, 152, 169
Radical Reformation, 38, 39, 174
Renaissance, 12, 18, 22, 156
reverend, 107, 183
Rheims translation, 129, 145, 156
Ridley, Nicholas, 78, 79, 80, 94, 113
Ryle, John Charles, 86
sacerdotalism, 87, 89, 161
Sampson, Thomas, 105, 107
Sandys, Edwin, 95
Saravia, Adrian, 147
Separatists, 9, 37, 39, 77, 93, 110, 120, 130, 137, 140, 146, 147, 148, 152, 154, 158, 159, 170, 171, 172, 173, 174, 175, 176, 177, 178, 179, 180, 181, 184, 185
Simon de Montfort, 15
Somerset (Lord Protector), 45, 78, 81, 82, 92
Star Chamber, 22, 120, 147, 151
Stubbe, Anne, 120, 137, 178, 181
surplice, 81, 95, 96, 104, 105, 106, 108

Sutcliffe, Matthew, 148, 151, 155
Travers, Walter, 73, 117, 126, 127, 128, 129, 130, 131, 133, 138, 141, 142, 143, 150, 157
Tremellius, John Immanuel, 118
Trent (Council of T.), 34, 77, 103
Tunstall, Cuthbert, 92
Tyndale, William, 19, 30, 31, 61, 82
Ursinus, Zacharias, 118
Uttenhovius, Johannes, 67
Vermigli, Peter Martyr, 67, (see: Martyr)
Vestments' Controversy, 81, 95, 100, 106, 108, 109, 113, 125
via media, 31, 47, 57, 64, 66, 75, 102, 118, 154
Wandsworth (congregation), 116, 117, 118
Warham, William, 59
Warwick (Hospital), 120, 129, 142, 146
Warwickshire (Decrees of W.), 138, 146
Whitaker, William, 87, 88, 127
Whitby (Synod of W.), 14
Whitgift, John, 24, 36, 69, 81, 87, 89, 101, 106, 114, 115, 119, 120, 122, 123, 124, 125, 128, 130, 132, 134, 139, 140, 141, 143, 144, 147, 148, 149, 150, 151, 155, 156, 157, 159, 160, 161, 162, 163, 164, 165, 166, 167, 168, 169, 170, 171, 172
Whittingham, William, 95, 96, 97, 98
Wilcox, Thomas, 110, 111, 116, 117, 122, 126, 139
William of Normandy, 14, 15
William of Orange, 33
Withers, George, 107, 116
Wolsey (Cardinal), 19, 21, 59
Wycliffe, John, 16, 17, 18, 39
Zanchius, Girolamo, 118
Züricher Ehegericht, 42
Zwingli, Huldrych, 31, 32, 35, 38, 42, 43, 44, 45, 46, 59, 60, 61, 64, 79, 95, 107

www.ingramcontent.com/pod-product-compliance
Lightning Source LLC
Chambersburg PA
CBHW031552300426
44111CB00006BA/280